How to Manage a Successful Press Conference

How to Manage a Successful Press Conference

RALF LEINEMANN AND
ELENA BAIKALTSEVA

GOWER

Published by
Gower Publishing Limited
Gower House
Croft Road
Aldershot
Hampshire
GU11 3HR
England

Gower Publishing Company
Suite 420
101 Cherry Street
Burlington
VT 05401-4405
USA

Ralf Leinemann and Elena Baikaltseva have asserted their right under the Copyright, Designs and Patents Act, 1988, to be identified as the authors of this work.

British Library Cataloguing in Publication Data
Leinemann, Ralf
   How to manage a successful press conference
   1.Press conferences
   I.Title II.Baikaltseva, Elena
   659.2

   ISBN-10: 0 566 08727 8
   ISBN-13: 978 0 566 08727 1

Library of Congress Control Number: 2006931598

Printed and bound in Great Britain by MPG Books Ltd. Bodmin, Cornwall.

Contents

List of Figures

Foreword

Andrew Laurence
Chairman & CEO, Hill & Knowlton EMEA

Journalists will thank you for reading this book.

In today's digital economy where e-mail, SMS and blogging are increasingly popular forms of communication, press conferences may seem a little old hat. However, they continue to be a vital way for companies to share news – a real opportunity to show the personality behind the brand, for the people behind the companies to meet and build relationships with an increasingly powerful constituency.

From a journalist's perspective, press conferences mean they can get a complete view of a company and its innovations; they can handle the latest product and hear directly from company leaders and often customers – in a physical environment. However, in a world where time is precious, the press conference is overused: too often it is the default method for companies to disseminate news. The time is right to redraw the rules.

As PR and communications professionals face increasing pressure to maximize their budgets and deliver clear and measurable results, it is more important than ever to be able to determine whether a press conference is the right approach to a given situation. The simple rule of thumb is to stage them only when the story is likely to generate a high degree of media interest. But as PR and communications professionals know, it's not always that straightforward. This book provides both the criteria and a strong justification for press conferences, and equips its readers with all the tools necessary to get the most out of them.

The press conference has a one-size-fits-all format and, as such, has potential limitations. These days one size or message does not fit all and the content showcased must be of interest to every member of the audience; with the increasing diversity of the media, this presents a real challenge. This book highlights the importance of understanding the needs of those who will attend; an ever more critical skill as stretched editorial teams mean it is increasingly difficult to lure journalists away from their desks.

For those aiming to reach an international community there is another layer of complexity. It is not just a case of arranging plane tickets, translating materials, converting dollars to Euros or advising executives to speak slowly and clearly. Cultural variations and diversity of editorial approaches create additional requirements. Journalists from different countries have particular needs and can react differently to the same situation. Some seek an exclusive or a unique point of view; others want solid trends supported by facts and figures. To some, an aggressive sales pitch is a turn off; to others it is expected.

Interestingly, similar considerations apply to the selection and management of speakers, whether internal executives or from partner organizations. Ralf Leinemann and Elena Baikaltseva teach us that to ensure success, PR professionals need to take into account cultural variations at every stage of a press conference from the structure of the event, to speakers, style, content and tone, right through to the all-important task of obtaining feedback.

By combining theory with best practice and useful hints and tips, this book provides valuable insight into the work that goes into arranging successful press conferences. Sharing more than 20 years of personal experiences, Leinemann and Baikaltseva analyse every aspect of press conferences, ranging from strategy and planning, through to the tiny details that can make all the difference. An essential tool for all communications professionals, this book is the definitive guide to managing a successful press conference.

Andrew Laurence is Chairman & CEO of Hill & Knowlton – Europe, Middle East & Africa. A specialist in corporate communications, he had advised organizations including BP, Shell, EDS, Motorola and the Institute of Chartered Accountants of England & Wales. He has lectured on aspects of corporate reputation at Leeds University and the Judge Institute, Cambridge.

Objective of the Book

This book is intended to be a handbook for PR professionals containing food for thought and recommendations as to what to consider when planning and executing international press conferences. The book should also be a good resource for event managers who are managing press conferences on different scales. We hope that they can also leverage some of the ideas discussed on the following pages for other events. Finally, we hope that marketing professionals and communications managers in general find this book useful.

This book is written by European PR professionals. It is based on experience in the European market. Since PR and media patterns differ from region to region (sometimes even from country to country), not everything discussed on the following pages is for consideration outside Europe.[1]

Turning this argument around, however, results in this book being highly appealing to audiences outside Europe.[2] In particular it may be of great interest to companies from outside Europe that are expanding outside their home market. Marketing managers, PR and non-PR communications professionals in those companies may want to learn what media work is like in Europe. Also, non-European PR professionals who do not have sufficient public relations support in Europe may want to supplement their knowledge. And finally, small PR agencies or individual professionals based outside Europe who need to gain some education about the European market, and even larger PR agencies that want to use this as part of their training with non-European staff, may be interested in learning about executing press conferences in Europe.

The goal of the book is to provide tips that make any conference successful and a memorable event for *all* participants.

It should be noted that the participants of a press conference typically have different individual needs. As a result, they have individual agendas and objectives and they will pay particular attention to different parts of the conference. Thus, different participants could easily walk away from the event with very different impressions and thus with very different perceptions of what has been communicated and if the event was successful.

It must be in the interest of the PR manager organizing a press conference to ensure that most participants of a press conference have a pleasant experience and, most importantly, that they understood the messages and, ideally, received them in a positive way.

It is obvious that the audience at a press conference are representatives of the media. It should be noted that this community is not homogeneous. Depending on what audience they communicate to in papers, radio, television or online, the individual reporters have different needs.

But it is also important to understand that there are additional participants at the conference, such as your own executives, who deliver the news in speeches and interviews. They probably pay attention to different aspects of a press conference. They want to be briefed

---

1   See, for example, Appendix B on cultural influences on PR.
2   This paragraph is based on discussions with Helen Ostrowski, CEO Porter Novelli.

properly, they want to leave a good impression, they want to meet interesting people. And, of course, they want to ensure that the journalists write positive stories about their message – and ideally also about themselves. Also, you need to take into account that for a company executive, the internal impact of his or her performance at a press conference is important. Success certainly strengthens an executive's position in the organization.

Finally, the organizers of a press conference are the third group of participants. You as the organizer want to ensure that everything runs smoothly and you are not caught by surprise during an event or during the preparation. You want to be prepared for everything. You are happy when everyone else is happy.

So, there are at least three different parties at a press conference who should be able to enjoy the event: the journalists, your executives and yourself. Nowadays, however, there is typically at least a fourth party involved in a press conference. This could be a partner company, a guest speaker, or another external organization or individual that endorses the news of the day. An example may be a software vendor who endorses the introduction of a new hardware platform (for example, a company developing games endorsing the introduction of a new game console, or a database vendor endorsing the introduction of a new processor generation). Another example may be the endorsement of a strategic company decision by an analyst company. And finally, your product launch may be supported by a customer who signs a significant order right away. Regardless of who the fourth party is at your press event, it is important to ensure that they enjoy the event as well.

Creating a perception

But what is the objective of a press conference? Well, you want to make an announcement to the public. But not only do you want the message to be heard, you also want to ensure that your announcement is received in a positive way.

You want to create a positive perception.

This book is about the PR tools and communication processes that should be used to support the news you want to announce, in order to get the public interested in the news and to leave them with the most positive perception.

1 *Introduction*

Introduction

1 Why is a Press Conference Special?

All conferences have one thing in common: the message disclosed at the event is intended for the audience of the conference. This is so obvious that it need hardly be mentioned.

A conference for physicists will address scientific topics.

An oil and gas conference will address companies and research organizations in that industry.

And how about a press conference? Well, you will argue that the audience is obviously the press and thus there is no exception to the rule, but this is true only at first glance – the true audience is not even in the room during a press conference! The true audience is the readers of the magazines and websites, the viewers of the TV channels and the listeners of the radio stations – your customers!

A press conference is a bit like a game of Chinese Whispers: the speakers present to the press, who in return deliver the content to their readers. In other words, a press conference is all about presenting to the presenters.

An immediate result of this fact is that you need to be prepared to measure the success of a press conference on two levels after the event. The first level is obviously the impact you made on the participants, the journalists. You need to ask questions like 'Did they attend in the first place?', 'Did they like your news?' and 'Did they write what you expected them to write?' The second level is the impact you made on the 'true audience' that the journalists wrote for or broadcasted to. When measuring the results of your press conference on this second level, you need to ask questions like 'Did you create increased awareness for your company or your products?', 'Did the customers change their behaviour towards your company or your products?' and 'Did the customers ultimately buy your products because of what they read?'.

We will discuss the topic of measurement in Chapter 28. For now we want to keep in mind that it looks straightforward to measure on the first level, but it may be complicated to measure on the second level, since measuring customers' behaviour is influenced by many parameters, with PR being only one of them. And it indeed looks difficult to single out the influence of a press conference on customers' behaviour.

Reach your audience

Vendors want to reach their customers. They want to convince them to buy their products or services.

There are several ways to get to customers. The direct one is through trade shows or events, addressing customers directly. These events could be presentations to consumers in supermarkets or user conferences typically addressing commercial or industrial customers.

The disadvantage of these events is that the number of reached customers is very limited. Only a few hundred people visit the supermarket per day or fit into the presentation room during the user conference.

At a press conference every journalist represents thousands or millions of customers, depending on the circulation of the respective publication. This makes a press conference so much more powerful than a customer event – and at the same time so much more challenging. On the one hand, it is a chance to get a strong message across to a large audience; on the other hand there is the risk that the message is misunderstood by the press and communicated in a negative way to customers. And if that happens, the idea of doing a press conference has back-fired on you.

It may be argued that advertising reaches the same audience. It is also considered safer since the advertiser has full control over the message – the content is not filtered by a journalist, or dependent on a journalist's opinion. While this is correct, it should still be noted that a positive article – and even a neutral one – is much more powerful than any advertising. According to media analysis research, an article generated by PR is up to ten times more effective with the target audience than an advertisement covering the same space in a publication. The reason is obvious: it is in the nature of advertising only to tell positive things about a product, while a positive article from an independent or neutral journalist is much more convincing.[1]

The fact that the press is neutral – or at least should be – is one of the differences between a press conference and a customer event.

The press should approach a presentation in a neutral way, be open, but also critical. After having collected all the information, journalists should come to a certain opinion that they then express in an article for their readers.

A customer, however, is typically prejudiced. In the case of a user group conference, customers meet who have already bought certain products; they should already be loyal customers. These customers should have a positive attitude towards messages from a vendor at that conference. Presenting to the customer base of your competitor, however, will be significantly more challenging ...

Competition

Any conference is also a battle for mind share. In business, you compete with your direct competitors, namely, vendors who address your customers with products and solutions that compete with your own. At a press conference, however, you should be prepared to also compete with vendors from different industries.

This is in fact a significant difference between a press conference and those 'normal' conferences where the true target audience is in the room.

When you talk to your customer directly, you very openly compete with your direct competitors. You want to sell your product, and they want to sell theirs. But you certainly do not compete with vendors who offer different products to the same customer. If your company, for example, sells CD players, you would like your customer to buy a CD player from your company. But since you do not sell CDs, you do not mind which CDs the customer actually runs on your player afterwards.

This approach is obvious, but it does not hold true any more when competing for mind share of the media.

---

1   In this context it is interesting to note that this circumstance makes measuring PR results by AVE (advertising value equivalent) or advertising equivalent a meaningless effort. The effect of a square inch of advertising can hardly be compared with the effect of a square inch of an independent article. Even though financial departments like this measure, PR professionals should not accept this as the measure of their success.

An almost unlimited number of news announcements hit any journalist on a daily basis. The typical scenario is that there are more news stories available than can be printed. This means there has to be a selection and that you compete for space in a publication with any other vendor who wants to reach the same target audience that is reached with that publication – in other words, you compete with *any* other news.

A magazine on music and audio would publish news, for example, on CD players, but also on new CD releases. So, in this case, a potential article on your new CD player would indeed compete with articles on other vendors introducing new CDs.

In women's lifestyle magazines, for example, the situation is similar. Coverage on fashion designers competes with coverage on diets, and hair stylists compete with make-up artists and cosmetics.

In car magazines, car manufacturers compete with tuning companies or the supplies industry.

In the IT press, computer vendors compete with manufacturers of peripherals, supplies, software or services.

In the daily press almost everything competes with everything: politics, sports, society news, technology news, and so on. If your company announces ground-breaking technologies, it may still be overshadowed by an economic crisis or a surprising political development or maybe an unforeseen natural disaster.

You should be aware that your own company could overshadow the visibility of announcements. For example, if you make an interesting product announcement on the same day that your CEO is replaced, then your product announcement may not be picked up at all. Your new CEO may make the headlines instead.[2]

---

2   It is obvious to avoid competing with yourself. But especially in larger corporations with many independent business units, these uncoordinated approaches can indeed happen.

2 *PR Tools*

Selection of the appropriate PR tool

A press conference is only one of many ways of communicating news to the public. In this chapter we will examine all the tools in order to identify criteria for or against executing a press conference for a given challenge.

Often enough, when requesting a PR activity, marketing professionals or business managers request either a press release or a press conference. These two tools are very good PR tools, but they are not always the best or most suitable tools for a given communication challenge.[1] Throughout this book we will demonstrate when and how a press conference can best suit your PR needs. We will discuss how and when a press conference should be used depending on the respective PR objective. Only in a minority of cases is executing a press conference in fact the best solution. 'Best' can have several meanings in this context depending on the objectives. The best tool can be the tool that is most cost effective or the tool with the biggest impact. It may be the tool with the best effectiveness for a very focused PR activity or the tool with the broadest outreach. You can certainly think of many criteria, but for a commercial enterprise cost efficiency is certainly the most important one, with all other parameters being defined.

In this context it is important to note that the value of a press conference can be perceived differently from region to region, and from country to country. While in some countries a press conference may be the best tool to reach the media, in other countries it may be more appropriate to run a press tour to the editors or to offer one-to-one briefings or interviews. It may be dangerous to make general statements, but it seems to be fair to say that there is more openness to attend a press conference in eastern European countries than in the west.

In this chapter we will enlist a collection of PR tools to select from – depending on objectives and on market needs.

It should be common practice to evaluate all possible options before deciding on a press conference. We will approach this topic in four sections. The first will look at tools as appropriate per the life cycle of a product. The second will look at additional generic tools that are not necessarily dependent on the state of a product in its life cycle. And the third approach will examine the life cycle of a product category. Here we will identify PR tools and tactics dependent on the life cycle state in accordance with Geoffrey A. Moore's ideas shared in *Crossing the Chasm* and *Inside the Tornado*. In the fourth and final section, we will ask journalists themselves what they believe is the best PR tool for each task.

---

1   In their book *Getting Free Publicity*, Pam and Bob Austin point out that the high-tech industry in particular is often guilty of misusing press releases. Only too often is this tool used to disclose minor news to the press. In fact, it is not only ineffective for the journalists, but also too expensive for the vendors in comparison to the expected return. Press conferences should be saved for major announcements only. This is in line with findings by Bettina Schoeppe in her Diploma Thesis (2003) – see Bibliography for complete reference. According to her surveys, journalists would only expect up to two press conferences per vendor per year at a maximum.

Tool portfolio for product-related announcements[2]

We assume that you are responsible for the PR work covering a portfolio of products, services and solutions. For simplicity's sake, we will consider in this first approach that the portfolio consists of commercial solutions targeting businesses. Nevertheless, we will discuss several times the respective equivalent for PR activities addressing consumers rather than businesses. In the following, we will list additional PR tools that are not necessarily linked to a specific state of a product in its life cycle.

It can be argued that the selection of the appropriate tool depends on many parameters such as your company's competitive position, the state of the economy or geographical aspects. These parameters – and many more – indeed play a role when defining the appropriate PR tool for your announcement. But it turns out that it is a good approach to make the appropriate PR tool primarily dependent on the current state of the product during its life cycle.

A few obvious cases show that there is indeed a strong correlation between product life cycle state and the appropriate PR tool. For example, you do not want to run a high profile campaign shortly before the product is discontinued. Also, you will have difficulties in executing a press visit to a customer installation when the product has not even been shipped yet.

We start with a matrix for selecting the appropriate PR tool for the announcement. The matrix is in fact a mapping of the product life cycle state to PR tools. The objective is to properly match messages and announcements with the appropriate PR tool.

In Figure 2.1, we are considering only company-initiated PR activities related to products and solutions over their life cycle. In other words, we do not consider PR activities arising from competitive or external pressures. The assumption is that you are responsible for a technical product. But you will also find several hints in the text for a transfer of this concept to other industries.

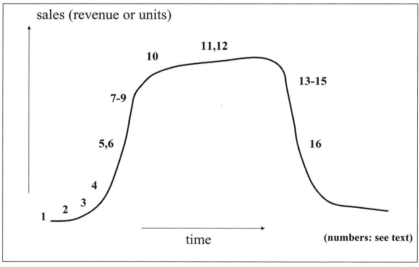

Figure 2.1   PR tools in product life cycle

---
2   This section is based on HP company internal communication in Boeblingen, Germany, with Tatiana Fish (1999).

1.   PRE-INTRODUCTION TECHNICAL ARTICLES, MEDIA ALERTS, NDA[3] BRIEFINGS

Before actually announcing a new product, it may be appropriate to 'pave the way' or create excitement for it within the industry. One way of doing that is to launch technical articles to the press about the new technology that your company will introduce in future products. This should be done on a fairly academic level without pre-announcing the product itself. To some degree the difference is similar to scientific work on a theoretical level versus an applied level.

Nowadays, this approach is also used in the consumer space to get customers excited about the new product. Often enough the product itself is, however, already pre-launched. This can be done as long as the forthcoming product does not cannibalize your current product portfolio, that is, customers not buying your current products anymore but waiting for the new one. If it does have an impact on the sales figures of your current product portfolio, however, this approach can cause a significant dent in your company's revenue stream. Pre-launching your product, however, can be particularly successful when your competitors already have products in the respective area and your own product is late to the market. In that case, a strong pre-introduction may convince customers to wait for your product rather than spend their money on your competitors' products today.

Pre-introduction activities can also focus on creating awareness of the need for your forthcoming product. Your research may show that your new product can create significant savings for your customers. However, the issue addressed by your product is not necessarily on a priority for your customers. In that case, your initial communication should create awareness for the issue you will address later with your product; your focus should be on educating the market.

NDA briefings are a special tool. Journalists who are invited to an NDA briefing are requested to confirm that they only disclose the news to the public after a given embargo date. In return for that favour they receive information at a very early stage so they can prepare their coverage well in advance; in this way they have a head start compared to journalists who only receive the news at the formal embargo date. You should hold these NDA briefings with a select group of very influential media only.

2.   EVENTS, PRESS TOURS

The introduction of a new product may indeed justify a major event like a press conference or some other significant investment like a press tour of appropriate executives to journalists' offices. The execution of a press tour can be a significant investment on your executives' time and should be thought through carefully. However, since it minimizes the journalists' investment, it is typically highly appreciated by the press and it has a significant impact. Not only is there no 'time out of the office' for the journalist, but also it allows your spokespeople to tailor the message for the individual journalist – or a small group of journalists working in the same publishing house. If you have the necessary staff resources to allow you to take this approach, you should seriously consider it, since it shows your dedication to the respective publishing house(s).

---

3   NDA = non-disclosure agreement.

3.   NEW PRODUCTS/SOLUTION PRESS RELEASES/PRODUCT TESTING

The introduction of a new product is accompanied by the issuing of a press release. This release is distributed directly to all journalists who may be interested in the content, and indirectly by making use of wire and news services. It should be noted that a press release alone typically has little impact, since it is often sent out anonymously – and the average journalist probably gets at least ten times as many of these press releases than he can cover in his publication. If there is nothing in the release that captures people's imagination, the impact is indeed only very low.

Depending on the announcement, another activity may be appropriate: you may want to provide journalists with test units so they can run their own tests on it. Making test units available to selected press is a common procedure in several industries such as home entertainment, IT and the automotive industry (see also 'Other PR tools', below).

4.   PHOTOS

Press coverage increases significantly in relation to the availability of picture material. Photo opportunities should be offered to journalists at specific activities, or prepared photos distributed. The minimum offering is product photos, but this should be a given for most products. An enhancement is the so-called environment shot, namely, photos that show your product in use.

Here are two examples: A mobile-phone vendor should provide photos of its products, but also photos of, for example, consumers making calls on a train with a mobile phone. A computer vendor should provide photos of its product, but also photos of, for example, the computing device controlling a grinding machine on the shop floor.

In consumer PR, one of the most used tactics is to show a celebrity using one of your products. Depending on the celebrity, the probability of this photo being published is typically extremely high. If you select the right VIP, then strong press coverage is almost certain. Even though the focus of the coverage tends to be more on the celebrity than on your product, the image gain for your company can be tremendous.

In a more generic context, you should not only think in terms of product photos. For some services, showing a picture will be difficult anyway. How do you want to illustrate a bank transfer, for example? In cases like this, you should consider making photos available of your company in a more generic sense. This could be photos of your executives, historical photos of your company such as the first office it opened or an image of the company founder, or simply your company logo outside one of your main buildings or a photo of your sophisticated R&D department.

5/6.   BACKGROUNDERS, INDUSTRY ANALYST REPORTS

The portfolio of documents or reports supporting your message is endless. Some of these documents are developed by your own company, some may be commissioned to external institutions and some are independently carried out by external organizations.

Documents developed by your own company include backgrounders that can focus on several topics. You can focus on certain product features, you can write a backgrounder on certain technologies, you can write a document on market developments or trends your company has observed. You can also focus the backgrounder on your company's involvement in certain industry associations or you can write a history of your company's involvement in certain customer solutions.

In a similar fashion you can make white papers available to the press. In fact, there is no clear division between a backgrounder and a white paper. A white paper can be considered to focus more on topics such as the implications of new technologies, for example. It typically addresses the specialist, while a backgrounder is for a broader audience.

You may also want to decide not to appear as the messenger of news yourself, but commission research out to a third party. This third party can be an independent research laboratory, a company that conducts customer surveys or industry analyst firms.

You want external resources to disclose this information, since external announcements can work like customer references. However, you need to understand that commissioned research is always suspicious, since its results may be influenced by the funding company.[4] It is especially suspicious when it only confirms your own message. It does work, however, when it is not directly related to your message.

Here are two examples to illustrate the above. If your commissioned work only reveals that your own products are the best, then it is basically useless for PR purposes. If you are a manufacturer of digital cameras, however, and a commissioned customer survey reveals that a certain percentage of the population use their digital cameras in an unexpected way, then this is interesting news for the media – they may not cover your products as a result, but you have positioned your company as a thought leader in this specific field.[5]

Truly external reports are the most rewarding. Industry analyst reports on your products or on market share data being favourable for your products have a significant impact on your customers and you want to refer to them in your PR work. Note, however, that you need to respect their copyrights, and you may need to purchase the report for reprints; if so, you may need to follow certain guidelines.

In consumer PR you have external news on a similar level: positive product reviews or product awards from industry institutions or associations can have a strong impact on customers' buying behaviours, and you certainly want to reference them in your PR work. (But think twice when you want to use awards from the media in PR! Awards from independent industry institutions are not an issue – but will magazines actually write about awards in potentially competing publications? In some cases it works, in some cases it doesn't. It typically depends on how well the award is recognized in the industry.)

7.   ROUNDTABLE DISCUSSIONS, SPECIAL INTEREST GROUPS (SIGS)

Once a product is launched and it is having some initial success in the market, you need to keep the momentum. One of the options is to reveal more technical details or background information to an audience that is specialized in these topics. You can also try to identify controversial aspects that specialists are interested in.

With a brand new technology, for example, you want to stimulate a discussion about the influence of the new technology on society or on the economy. You can also discuss potential future development or use of the technology. You can also define business topics that can be addressed in roundtable discussions.

---

4   Especially in politics and in legal cases the involvement of external resources has become very suspicious, since the results of these external experts almost certainly reflect the opinion of the commissioning party. If the results contradict their opinion, the results are typically hidden and not published in the first place.

5   Sometimes you have unexpected results: an online survey commissioned by a vendor of digital cameras in the Netherlands in 2004 revealed that 10 per cent of the male population use digital cameras to take erotic pictures. This finding even made it to the national TV news.

You can arrange formal roundtable discussions with interested journalists or informal meetings of groups. Formal roundtable discussions can be arranged at industry events such as trade shows or industry conferences. Informal roundtables or special interest groups can be set up with journalists from one city. You may, for example, want to invite journalists to a restaurant on a monthly basis.[6]

It is interesting to note that roundtable discussions can also be held at press conferences after the initial announcement. They can be used to discuss special topics related to the disclosed news. For these discussions you need to avoid doing presentations, but only stimulate the discussion, for example with controversial statements. Roundtable discussions should be an open information exchange, a dialogue that every participant benefits from. In order to maximize the value for the participants, you should select the audience carefully. Avoid placing competing journalists at the same table: their contributions would be small to avoid sharing their thoughts with their competition.

8.   TECHNICAL FEATURE ARTICLES

We have seen earlier that interest in new products can be maintained at a high level, when you allow more and more technical details to be disclosed over time. You can do this face-to-face in roundtable discussions as we have seen above, but you can also distribute technical feature articles focusing on certain topics that are of interest to the public. Basically, you can talk about the science behind your product, requirements during the production process of the product, compliance with environmental demands, and so on.

Especially when your product is a commodity product, you should select features that make your product unique or superior to others. Or, if your company follows a high road business strategy, you want to focus on features that would justify a premium.

If you do a refresh of the product, you want to talk about its new integral features. For commodity products like washing powders you may want to address the effects of new ingredients. For cars this could be a new design. For computers this could be a more powerful processor or memory, for example.

9.   ORDER STORIES

At some point in time you want to show that there is a strong momentum behind your product. You can do so by announcing market share data, but for individual products this may not be appropriate – unless the market is dominated by just a few products.[7]

In addition to using external data from industry analysts you can also use data directly from your sales organization as evidence of your products' acceptance. It is a common practice to share significant deals with the public. This is particularly used in the B2B ('business-to-business') space. Examples include multi-million dollar outsourcing deals, significant orders of airplanes, signing up major suppliers or subcontractors, purchase of entire power plants or airports, and so on.[8]

---

6   In Germany, a so-called 'Presse-Stammtisch' is a common practice. Directly translated, a 'Stammtisch' is a table reserved for regular guests. But the idea of a 'Stammtisch' is a social institution going beyond just having a beer together at a bar. In the UK, breakfast meetings in London have a similar function in that they are used to provide news updates to the media or clients on a regular basis.
7   For example in the aerospace industry, the PC processor chip industry or the game console industry.
8   Announcing major deals is particularly interesting at trade shows, especially when you have no other significant announcement for creating awareness for your company. Trade show organizers like order announcements, since they often measure the success of their event by the number of closed deals.

On the consumer market, you can celebrate the one millionth visitor in a museum or a theme park or a deal with a major retailer, and so on. You can also celebrate the shipment of the 10 000th unit from your factory.

10.   PARTNER AGREEMENT MEDIA ALERTS

Any partner agreement endorses your product. Typical partner announcements cover channel partner agreements or partnerships related to the supply chain. Others address partnerships resulting in joint ventures or those between companies working together to provide customers with complete solutions.

For example, providers of game consoles are interested in partnerships with manufacturers of games, or computer manufacturers are interested in partnerships with independent software vendors (ISVs). They not only endorse your product, but also create actual demand with customers. A computer without software running on it would be as useless as a game console not supported by any games – regardless of how powerful the hardware may be.

11.   ALLIANCES MEDIA ALERTS/PRESS RELEASES

You may want to agree with other players in the market on standards. Ideally, those standards incorporate components that you have already introduced to the market. An alliance of vendors endorsing these standards including your company's contribution is obviously helpful to your company's reputation. Examples include agreements on hardware or software standards in the IT industry, environmental standards, interfaces between components, quality standards, standard parameters describing the cost of bank loans, and so on.

Other alliances include, for example, airline alliances or alliances of companies in the same industry to leverage resources or share results benefiting both companies. They could, for example, share an IT service centre, or even more if they are not directly competing (for example, they operate in different geographies).

12.   APPLICATION ARTICLES

User stories are some of the most effective PR stories. Journalists and the public are typically more interested in the actual use of products than in the products themselves. In the 1990s, there was a strong trend away from product articles towards applications articles. This is particularly true for the lifestyle press, where the product itself is almost irrelevant nowadays. What counts is style, design, value for life, or maybe a celebrity endorsement, making it an icon consumers want to have.

But even when you don't have a (famous) user referencing your solution, you can communicate similar news to the public describing unusual or surprising applications. You may want to discuss technology enabling entire airports to run flawlessly or printing solutions that allow museums to provide print-on-demand solutions of their masterpieces for visitors or industrial solutions allowing manufacturers of popular consumer products to produce these items. In the latter case – selling some manufacturing devices for the factory floor – you may even benefit from the brand recognition of that popular brand that uses your devices.

13.   SPECIFIC TECHNICAL ARTICLES ON TECHNOLOGY COMPONENTS

Similar to those articles discussed in the item on technical feature articles above, you may want to release more details of the technology you are using in your products at a time when you have reached the 'midlife crisis' of your product. Once you have reached maximum sales activity you want to keep sales at this high level for as long as possible (depending on competitive pressure and new product generations).

14.   MEDIA ALERTS ON PRODUCT ENHANCEMENTS

Towards the end of the lifetime of your product, support it with some final 'kickers' or enhancements. Maybe you have to do so, since the next-generation product is not yet ready and you need to bridge the gap or to provide support to retail selling their stocks.

You may have introduced a revised set of components that you want to draw attention to. There are many examples in the computer industry of this approach: the introduction of a faster processor, more memory or a better CD or DVD player. In the car industry it could be an enhanced engine, an improved safety package – or bundling a component to the base product that was an extra at an additional price on a previous occasion.

Media alerts on product enhancements are a common practice and an appropriate and inexpensive tool to get the news out to the public.

15.   SALES MILESTONES MEDIA ALERTS

'Ten million customers can't be wrong...' This is exactly what you want your potential new customers to think!

You have several options when announcing sales milestones. You can issue media alerts. But you can also escalate this all the way to a giant celebration with major events, advertising and raffle prizes for the public. If appropriate, you can also use a sales milestone to position your offering as superior to the competition. Maybe you want to reiterate market leadership.

There is one challenge with celebrating sales milestones. In accordance with its definition, it requires a look back into history. You will provide a reminder of the first units to leave the factory some time ago and you will probably share anecdotes from the past.

A significant sales milestone may also justify a press conference. But if you decide to do so, you need to make sure that your message contains a strong forward-looking component.

16.   CUSTOMER INSTALLATIONS/CASE STUDY STORIES

As already briefly discussed in the item on application articles, an external reference for your products or services is one of the strongest messages for the press and your target audience.

On the commercial side, a customer who is willing to share publicly his or her experiences of a product installation with your company is such a strong message that you do not need to actively 'sell' to the press, but you should expect a 'pull'. The best you can hope for is a customer who is willing to give press representatives access to their site and especially a customer who is willing to discuss financial aspects of the deal. The business press is always very interested to understand the overall cost of an installation and the return on the investment.

On the consumer side, the situation is more challenging. Take cookery ingredients, for example. There is not necessarily a story on the return on the investment in buying yeast or spices. But you may want to invite your customers to contribute their favourite recipes to your company in view of publishing a cookbook based on their inputs. You can then publicize the release of the book with a strong PR campaign.

Other PR tools

In the following, we look into a few more options we have in our PR toolbox. They are not necessarily linked to the life cycle of a product, but may be executed at any time. Actually, they may not be related to a product announcement at all.

INTERVIEWS

An interview is in fact the most effective PR tool! It requires skilled spokespeople who are ready to dedicate time to the activity. But the outcome of an interview normally justifies the investment. The journalist has received exclusive information and almost certainly will write a story about what he or she has heard.

Interviews can be carried out in many formats. They can be done face-to-face, or on the phone. They can be done almost anywhere: at your company's site, the journalist's office, at a trade show or at a press conference. They can be done during a stopover at an airport or during a joint dinner. Note that the schedule of a press conference should always leave time for interviews.

FACTORY TOURS

If your company has an open-door policy, you may want to invite journalists to your company's manufacturing site, the laboratories or the R&D department to demonstrate your leading-edge technology or the complexity of the process, which may not be visible in the end product.

When you allow those visits by technical journalists, you need to ensure that your open-door policy is consistent. You need to provide the journalists access to your engineers and at least to the department heads. The event could be extremely counter-productive if you limit access to specialists, but only communicate with the press through marketing managers. By issuing an invitation to a factory tour you set the expectation to get information directly from 'the horse's mouth'.

You need to select a factory tour carefully, though! It may be the appropriate solution if the trip supports the message you want to disclose. There is a danger as well, however, if it does not support your main message. In that case the impression of your factory facility may be distractive or it may even overshadow the topic of the press conference, in which case the coverage resulting from the activity may not have the focus you intended.

BY-LINED ARTICLES OR OPINION PIECES

By-lined articles and opinion pieces are typically written in the name of a specific executive. You can consider them to be long answers to a question that has not been asked, but are either expected if the journalist had an interview with the executive, or they cover a topic proactively on which your company has a strong opinion. If journalists consider your standpoint to be interesting to their readers, they may cut and paste it into their publication. They can make it look similar to an interview they had with the executive, or their comments on it.

ADVERTORIAL OR JOINT PROGRAMMES

As the word 'advertorial' signifies, we enter the grey world in between PR and advertising.[9] Advertorials are an appropriate tool in which to deliver information to your customers. However, it is important to avoid crossing the line and pay for PR, that is, pay a journalist or a publication for an article that you contributed, but which is disguised as an independent text.

An advertorial could be the result of a joint programme with the publishing house. Assume your company and the publishing house jointly run a readers' competition. This could be a photo competition, if your company sells solutions for photographers. This could also be an award scheme, for example you want to identify the best innovation in the industry or the most successful CEO over the past 12 months. The text in the magazine of your publishing partner would be clearly recognizable as contributions from your company.

You could also embrace sponsorships under the umbrella of advertorials. For example, you may want to sponsor a certain section in the publication such as a user club in a magazine or a special series on TV.

An advertorial could also be any text delivered by your company, but it will always be declared as text delivered by your company; they are not disguised as editorial content of the respective publication.[10]

So, what is the difference between an advertisement and an advertorial? An advertorial is much more factual than an advertisement, and it is typically tailored to the specific magazine in which it appears. In fact, advertorials normally appear exclusively in individual magazines only. Advertorials are often text-only rather than containing pictures or other images which you normally see in advertising.

PRODUCT TEST UNIT PROGRAMMES

A test unit programme addresses the needs of journalists who evaluate products. You provide test units typically very early in the life cycle of the product, potentially even before it is publicly available. The journalist can then test the product and write a report on it.

In the IT industry, the automotive industry and most consumer industries, providing test units is a very common practice. You can expect products that have a significant financial impact on the customer to be primary targets for reviews. Customers do not want to run the risk of making a wrong decision. They want an independent opinion not only based on theoretical comparison with other products or services, but also based on practical use. They want to know, for example, if a professional driver considers the performance of the car to be safe or if the value of the car justifies the price.

SPONSORSHIPS, LEVERAGE FROM SPONSORSHIPS AND PHILANTHROPY PROGRAMMES

Sponsorships are a very common practice in PR. They can range from sponsoring local schools or communities all the way to multi-million dollar sports sponsorships. You can support the arts or sciences or you can help underprivileged children to receive a proper education. The number of ways to get attention in the press through sponsorships is endless.

---

9   Advertorial is a mix of advertising and editorial.
10   This also applies to opinion pieces (see previous section). If they are indeed cut and pasted into a magazine, editors often separate them out into separate boxes clearly marking them as an unedited contribution direct from a vendor.

The actual sponsorship you select – if any – is dependent on the objective of your company. You may want to focus on generic brand recognition, or you may want to reach your target audience and be identified as a company sharing their values and ambitions.

Sponsorships of sport teams may not only be executed to make your company logo visible, but also as a hospitality opportunity (see below).

Companies tend to take very different approaches to sponsorships. Some include them directly into their PR activities; some manage them outside the actual PR teams. It is probably fair to say that consumer companies have a stronger tendency to drive a sponsorship just like any other PR activity. It is mainly a tool to reach the masses. Companies addressing commercial customers often tend to use sponsorships to provide a hospitality environment for their customers or business partners. In that case the sponsorship may be driven by other entities than the PR department – if company processes allow, they may even be driven by the sales department.

Leveraging from sponsorships for PR purposes should be reasonable. Assume you run an IT company, and you decide to sponsor a school or a university. Just sponsoring equipment to be used in the classrooms may not be worth the effort of writing a press release. But if you equip the classroom with a unique (new) IT solution that elevates the educational process to another level, then this may be an interesting PR story that deserves some publicity.

Philanthropy programmes may include supporting local communities, public projects, museums, research, health or educational organizations, or others. A PR programme leveraging from such a project may be appropriate in some cases. In some other cases, though, you need to ensure that 'advertising' your good deed is not in conflict with basic ethical considerations.

HOSPITALITY PROGRAMME

If your company is actively involved in certain sponsorship activities or has partnerships with certain institutions, then you may want to invite journalists (or analysts) to events related to those sponsorships.

Typical examples include visits to games (football, baseball, basketball, and so on) or other sports events (such as motor races, athletics). But you can also invite journalists to exhibitions or music events that you sponsor. The events should be considered as a backdrop to an informal meeting. You do not really want to disclose news at these events; the main purpose is to develop a closer relationship between executives and influential and senior journalists.

WORD OF MOUTH

In the past ten years or so, word-of-mouth tactics became popular for the promotion of selected products or services. Learning about products from friends solves two problems for consumers right away: they can be sure the product is good, because they can trust their friends, and knowledge about the product or service makes them a member of an elite group of people, so they will feel special. This, in return, will stimulate their willingness to share the interesting news with others; in this way the news continues to spread.

PR tools per product category life cycle[11]

The curves describing the product life cycle and the product category life cycle look very much the same. Yet they should not be mixed up since they describe fundamentally different facts.

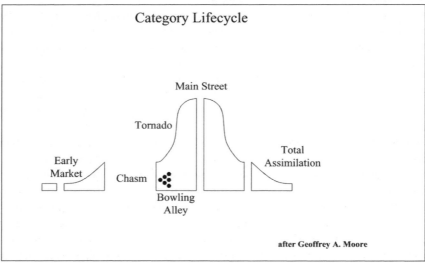

Figure 2.2   Product category life cycle

One product category may be record players. We have seen record players coming and going in the past century. Today it is in its end stage ('total assimilation') replaced by the category CD player. This category may be broken down into several individual categories of products that had interrupted the market (such as the move from mono to stereo), but for simplicity's sake we will ignore these details. It remains important to note that the category was alive for a considerably long time frame, while the products within that category had significantly shorter product life cycles. Also, not every single product needs to go through the entire category life cycle (but through its individual product life cycle). A product intended for main street replacing an earlier version will immediately start on main street and probably also be taken off the market when the category is still on main street. Only products that interrupt the market will have to start again in the early market phase.

A product category life cycle can be broken down into six stages that require very distinct behaviour by the vendor. The stages require different go-to-market approaches and a different communication approach. PR plays an important role in four of them. We will discuss all six stages here briefly.

EARLY MARKET

During the early market phase your products will attract customers who are referred to as early adopters. They are fascinated by the technology and will want to buy a product to explore it and test it out. They are driven by features, not benefits. They do not need references and are not discouraged by complexity. Often enough, the complexity of the product is actually one of the criteria when choosing it.

---

11   This section is based on discussions with Michael T. Eckhardt, Director, Market Strategy Consulting, EVEREST Advisory Group.

PR plays an important role in this early stage. It is actually much more important than advertising. You may even want to build your communication strategy on a word-of-mouth campaign at this stage.

PR can make a strong contribution to communications in the early market stage. Press conferences to trade press (or speciality press for insiders) and making test products available to the trade press can be strong components of a PR campaign at this stage. In addition, the communication of technology white papers or technology backgrounders will be very attractive to your audience.

CHASM

During the chasm phase you prepare for focused communication to the identified target markets that you want to address as first 'bowling pins' in the bowling-alley phase. You may want to identify ambassadors or advocates for your products and work with influencers in the particular industry or market segment. Influencers could be industry analysts, celebrities, university professors, selected media or others.

During this stage you also tailor your message to the selected market. Replace features with benefits. Sign up partners that add value to the selected segment and develop PR campaigns around complete solutions. These solutions must be specific to the selected market.

BOWLING ALLEY

In the bowling alley you execute a very focused PR programme on a selected market segment. You target specific media that are relevant to the selected segment. In other words, you go specifically for the press that is read, for example, by the manager of CAD departments in the automotive industry instead of generic IT publications. Or you address specifically the media addressing young parents instead of generic consumer press.

It is important to address the whole story when you are in the bowling alley. You want to offer a complete solution, potentially the complete value chain. Partners complementing your product may be necessary in this phase. These could be other manufacturers similar to your own company adding their products to yours, or value added resellers (VARs) knowing the addressed market. They may not only help in the presales activities, but also during installation and support.

TORNADO

The tornado phase is not really a domain for PR. During the tornado phase, the communication mix should be dominated by advertising. The whole intention during this roughly two- to four-year phase should be to keep things simple for the customer. Less is more. Complexity of the product and in the product's messages is counterproductive. Things should be kept simple – without 'dumbing down', however.

MAIN STREET

On main street, PR again contributes significantly. You deliver a consistent message over time focusing on the benefits for the customers. In comparison to the early market phase, you need to segment your customers and deliver messages per segment. This means that you may not want to run large press conferences, where 'one size fits all', but smaller events addressing the media per segment.

TOTAL ASSIMILATION

In this phase, there is no longer any justification to invest in PR. You may instead focus on other areas where the return on investment (ROI) is more appropriate.

PR tools as perceived by journalists[12]

In 2003, a survey was carried out with almost 100 journalists in Europe following the IT industry. The journalists represented both trade press (about 75 per cent) and business press (about 25 per cent).

The survey was based on a questionnaire and face-to-face interviews with journalists who attended press conferences of Hewlett-Packard in Europe. The actual focus of the research was on cultural influences on PR in Europe. But one specific question of the questionnaire was dedicated to PR tools.

The journalists were asked 'Which public relations tools do you find most useful for which announcement?' They were given the option to select one or more options given to them:

- international press event
- local press event
- online press conference
- one-to-one interview
- press releases
- web news room.

	International Press Event	Local Press Event	Online Press Conference	1:1 Interview	Press Release	Web News Room
Strategy Announcement	65%	35%		30%	35%	
Significant Product Launch	61%	61%			49%	30%
Industry Partnership Announcement		33%			58%	26%

Figure 2.3   PR tools by announcement type, per review with journalists

12   The results presented in this section are based on the Diploma Thesis of Bettina Schoeppe (Fachhochschule Aalen, 2003), in cooperation with Hewlett-Packard GmbH, Germany. More details of that survey are discussed in Appendix B.

The journalists were also allowed to tick the box 'can't judge', but this option was hardly used.

A graphical display of the results is given in Figure 2.3.

The findings can be summarized in the following three statements:

- Strategic announcements should primarily be announced at international press conferences.
- Significant product launches can be carried out either at local or at international press conferences – or covered with a press release only.
- Industry partnerships should be covered in press releases – or at a local press conference, if a press conference is considered at all by the vendor.

Interestingly, more than three-quarters of the interviewees did not consider an online press conference to be an option replacing a face-to-face press conference.

For vendors, the findings mean that local press conferences should focus on product launches and less strategic announcements, while international press events should focus on strategic announcements including significant product launches. Or, in other words, international press conferences should be reserved for significant news only.

3 *Types of Press Conferences*

In the previous chapter we have shown that a press conference is not the only tool in our PR armoury. Often there are good reasons not to use a press conference to make an announcement. But there are also good reasons from time to time to make a major announcement at a press conference. Let's examine the list of key reasons why you should hold a press event.

In our everyday life we all have important events when our friends and family get together. It can be our birthdays, Christmas parties and New Year celebrations, graduation from university or weddings. We do not invite people too often, otherwise it may become boring. And we do not invite people for little things but for bigger occasions. A similar approach can be taken in our business. We create the following list by 'translating' the above examples into business terms:

- *Product/services portfolio announcement.* We have talked already about new products announcements. A significant change in your product or service portfolio, which impacts your market and the competition, can be a good reason for a press conference.
- *Financial results of the company, earnings announcement.* Companies very often announce their financial results to journalists – either because they are obliged to share their results with the public, or because they follow a tradition of success with the public. They normally issue a press release and often also invite journalists to a press conference. These press conferences are more often held for annual results announcements but they can also be done on a quarterly basis.
- *Major partnership or company acquisition.* Nowadays industry partnerships and acquisitions happen more and more often. The acquisition of companies by others and major alliances of companies influence the competitive market landscape. These types of announcements are often done as joint press conferences where all parties present together and are open for questions from journalists.
- *New company strategy announcement or strategy changes.* This announcement sometimes happens when, for example, a new CEO of a company is appointed. A strategy announcement is also appropriate when a company (with the same management) decides to change the company business focus or to increase its presence in a particular market segment.
- *Opening of new facilities.* Your company opens a new production facility. You announce the new plant or factory together with a good story about new business opportunities arising from the extended production facilities and new jobs in the region. You may also want to invite the press directly to the production facility, which may leave a positive impression on your journalists since, as the proverb says: 'A picture says more than a thousand words'.

Criteria defining a press conference

One press conference is never identical to another one. All press conferences are unique. Press conferences can indeed be *very* different. And in fact they have to be. If all press conferences were following the same scheme, then the element of creativity would be missing. But this is exactly what is needed at a successful event. You need to catch your audience by surprise. You need to deliver the content in a way that it is well remembered. You need to ensure that your main messages are picked up. Different agendas, different communication tools, different effects, different speakers and many other parameters help to create a memorable event with memorable messages.

Nevertheless, press conferences can be segmented into several categories that embrace common features. For example, we would argue that all press conferences disclosing a company's financial results are somewhat similar. They cannot be compared with press conferences of football coaches after games, which again are all somewhat similar.

Press conferences can indeed be sorted according to several parameters. In this chapter, we will have a closer look at the various types of press conferences. We also come to some conclusions about what to do differently for each type of press conference.

Here are some criteria that define a press conference:

- demand
- objective
- content
- size
- geography
- infrastructure.

We will discuss these parameters in turn. Still, we should not forget that there are more criteria that could be mentioned here, such as style, audience, industry, available budget and length of the event.

It is obvious that many of these criteria are not independent, but interlinked. In Figure 3.1, some of the interdependencies are shown for the parameters defining a press conference.

DEMAND

Who drives the transfer of information?

We typically have two scenarios: either there is a strong public interest in receiving information, or information is actively pushed onto the public from an individual, a group of people or an organization.

In several areas, the public has an interest in learning about something. One of the most obvious areas is politics. As a citizen, you have a strong interest to learn about political decisions since they can affect your life directly. This could be introductions of new laws, changes of tax policies or any other announcements. It is particularly important for you, since you base your vote at the next election on receiving this kind of information.

At the same time, however, it should be noted that all politicians have an interest in creating visibility for themselves by packaging information according to their own agendas. So, even though there is a strong demand by the public to receive information, it may not be delivered in a single press conference by a politician. You may need to listen to all parties

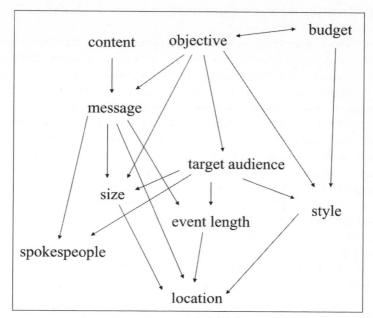

Figure 3.1   Interdependencies of parameters defining a press
conference (Example: the size of an event depends on the
message, the objective and the target audience)

involved to obtain a complete picture. Joint press conferences with representatives from all
political camps are very rare. An example may be representatives of employers and trade
unions announcing the results of salary negotiations.

Other areas with a strong public interest driving announcements and press conferences
include sports and cultural disciplines.

The public has a strong interest in learning the latest and greatest from their stars,
regardless if that celebrity is a Formula 1 driver, a rock musician or an actor. The fans want
to learn everything about their stars, the latest gossip, news about upcoming projects, and so
on. The demand for new information often meets the stars' need to create more publicity for
themselves.[1]

Press conferences especially with artists reveal very quickly where the initial demand
actually came from. If celebrities have a prepared presentation that takes up a considerable
amount of time, you can assume that the driver was actually them – or their manager or
record label – trying to generate some publicity for the star. If the celebrity primarily reacts to
questions from media representatives, then the driver was mainly the public, represented by
a journalist.

The typical situation in sports is the regular press conference with either an individual or a
team at a major event. For example, the public is interested in knowing every detail about their
football stars during a World Cup. And often even a daily press conference is not sufficient to
fill the papers or the TV programmes. These press conferences are typically brought down to

---

1   The fact that some stars consciously decide to stay away from the public eye and not be available for press
conferences or interviews does not contradict the need for a celebrity to stay in the limelight from time to time. If the
public interest is indeed high enough, then this behaviour is a proven tactic to create even more awareness and ultimately
create even more demand for being present at press conferences or in interviews. Or their unavailability itself is already
sufficient to get the publicity they want.

only minimum news being disclosed in a prepared speech. Most of the time is dedicated to a lengthy question and answer session.

In this context, we need to remember that good news is no news. Far too often, the public interest is triggered by the search for some bad news. This could be the suspicion that an athlete took steroids or a celebrity took drugs or a company was manipulating its financial statements or a politician was bribed. It could be anything that requires a PR department to initiate a crisis communication process. We do not want to discuss crisis PR in this book. It is a topic of its own that already fills dozens of dedicated books. We just want to stress the fact that in some cases it is not at all appropriate to initiate a press conference in a crisis situation. In some other cases, however, it is highly appropriate to go on the offensive and proactively hold a press conference disclosing news in favour of your case.

Commercial press conferences are typically on the other side of the spectrum, that is, they are triggered by the respective corporations and not by the public. Journalists have probably ten to a hundred times more information from vendors on new strategies or new products than their publications can swallow. There is an information overload and it is up to the vendors to stimulate and drive the communication.

The interest of the public, however, can drive the need for a commercial press conference as well. In that case, the PR machinery of that respective vendor has probably done a very good job in 'wetting people's appetite'. Especially in the area of consumer goods, it can happen that the public is interested in learning more about an upcoming product.[2] Maybe conscious leaks generated that interest – and then the excitement is kept high by only revealing bits at a time. Best examples are probably the way electronic games are often launched to the public. Market leaders can afford to leak information about their new upcoming games months in advance. Lifestyle gadgets such as mobile phones with ever-increasing functionalities or new movies with ever improving special effects can also be introduced in the same way.

Companies selling commercial products also have an audience that pays very close attention to their announcements. It may not primarily be the introduction of new products that drives their interest. It could be the investment community that demands regular earnings and strategy announcements to the media, especially from companies that are listed on the stock exchange for whom regular announcements are even mandatory.

OBJECTIVE

Your decision to run a press conference may be driven by one or many objectives. These objectives drive more or less all parameters of the press conference, such as target audience, involved executives, venue, style, and so on. And ultimately, they drive the budget.

Before we look into typical objectives, we list some of the most common ones: education, information, awareness creation, relationship building.

For a commercial vendor, the most common scenario is to bring new products or services to the market. Their objective is clearly driven by making the products known to the public to create awareness and demand for them. Please note that the tactics used to achieve this goal could be very different.

Another objective could be to educate the public. Public institutions may want to provide information about health dangers with the aim of reducing smoking, avoiding drinking and driving, endorsing the wearing of safety belts, and so on.

---

2   If your PR machinery is indeed very powerful, then 'it can happen' should instead read 'interest has been generated'. You are not in the role of a reactive organization, but you operate actively and generate demand for information.

Commercial companies may do similar activities; however, there is a commercial intention behind their running press conferences on topics like the above. They may want to stimulate the demand for substitutes for cigarettes, or to sell soft drinks instead of alcohol, or to sell their cars featuring the latest generation of safety belts.

Commercial companies may also execute press conferences focusing on trends in the industry – and then of course position themselves not only as thought leaders, but also as organizations that are well prepared for those trends. For example, if you run a TV service that sells movies on demand, then you may want to educate the public on potential cost advantages over buying or renting movies.

It is obvious that a press conference introducing new products and a press conference focusing on a market topic will differ significantly. Product news should primarily interest your respective trade press; market news may be more appealing to the business press.

But even press conferences on new products that may be considered to be straightforward with clear objectives can differ significantly, since your objectives may still differ. For example, your primary objective may initially be to create awareness for your new products or services. They may be so innovative that you cannot expect to generate demand right away, but you initiate a PR campaign with a press conference that clearly is focused on generating awareness. Only in a second wave is your objective based on generating demand and directly impacting short-term sales, if that is possible.

CONTENT

Several of the parameters we describe in this chapter are not independent. The content that you want to disclose to the public, for example, cannot be independent of the objective. For example, we assume that you work for a company with a diversified product portfolio. You want to introduce a new product, which is a milestone in the respective target market. But since the market opportunity is comparatively small for your company, it will have no significant impact, neither on your company's top line nor on your company's profit.

In this example, you have a message that is product driven. You can make it a straightforward product launch targeting the respective trade press. This approach would be fairly tactical. It would be appropriate if your objective is simply to create awareness for your new product.

You can also take a different approach and embed the product launch into a more generic message targeting the respective market. The objective for this approach would be to position your company as a thought leader in the respective industry. For example, you may want to talk about a paradigm shift in this market, which is either caused by your new product, or it is a change that you anticipated and which you are now well positioned for with your new product. In that case you may be able to address a different audience with your message.

However, since the financial impact on your company is only minimal, you will probably not be able to position the product launch as a milestone in your company's progress. In particular, it will probably be a long stretch to make this a strong story for the business press.

The above example shows that a given content can be embedded into different messages that would support different objectives. The different objectives would then define and target different media and necessitate different approaches from the press conference. A straightforward product launch, for example, would address the technology and product features. You would also talk about how the product would meet customers' needs. You may want to run respective breakout sessions addressing these topics. If you take a more generic approach, however, you may want to consider bringing in external specialists who can talk about market trends and position your company appropriately. It is always best to hear such a story from an independent capacity in the industry, such as an industry analyst. After the analyst has set the scene, you can then do your product introduction, positioning it accordingly.

The above example also shows that a given content does not allow you to 'bend' your message in any direction you want. If you push it too far, then you will not come across as very trustworthy.

We should look at another example as well:

Let us assume your company delivers products and services both for consumers and for businesses. You come to realize that bringing a consumer product to the market is very different to bringing a B2B product or solution to the market. Your target audiences are different, the messages are different, there will be a strong impact on the style of the event, and even the size of the event may be impacted. Finally, you may need to position different executives depending on your message.

To compare two very different audiences, let us look into running an event addressing business press versus running a press conference for consumer/lifestyle press. In fact, the first question you should ask yourself is if you want to run a press conference for the business press in the first place, or if you want to address them individually. But you should also make sure that your content is tailored accordingly. For the business press you need to address financial aspects, projections of your business and, for example, your go-to-market model. The lifestyle press, on the other hand, would not care for these items at all. They want to know what the benefit of the new product would be for their readers and they want to experience the use of the new product.

SIZE

Size matters!

Once you have decided to deliver your content via a press conference (and not by using another PR tool), you need to ask yourself the question, *how* you want to do this, since you have several options. One of the parameters that defines the size of a press conference is the amount of available budget. But this is not the only aspect that needs to be factored in.

You need to make a conscious decision how many journalists you want to reach with your press conference. If the number is too small, then you should reconsider your decision to run a press conference. Spending a lot of money on a press conference for only a small number of journalists may not be justified. The cost per participant may be significantly too high.

On the other hand, you should not run an event with too many participants either – unless you have a sufficient number of hosts looking after the journalists. Even with an unlimited budget, you should not go for too big an event, since one of the important aspects of a press conference would be violated. You want a press conference to be personal. You do not want to lose contact with the journalist, but to use the event for relationship building.

One reason for running a big event with many participants, however, is to disclose your news to a large audience and to leave a strong impression with that audience. It is impressive for a journalist to see how many colleagues you were able to mobilize. Making a significant impact by running a large event could even be a self-fulfilling prophecy. However, you should not do this at the price of risking a good relationship.

You may consider taking the best of both worlds and leverage the set-up of the press conference for several smaller events, one after the other. One way of doing this is to invite a certain set of journalists to the first day, maybe the trade press. On the second day you invite the lifestyle press. This even allows you to tailor the content for the different audiences.

You may also split the audience according to geographical aspects (see also below). If you want to disclose information on Europe, you may want to run a central press conference somewhere in Europe with Western Europe participating on the first day and Central and Eastern European journalists attending on the second day. Again, this segmentation of the audience would allow you to tailor your message.[3]

Be aware of one very important prerequisite if running press conferences in sequential order: You should only run multiple events if the embargo date (see also Chapter 6) of the news is set in a way that no group of journalists has an advantage over the others. In other words, if the group on the second day receives information that has already been published by the first group, then we predict that you will have a significant issue with the second group, who will feel that their time has been wasted in attending a press conference where information is disclosed that is no longer news.

Events running one after the other only make sense if the embargo date is still in the future (so all journalists can publish simultaneously), or if the information is not time critical.

A second option when running multiple press conferences is to avoid a central event, but run events per country in parallel, for example – assuming you represent a company with an international presence. The advantage of this approach would be lower costs, since you would not have to cover expensive flights for the participants. The obvious advantages, however, are the fact that you can address the audience in their local language (no translation service required) and you can host more journalists than you ever could in one central event. Also, you can give your news a local spin. You can, for example, put the announcement into a local context. Overall, relationship building between yourself, representatives from your company and your journalists would benefit from local events.

A disadvantage, however, is the fact that local events are typically scaled-down events, that is, you would not be able to leave a strong impression like you could with a central event. Also, you would not be able to reach high-level executives with international responsibility at all locations at the same time. Nor could you have guest speakers at every location similar to what you would be able to offer at a central event. Again, this may impact the perception of the audience.

	central (international) press conference	local press conferences
pros	• impact (impression, hype) • applicable for higher level messages • suitable for strategy announcement • high-level speakers/executives • aligned with embargo date	• less cost • event in local language • message tailored to local needs • more interaction with individual journalist, more personalized • ability to adapt to local legal requirements
cons	• higher cost • language barriers • news may be different per country • news may be of different significance per country	• time/resource-consuming • limited availability of high-level international spokespeople

Figure 3.2   Local versus central (international) press conferences

3   One potential scenario could be that you introduce products that are addressing a mature market in Western Europe, but the market for these products in Central and Eastern Europe is only developing. In that case your messaging should be different for the two respective press conferences. The event addressing the East may require some educational components that would be irrelevant at the event addressing the West.

It becomes obvious that the content and the message you want to share with your audience drives the decision to execute a central event or to have smaller local events happening per country. If you want to stress your commitment to a certain topic, or if you want to announce a major breakthrough for your company and the industry, then you should run a central event. The same is true for relationship building with senior media representatives like, for example, editors-in-chief. You may want them to spend time with your senior executives at central events.

Normal 'ongoing PR', such as standard product introductions, is, however, probably better addressed in local press conferences.[4]

GEOGRAPHY

We have already discussed several issues related to geographical aspects. We have seen that there may be advantages for or against local or international press conferences. We will now delve a bit further into this issue.

In fact, geographical aspects can even have fundamental influences on the communication strategy itself. A decision for or against holding a press conference could be taken differently from country to country. For example, a press conference may be justified in larger countries, but due to lack of critical mass you may prefer individual interviews with leading publications in smaller countries. Also, the content of your announcement may be particularly important in some countries, but irrelevant in others.

As always, your message drives almost all decisions related to the press conference you will run. Geographical decisions are no exception.

There are some obvious reasons for local events like, for example, a strong requirement to localize the content delivered at the press conference. Unlike hardware products, services typically have a strong local component. Different local requirements or different legal environments may require localization or customization to a degree that makes a centralized event not really an option at all. But even product introductions may be different from country to country. For example, they may only happen in certain countries initially. Your company may have decided to test a product in a few countries only before rolling it out across the globe. In that case you need to ensure that you do not set false expectations by running an international event – or if you do so, you need to state clearly where your announcement is valid.

But there are other criteria that help define the type of press conference in relation to geographical aspects. We already mentioned the available budget. But we also need to mention aspects like suitability for the message or suitability for the target audience.

If, for example, you want to stress your company's heritage and its long and stable existence, you may consider running the event at a location linked to the history of your company.

If you want to introduce a new fashion collection, then you may have no option but to run your event in places like Milan or Paris – unless you consciously want to be different.

Another example of the message influencing the location: if your company faces challenging times, you should hold a press conference in a modest venue. Using an expensive place will make everybody immediately understand why your company is in financial trouble!

Geographical aspects with regard to venue selection are also covered in Chapter 12.

---

4   See also the section 'PR tools as perceived by journalists' in Chapter 2.

INFRASTRUCTURE

There is a common perception that a press conference always has to happen face-to-face.

This is incorrect.

The majority of press conferences indeed happen in the old-fashioned way with all attendees gathering in one location, with presentations, a Q&A session, interviews, and so on. However, more and more press conferences happen on a 'virtual' basis nowadays. Attendees no longer meet physically, but are connected via phone conferences or web-based broadcasts.

The advantages are obvious: less time out of the office and more flexibility for the journalists (they can connect to or disconnect from the conference at any time).

The advantages for the presenters are as obvious: less cost and less travel time for the executives.

However, the disadvantages should be looked at as well. The 'human factor' is removed from the equation. You no longer interact – if interaction is planned for at all – with humans in the same way, but you have a device in between that makes the exercise very anonymous. Even though you should still offer a Q&A session, that interaction is no longer as intensive as a face-to-face discussion. You would still hear a question and be able to respond to it, but you would not be able to see the face of the person asking, nor would you be able to see his or her body language.

Our own opinion is that a lot of what is intended with a press conference is indeed lost with a webcast or a phone conference. And it is interesting to see that journalists vote in the same way. According to a survey in 2003,[5] only 3 per cent of them consider an online press conference to be appropriate for a strategic announcement (9 per cent found it acceptable for a significant product launch, 11 per cent would consider it for the announcement of an industry partnership).

A more detailed discussion on online press conferences can be found in Appendix F.

---

5   Bettina Schoeppe, Diploma Thesis, 2003 (for details see Bibliography).

4 *PR Plan*

The basis for all further work on a press conference is in the PR plan. The PR plan contains all the information required to plan and execute the event. The PR plan, however, should not only be written as a document for the PR community; it should also be used in a similar way to a contract or a service level agreement (SLA). All stakeholders in the PR work should have access to the document and, if appropriate – depending on reporting lines and lines of accountability in the company – sign or approve it.

Writing a PR plan is sometimes an art in itself. We have seen documents declared as PR plans that were actually project plans or loose descriptions of vague intentions.

There are certain rules that should be taken into account when writing a PR plan for a press conference. The first question you should actually ask yourself is whether the term 'press conference PR plan' is actually appropriate. The term could indeed be questioned, since a PR plan should in fact be the result of a business and a marketing plan. And a press conference should not really be the topic of a PR plan, but a tactic developed from a PR plan and supporting an objective outlined in a PR plan.

A proper PR plan should address a certain time window, for example one calendar year. However, the term 'PR plan' is often also used for a specific campaign, which is embedded into a time window. Since a press conference is a special form of a PR campaign, the term 'press conference PR plan' is in fact a common term.

Coming back to the rules that should be taken into account, the first very important rule ensures that this specific PR plan does not stand alone. It depends on the overall objectives, that is, on the overall PR plan that has been written for your business for the specific time window you are operating in.

Rule 1: The press conference (project) PR plan is embedded into the overall PR plan for the business.

A first significant portion of the press conference PR plan should therefore be dedicated to setting the scene within the given framework. This 'introduction' to the plan should certainly contain the following topics:

- business objectives
- marketing objectives
- PR objectives
- messages
- situation analysis (potentially including SWOT analysis)
- challenges
- metrics.

Within this framework, you can develop the parameters of your project, namely, the press conference. In this context, the press conference is indeed a media tactic, which requires you to address the following topics:

- time
- location
- target audience
- audience expectation
- spokespeople
- objective/intent (specifically for the press conference)
- message (specifically for the press conference)
- set-up
- agenda proposal
- PR team
- roles and responsibilities
- budget
- measurement (in line with overall metrics).

In the following we will go through the individual items – and also develop a sample plan. Before we do so, however, we would like to return to the basic rules that you need to take into account when developing a PR plan.

Rule 2: The results of the project described in the PR plan must be measurable.

If there is no measure, then there is no accountability. Note that not only must you define goals that you want to reach with the press conference, but also they must be measurable and they must be relevant. And they must be realistic, that is, achievable.

This final request is based on reality. Especially in times of tight budgets it is often remembered that PR can actually be a comparatively inexpensive tool compared to some other communication tools, in particular compared to advertising. In those cases, it is very tempting for marketing managers to try to cover all kinds of communication objectives with 'cheap PR'. It is important to understand then what PR can do and what the limitations of PR are.

We would question a goal like 'as a result of the press conference we will sell 50 per cent more product units compared to a scenario where we run no press conference'. This measure has a nice business angle to it. But it is not useful for two reasons:

- The goal cannot be measured, since you do not know how many units you would have sold without a press conference.
- Even if you knew how many units you would have sold without a press conference, it is not useful, since you would still not know how many units you would sell as a result of having run the press conference. Customer behaviour is influenced by many parameters. A press article is only one of them. Others include, for example, advertising or point-of-sales activities. Typically it is a major challenge, if not impossible, to single out the influence of PR on customers' buying behaviour.[1]

---

1   You may want to run a dedicated market research project to test the customer reaction to an article. Such research is typically very costly. It may not provide an appropriate return on investment. And it typically does not provide a full answer to the question asked.

But not only is measurability important; relevancy is too. We would argue that a goal like '50 journalists must attend' is not relevant at all, since we may reach the wrong ones and we would still not know if they have written anything (positive) about the content delivered at the conference. A goal like '50 positive articles are written as a result of the press conference' is more like it as long as you have defined the target press in parallel.

A final third rule addresses the completeness of the plan.

Rule 3: The PR plan contains all parameters to ensure approval by stakeholders.

The PR plan should not refer to other documents that may not be available to the stakeholders. The main reason is that these other documents may be so-called 'living documents' that change over time. This would mean that these other documents would contain different data at the time the plan is approved and at the time the press conference is executed or evaluated.

Typical examples that could cause confusion include:

• Marketing messages can change over time. For example, competitive pressure requires your company to change the messaging. Document clearly what the initial plan was, so you can adapt as needed and communicate changes clearly to all involved parties.
• The available budget is not spelled out in specific enough terms, but the PR plan refers to an external document defining budgets. These may be subject to change (reallocations, budget cuts, budget transfers, and so on). As a result, you may all of a sudden have less money available for your event than initially planned. These surprises can be avoided when you work within defined absolute amounts set out in your plan and allocated for your project.
• The methodology of your media analysis changes. Make sure that your metrics remain relevant in such a changed scenario. The above goal to generate 50 positive articles would be okay. A relative goal like 'we increase coverage by 20 per cent' could cause some concern, for example when the base of your media analysis all of a sudden changes because you amend the reading list.
• Ensure that the document defines roles and responsibilities clearly. You want to avoid redundant work and you certainly want to avoid gaps.

Introduction of the PR plan

The introduction of the PR plan should embed the project into the overall business and marketing plans; it ensures that the press conference is consistent with the overall planning and does not appear as a stand-alone project.

Not all plans need to be 'cut and pasted' into the PR plan. It is sufficient to list the business and marketing objectives. From the overall PR plan again you pick the PR objectives you have defined for the current time window.

Since you may not be at the beginning of the time window addressed by the PR plan, you may have more information now than what was available at the time when you wrote the generic (annual) PR plan. Maybe you have already observed reactions to earlier PR projects, or you have information on competitive moves. It is therefore very useful to include a situation analysis into the introduction of the PR plan.

For completeness sake, you should also include in your introduction your generic messaging framework. Note that your press conference message may not be identical to those overall messages, but it certainly must be consistent with the overall framework. This means you may want to address a subset of the overall messages, or you address a tailored version of the messaging for a selected market segment, an industry or a selected geographical region.

A situation analysis can be carried out using a description of recent observations of developments and trends. A standard would be to make use of a so-called SWOT analysis (see Figure 4.1). In a SWOT analysis you list strengths, weaknesses, opportunities and threats for your business – from a PR point of view.

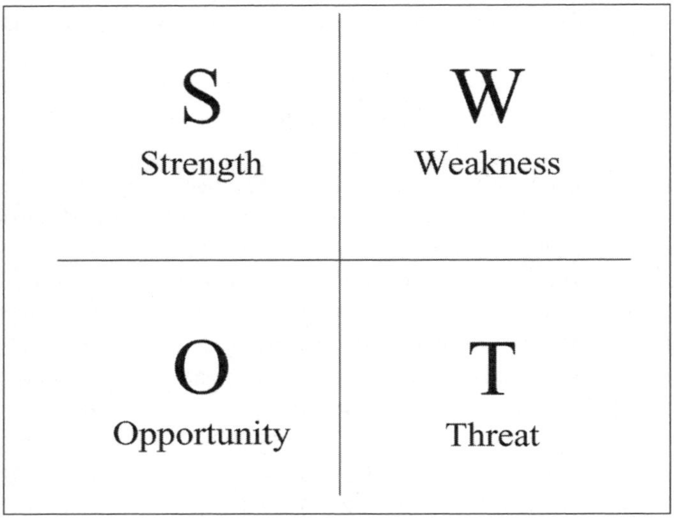

Figure 4.1   SWOT analysis

Strengths could, for example, include product differentiators or strong business partnerships. Weaknesses could again be related to the products or include potential delivery problems or a lack of brand recognition. Opportunities could be related to weak competitors or growing markets. And, finally, threats could, for example, be caused by anticipated moves by competitors, an anticipated decrease in profit margins or even an unstable political situation.

Articulating all these facts at least once typically helps tremendously in the planning of your PR activities in general, and specifically your upcoming press conferences.[2]

In the list above we also referred to 'challenges' to be included in the introduction of the press conference PR plan. You may ask the question what is the difference between objectives and challenges. Here is an example:

In your annual PR plan your defined objective is to grow your presence in the business media. You have discovered earlier in the year that you struggle to achieve that goal; although your company seems to have good product messages, there is no compelling news to get you a foot in the door of business publications. You want to stress this fact in your press conference

---

2   You may need this documentation for your PR agency briefing.

plan since it is an important input for your content providers, in case your press conference is supposed to address business press journalists.

Your overall metrics should be listed here as well. You may not want to go into every little detail at this point. It should be sufficient to reiterate your business fundamentals in PR in this section. But it is vital to translate these business fundamentals or long-term goals into measurable objectives for the press conference (see below).

The core of the PR plan

The time of your proposed press conference should already be assigned. Maybe you already know the exact date (for example, if it is a worldwide launch date that you need to comply with or if it has been assigned by a business partner) or you know it falls within a narrow time window, such as a specific week.

The location is most likely 'to be assigned'. In fact, part of the later process will be to assign a location and a venue. Only in some selected cases will the location already be decided upon at the time when the PR plan is put together. An example may be that it is your explicit objective to bring the journalists to your R&D facility. In that case the location would obviously be specified up front. Likewise, the location would be specified up front if you wanted to demonstrate a specific customer installation on-site.

Your target audience must be listed in the plan. You need to define the audience very well. Something like '25 journalists' would be completely insufficient. Not only do you need to define the media type (for example, photo trade press or channel press), but also you need to specify the individuals you want to attend the press conference. You may want to specifically address editors-in-chief or you may want IT editors of business publications to attend. You may want to issue non-transferable invitations to individuals.[3] You must also define the region the journalists should address. You may only want to address developing countries in Africa or selected Western European countries or maybe just those countries that recently joined the European Union. Nothing is worse than delivering news to an audience for whom it is irrelevant.

You should know the expectations of the target audience – and you should document them for your content providers and for your spokespeople. The audience may have very specific needs that you will have to address. Also, they may have certain concerns that you want to share with your content providers and with your spokespeople immediately, so that you can plan proactively how to address them.

The spokespeople themselves should be listed in the press conference PR plan as well – or rather the proposed spokespeople. You should leave room for changes at this point in time. Your spokespeople may change depending on availability or on final content.

Even though the content may still change over time, the overall message of the event should be defined in the PR plan right away, as it is closely aligned with the objective and the intent of the press conference. These items basically define the justification for running a press

---

3   Example: You develop a press conference for senior editors-in-chief. You specifically invite those individuals to the event. You certainly want to avoid your invitation being passed on to another member of the publication's staff. And in fact, there are several reasons for that. The most obvious one is that the content you put together is not appropriate for a regular staff journalist. The not so obvious reason is that you do not want senior editors to feel misled if they attend an event with too many junior journalists attending on behalf of their invited editors-in-chief. They would question why they came. They may even question the strategic importance of your news.

conference in the first place (rather than making use of another PR tool). If you start to change them, you may actually remove the justification for running the press conference itself.[4]

The PR plan for the press conference should also include a proposal for the set-up (speeches, breakouts, roundtable discussions, interviews, and so on) and the agenda. That may still change slightly, but you need to set the expectation properly. A speaker at the main press conference, for example, would then understand clearly that his or her message is to be followed up by a breakout session. He or she would not need to go into all details of a certain topic but refer to the additional sessions for specialists who want to know more.

Finally, basics like the budget and the PR team are included – and roles and responsibilities defined across all involved entities (within the company and external resources such as subcontracting staff from a PR agency).

Typically you conclude the PR plan with the measures for the project which drive the behaviour of all involved individuals. As previously mentioned, these will be in line with the overall metrics; they should be measurable and relevant.

When setting out your objectives for a press conference a common practice is to define what are the intended headlines of articles published after the event. This approach has several advantages. It shows you if you got your content successfully across and it shows if the journalists actually understood your main messages. During the media analysis phase, this objective setting helps significantly (see the section 'Outgrowth level' in Chapter 28 Media analysis).

An example

We want to illustrate the above with an example that can be used as a template for your own press conference PR plan. We recommend you do not take all the content in this example literally. It is expected to be a trigger for your own thoughts, ideas and set-ups only. In addition, some parts may differ significantly from company to company in accordance with their internal processes and the industries in which they operate.

---

4   Example: We assume that your company's objective is to use the next product introduction to grab market share from your competitors. The plan is based on the assumption that you will be able to offer the lowest price of any vendor. The press conference therefore is based on a messaging framework that is focused on affordability and price. As you get closer to the intended launch date, your company realizes that the margin on the product does not allow you to offer the aggressive price point you intended. Consequently, you change the messaging of the intended press conference. It would now be based on a product feature or a customer benefit. This change obviously does not support the overall marketing objectives. As a result, the press conference should no longer go ahead, since the news value has decreased significantly. The new product may still be an excellent product that will be successful in the market. But it would no longer support the main promotional message. It may be more appropriate to spend the money that was planned for the press conference on a different PR activity.

NEW PC INTRODUCTION – EUROPEAN PRESS CONFERENCE PR PLAN

Time:
Week 1 November 2004 (most likely 2 November to avoid European holidays and to be in line with product availability in stores).

Location:
To be assigned (an option is Helsinki to stress the mobile components in the product, since Finland is seen as the centre of mobile communication).

Target audience:
50 IT trade press journalists. Focus on product reviewers. Journalists must come from the 12 Western European countries where the product will become available.

Audience expectation:
After recent introductions from competitors, journalists expect a PC with a built-in wireless Internet access. They also expect us to share observed trends in mobile technologies. In particular, they want to learn about our own technology.

Spokespeople:
European product manager and technical engineers. Proposal: Keynote from John Smith, Product Marketing Manager, EMEA.

Objective:
1.   Position our technology as superior to that of the competition. Especially, our technology is more powerful and offers a stronger growth path.
2.   Introduce John Smith to the public and position him as a thought leader in PC wireless technology.

Message:
The XYZ technology is scalable and grows with consumers' demands.

Set-up:
One-day event with a 60-minute press conference, roundtable discussions with John Smith on trends in wireless technologies and 1:1 interview opportunities with technical engineers on product features.

Agenda:
Journalists arrive until 10:30am. Press conference at 11am followed by lunch. Two roundtable discussions with John Smith (1-2pm, 2-3pm), interviews with engineers running in parallel from 1 to 3pm. Return to airport at 3pm.
Optional: Extend agenda to include dinner and one-night accommodation.

PR team:
Overall lead: Joe Miller
Event management: Julia Kwan
PR support: PR agency *Convincing*
Logistics: to be defined – per request for proposal

Roles and responsibilities:
Overall project owner: Joe Miller
Content providers: Product marketing, business intelligence
PR collateral development, speech writing, press kit: *Convincing*
Logistics: Julia Kwan
Invitation process and hosting: Country PR managers

Budget:
$150k (to cover all costs)

Measure:
- One article written per participant.
- All articles are rated either neutral or positive per our current rating scheme.
- Expected headline 1: 'Company ABC shakes up the market'
- Expected headline 2: 'These products are a safe investment for customers'

2 Basics and Processes

5 *Planning*

The PR manager who operates as the project manager for a press conference must follow a clear timetable to have all contributing factors for a successful press conference in place at the right time. In this chapter we will discuss timelines and dependencies of various tasks that define or strongly influence when you will have to do what.

But before we dive into the timing aspects of conference management, we should look first at the best timing for the event itself. We have seen in the previous chapter that not all dates are equally appropriate. You certainly want to avoid holiday seasons and vacation times. You also want to avoid competing with other activities addressing the same audience (such as trade shows, industry conferences, other vendors' major announcements).

Planning of major press conferences must happen well in advance. Now, the term 'well in advance' depends significantly on the content and type of the announcement. We should have a closer look at a few examples:

- You run an annual press conference with a defined set of journalists. This annual meeting is not driven by a specific announcement on the day, but it is more an annual business update. You may want to link this, for example, to your annual earnings announcement. You may also do regular events like this per season or per 'window'. Fashion designers, for example, have their shows twice a year, that is, they operate with two windows per year. As a vendor of consumer goods that go through regular update phases, you may also want to do two such events per year, one focusing on the news for the spring window (Christmas/January to summer break), and a second one focusing on the news for the autumn window (summer break/'back to school' until Christmas).
- You launch a new product. New products do not 'appear' overnight. Your company's R&D department has probably spent months or years on the products. So, you should have plenty of time to plan the announcement scenario and in particular the press conference introducing the new product to the media – if you believe a press conference is the right tool to introduce the product (see Chapter 2). Experience shows that a lead time of three to six months should allow for sufficient time to set up a successful press conference.
- Press conferences as a reaction to external triggers may need to happen with significantly less notice. Here the lead time may only be a week or two. The disadvantage is that in this scenario you are in reactive mode. The advantage[1] typically is that there is a demand from the public to listen to you. Thus, you should not need to run a lengthy invitation process convincing journalists to attend your conference; journalists are already waiting for you to invite them.
- Business news may require very short lead times as well. A typical example is the announcement of an intended merger between two companies. Due to the sensitivity of

---

1   It is probably needless to say that such an advantage can easily become a disadvantage, especially at times when no news is good news and only bad news is news. In others words, the demand from the public is only there because they expect bad news from your press conference.

the matter, only a very few people are involved in the negotiations. And even though the corporate communications manager is potentially kept informed, you still may need to set up all the logistics around a press conference at very short notice. Maybe you are given days to schedule a press conference, maybe you are given only hours.

- We all know that in some cases press conferences take place only minutes after some special occasion. Examples include sports events, where an athlete or a coach is summarizing a game to the attending journalists, or in motor racing, where the winner is sharing his or her view of the race with the registered journalists. Others examples are in politics, where winners or losers of an election are attending press conferences very soon after the first polls are published on the night of the election.

It is important to note, however, that these examples describe a very special kind of press conference that can hardly be compared with press conferences driven by companies for commercial reasons. The objective behind these press conferences is very different from a product launch, for example. The driver for these press conferences is the public and the objective is to collect spontaneous and subjective feedback from public figures for a large audience.

And even though these press conferences happen right after an event, they are obviously planned well in advance. The entire infrastructure for these events is well set up in advance. A football stadium probably has a press centre, where these press conferences can be held. In politics, this prepared set-up would typically be a TV studio that is prepared to host not only initial interviews after an election but also entire press conferences for a larger audience.

We want to have a closer look now at the timescales for event management of a press conference. We will do this in two steps. The first will address smaller or local events; the second step will address larger or international press conferences.

Timescale for event management of a small or local press conference

The term 'local press conference' by definition means a smaller-scale event than an international press conference. The objective of a local event will obviously be to reach the local press and to deliver news related to local markets or country-specific news. Very often the presentations are done with local spokespeople and in the local language. The planned outcome of such activities will most likely be coverage in local media.[2]

We have already given some examples and discussed different triggers leading to press conferences. They indicate that we should be able to prepare a local event in a comparatively short timeframe.

Let's take the example of a product launch. Even in an international corporation where press releases covering product announcements are issued in many regions at the same time, the relevance of the announcement, and therefore the local press event dedicated to it, may be

---

2   Please note that this statement looks very innocent. Nevertheless, it can have major implications. Assume, for example, that you make a local announcement that is not valid outside a certain country or region. In our networked world, the news will still make it across borders. In order to avoid confusion outside the region you target with your announcement, you need to be very specific about your announcement. For example, you should declare very clearly that a new product or service is available in a certain country only; that way, you will avoid journalists from outside that country raising false expectations in their customers by writing about your news by copying from articles you generated at your press conference.

dependent on several local parameters. An obvious one is local product availability. Thus, even when you plan the product introduction well in advance, you may only want to start preparing the actual press event once you have confirmation of product or solution availability. This confirmation could come from your own manufacturing organization or from your partners; for example, those who supply your products to retail chains for customer availability or who provide solutions based on your product to end-users.[3]

Another example of a local press conference resulting in a shorter preparation lead-time may be the announcement of new board members or a special award received by your company. In other words, local news often requires a quicker reaction. As a result you have to be more flexible as a PR manager to make sure the news is still new and does not age because of long preparation time for the announcement.

It is also important to mention here that the preparation for a local press conference is normally not as complex as for an international press conference. The critical points for success in this case will be: good content and deliverables, well-organized logistics, well-selected spokespeople and – last but not least – availability of journalists to attend your event.[4]

There are factors that you can influence and factors you cannot influence. So, let's have a look at the preparation plan itself. The preparation plan can be used as a template for any local event. It may help not to get distracted by tactics, but to focus on content to be delivered at the event and on the relationship with the journalists (for example, track their confirmation and participation).

Below is an example of such a plan that is intended to help a PR manager in day-to-day business. The time 'T' in this plan is the actual launch date or event date (see also below in the next sub-chapter).

Timescale for event management of a large international press conference

In this sub-chapter, we will discuss the chronology of organizing an international press conference from the initial decision to run an event all the way to the execution of the event – and beyond. We will assume we are in a well-defined environment, that is, our own company drives the event. We do not need to react to external influences such as competitors' moves, accusations or other crises.

In an initial kick-off meeting, the decision is made to hold a press conference to support a product launch. All parties involved agree that an international press conference is the most effective way to support the product launch and it is agreed right away to hold the event in exactly four months. This date will be defined in accordance with the criteria discussed in the next chapter. It is common practice to look at the time remaining until the event itself just like aerospace agencies do. We do a countdown until lift-off, that is, press conference execution. In this case, the liftoff (that is, the press conference itself) is at the date T.

With four months remaining, we are now at 'T minus 4 months', or at about 'T minus 17 weeks'.

---

3   Examples are vendors of computer processors who are dependent on computer manufacturers integrating new chips into their computers or vendors of game consoles who are dependent on software companies supporting their latest games on a new console.
4   It may become a serious issue when you plan your local press conference to happen in only two weeks and find out only during the invitation process that most of your target media are already invited elsewhere or booked for this time and date.

Preparation Plan – PR Timeline:

Tasks	Owner	Deadline	Status
Confirm spokespersons		T – 3 weeks	
Confirm budget		T – 3 weeks	
Confirm all the parties including partners and so on		T – 3 weeks	
Event location/logistics to be confirmed		T – 3 weeks	
Communicate with partners		T – 3 weeks	
Press presentation		T – 2 weeks	
Talking points, press releases		T – 2 weeks	
Customer quotes identified for press releases		T – 2 weeks	
Invitations to partners		T – 2 weeks	
Invitations to press		T – 1–2 weeks	
Draft releases from partners		T – 1 week	
Technical requirements check		T – 2 weeks	
Giveaways production		2 weeks	
Q&A		2 weeks before	
Partner demos lists		1 week before	
Third parties confirmation		T – 3 days before event	
Press participants secured		During 3 days before event	
Press kit CDs and package for press		T – 3 days	
Pre-event briefing with spokespeople		T – 1 day	
Post-event debriefing		T + 1 day after event	
Launch coverage summary		T + 1 week after event	

We now need to carry out several tasks in the right order to allow later steps to build on earlier activities and to take into account certain dependencies.

Examples: You do not want to define the event venue before you have defined which regions you want to address, that is, what countries you want to address with your message. You do not want to define spokespeople before you have defined the objectives and target audience.

Many of the basic parameters have to be defined very early in the process, in fact in the very beginning. All these basic parameters are defined in the PR plan for this project, that is, the press conference. We describe the PR plan itself in Chapter 4. As to timing, we need to remember that the PR plan has to be developed before anything else is started.

The following list should be considered a guideline for creating your own planning table rather than being a complete planning table itself. Specific needs are different from event to event, from company to company, from industry to industry, from region to region. Still, this list covers the tasks that should be generic for all press conferences. It should therefore serve as a template for your own plan. Feel free to make adjustments to suit your own needs.

PLANNING TABLE FOR A PRESS CONFERENCE T – 17 weeks:
PR plan is developed and approved by all stakeholders.

T – 16 weeks:
Event agencies are briefed to start a venue search.
PR agency is briefed on plan and objectives. Content creation is started.
Time of selected spokespeople is blocked.

T – 15 weeks:
Product organization delivers detailed information on the product.
Production agency receives a first briefing.

T – 14 weeks:
Event agencies pitch the results of their venue searches.
Best proposal is selected.
PR collateral development starts.

T – 13 weeks:
Preview trip (with events and production agency) to the selected venue.
Venue is confirmed.

T – 12 weeks:
Production agency to submit first creative ideas.

T – 11 weeks:
Spokespeople are confirmed.
Speech writing starts.

T – 10 weeks:
Contribution from production agency is approved.

T – 9 weeks:
Final messaging is approved.
Final event branding is approved.

T – 6 weeks:
Invitations are sent out.
Registration website goes live.

T – 4 weeks:
First draft of all PR collateral.

T – 3 weeks:
Speeches are shared with spokespeople.
Follow up with journalists who have not responded to the invitations.

T – 2 weeks:
First rehearsal with spokespeople.
Tuning of speeches.
PR collateral is final.
Press kit development starts.

T – 1 week:
Second rehearsal with spokespeople.

T:
Press conference execution
Internal newsletter to employees about event

T + 1 week:
First wrap-up report of the event based on initial feedback.

T + 6 weeks:
Final event summary incl. coverage report and media analysis.

The above timetable is a good start to keeping control of your progress. However, for larger events it cannot replace a more sophisticated project plan that you will want to keep updated on a PC.

There are several good project management tools available on the market. You may be obliged to follow your company's policies when selecting such a tool. But if you decide to purchase one by yourself, pay attention to some features that you will find useful. The tool should be flexible enough to introduce changes at any time. It should provide a good graphical interface and graphical presentation of the tasks. You will find this helpful if you need to report progress to your management. Also, the tool should make interdependencies visible.

Finally, the achieved progress should be visible in the tool. You should be able to see immediately if some sub-tasks are not on time. You should then be able to see immediately the impact on other tasks. For example, if your online registration website is not available yet, you do not want to point journalists to that site in an invitation letter. If it is foreseeable that the problem can be fixed within a short timeframe, you will then want to delay sending out the invitations accordingly.

When you start planning in greater detail, you will find it extremely helpful to see dependencies. If you run into issues, you will be able to troubleshoot very quickly and identify the missing link almost immediately.

A very simple example is given in the Figure 5.1.

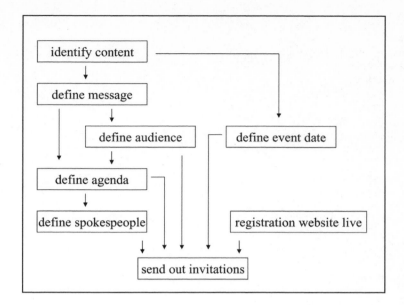

Figure 5.1   Simple example of interdependencies of project tasks

In Chapters 6 to 12 we will take a slightly more sophisticated approach to planning and break down the tasks into smaller sub-tasks. This becomes important as soon as you are embedded into a major organization with a large number of entities or even organizations involved. It also becomes very relevant as soon as you need to delegate more and more tasks to support staff and/or external agencies.

6 *Embargo Date*

In this chapter we want to find out how to define the best date for running a press conference.

Depending on country and industry characteristics, certain days of the week may not be appropriate for running a press conference. Mondays or Fridays[1] may not be appropriate, since the journalists either have to work on the backlog that has piled up over the weekend, or they want to leave early for the weekend. So-called 'bridge days' between a weekend and a holiday are certainly inappropriate, since many people take that day off for a long weekend. Also, some days during a week may not be ideal, since they are the deadlines or sign-off days for next week's editions. The same is true for monthly publications that often have their deadlines and editorial conferences on certain days. You need to take into account that the journalists will almost certainly prioritize these internal activities over your press conference.

Tuesdays or Thursdays have proven to be the best bet for running a central event on a pan-European or EMEA (Europe, Middle East, Africa) level. For international press conferences you also need to take into account local holidays in those countries that you expect representatives to come from.[2]

You also need to consider industry events, trade shows or other vendors' events targeting the same journalists. All these activities may overshadow your planned event.

In addition to these logistical aspects you also need to take into account when you actually want the news to appear in the media. You will have to make a decision at some point in time about the so-called embargo date.

The embargo date of your news is one of the most important criteria to define the date of your press conference. The embargo date defines the time when your information can be communicated to the public.

The embargo date is not necessarily the date when the information is shared with the journalist, but it is the time when they can write about it! Mostly, though, the date of the press conference is chosen in a way that journalists can write about the news immediately after they have received it and left the conference room.

But there may also be good reasons to share information with journalists prior to the actual embargo date. In fact, there may be quite a few reasons for taking this approach. We will discuss these reasons later in this chapter.[3]

---

1   Fridays do sometimes work for smaller local events, if you plan one of the main objectives of the event to be relationship building. In that case you may plan an entertainment programme for the participants which calls for them to stay until later in the evening.
2   Often enough this is a painful exercise since countries across EMEA tend to have a significant number of national holidays that are different from country to country. You sometimes need to make tough decisions about the date of your press conference that put some countries at a disadvantage, if their journalists are expected to travel on a holiday.
3   It is obvious that sharing information with the media only after the embargo date is not a good idea at all. In that case you may find strange scenarios such as products already being publicly advertised, but journalists not knowing about them. Or, products appear on your price list visible to everybody, but journalists do not know about them. In simple terms, news is no longer news if disclosed too late. And if it is no longer news, the press is no longer interested.

Considerations to be taken into account

It is the embargo date that defines the date of the press conference and not the other way round! But what criteria define the fixing of the embargo date?

The embargo date is driven by the objectives your company has chosen to achieve with the announcement. Typical criteria include:

- If your announcement is related to a product launch, then the availability of the product plays an important role. If you make information available too early to the public, then you may hurt your current sales. Customers would no longer buy your current products, but would wait for the next generation, which may offer new features, or simply be less expensive. If you make information available to the public too late, then press coverage of the launch will be too late.
- There is a strong dependency on the purchase behaviour of your customers. If the decision cycle to buy a product is long, then you can announce the information significantly before product availability to the public. Expensive commercial products require several approvals within the buying company. Depending on the value of the purchase, they may require the approval not only of the purchasing department and the functional department, but also of high-level management – potentially up to the CEO – and of the financial department. In these cases you want your customers to have early notice of your product, so they can make a purchase request in good time. If the decision cycle is short, as it is for most consumer products, then you should have an embargo date which is closely aligned with retail availability of the product. When consumers read about a product in the media, they want to go out and buy it straight away.
- The embargo date is also dependent on competitive moves. You may be forced by your competitors to launch earlier than initially planned. You may have to follow an aggressive move from another vendor very quickly in order to keep sales up, to maintain market share or to prevent a competitor breaking into one of your domains. On the other hand, a lack of competitive moves may also allow you to wait a bit longer than initially planned and continue to focus on current products. On a different note, your market research department may have picked up signals that a competitor is planning a significant move. You may or may not want to pre-empt that move by bringing your own embargo date forward.
- You may want to align your embargo date with industry events such as major conferences or trade shows. The advantage of making a significant announcement at a trade show, for example, is that you have a large audience at the event. Journalists are attending and covering trade shows anyway. You do not need to invite them to your own event. You should save quite a bit of money that way. The disadvantage of making an announcement at a trade show is that you compete for the journalists' attention against all other vendors who think like you and make major announcements at the same trade show.

    But you should carefully evaluate when you need to communicate to journalists in order to get your news integrated into coverage from that show. For larger trade shows, the respective trade publications publish special editions, or they dedicate a special section to the show in an edition. Be aware that these special editions or the special coverage are typically already published in advance of the show itself. So your embargo date needs to be compliant with the needs of these publications.

On the other hand, you may want to go out with breaking news at the trade show itself. The closing of a significant deal, for example, may be timed for the show itself. Immediate coverage in daily newspapers will then potentially drive visitors to your stand.

The important thing to remember about making announcements at industry events is that it is a double-edged sword. You have a large audience at the event, but you compete with a lot of other news items.

- Be aware of the lead times of your target publications. They may freeze the content of the next edition several weeks before the publication date. This lead time defines when you need to share the information with the journalists. The publication date has a strong influence on the embargo date. For example, if you focus your message on monthly trade publications that are available in the kiosks at the end of a month, then you should go with an embargo date timed at the end of a month. If you go only a few days later, you miss an entire month – and your announcement may already be old by the time of the next edition, because it will have been covered in dailies and weeklies.

  But let us reiterate that this does not mean that you run the press conference only at the end of that particular month. You need to run it before the final editorial conference. As mentioned above, this is typically towards the middle of the previous month; for the consumer lifestyle press it is often significantly earlier than that. So, if you expect the content freeze of your target publications around the 15th of a month, you want to run your conference maybe a week or at least a few days prior to that.

- When determining an embargo date, you also need to pay attention to seasonal aspects. In Europe, for example, you do not want to make announcements during the summer vacation period, since your target audience will spend time at the beach and publications may not even appear. Several publications, for example, merge their July and August editions into a single one. This means that you may reach neither the press nor their readers if you time your announcement badly.

- Larger corporations, especially, often face the challenge that they need to coordinate their outbound communication across the entire company. They must avoid competing events from separate branches in the company happening in parallel. It would be embarrassing to learn that a journalist had been invited to two events from your company at the same time. Proper coordination of PR in these corporations would not only avoid these situations, but also increase efficiency and even effectiveness. A single company message supported by all entities would be significantly more powerful than several minor messages per division.

Precise timing

Since the introduction of the Internet and the availability of online publications, announcements made somewhere on the planet become available almost anywhere almost instantaneously. It may no longer be sufficient to define just a day for the embargo date; unless you consciously want to give one region an advantage over others, you may need to give a precise time, so no region can pre-empt another one.

Here is an example: You may want to announce your financial results immediately after the stock exchange closes. If your company is registered at the NYSE (New York Stock Exchange), then you have a defined time based on the American Eastern time zone. Journalists around the globe can pick up the information at exactly the same time. So, European publications will cover the news the following morning.

Geographical aspects

An obvious challenge with the worldwide news network is that even information that is irrelevant to some regions makes it into that territory. You must therefore specify clearly where your announcement is valid. Otherwise you will have a confused press – and a confused customer.

If the geographical validity of your announcement is not specified clearly, you can even confuse your channel partners. Suppose that your products or services are different from region to region, but you do not mention that fact in your announcement; the channel press would then provide incorrect guidance to their readers in some of the regions.

Strategy announcements also need to be well defined, since you may run different strategies in different regions. Suppose that you want to address one market directly with your own sales force, but you want to operate with channel partners in another region; not making yourself clear could result in an upset channel in one region (where you left them with the incorrect understanding that you do not need them anymore) or in retailers approaching you in another region (where you may not want them).

One interesting geographical aspect in the context of timing a press conference is local customs. For example, you may not want to run events on certain days of the week, as we saw earlier in this chapter. But even the time of the day when you want to run your event may vary from country to country. In some countries it is preferable to run an event in the morning; in others it is more appropriate in the afternoon. And even an event starting in the evening is possible in some countries.[4]

Sharing information prior to the embargo date

In the introduction to this chapter we made the comment that there may be good reasons for sharing information with the journalists before the embargo date, sometimes well before.

At first sight, this statement seems to contradict the request to share with the press only news that they can immediately exploit, that is, write about. In fact, we have even seen cases in real life where journalists consciously decide not to participate in a non-disclosure presentation since they believe that they should focus only on news they can write about right away.

Nevertheless, a vendor may want to share information, under a non-disclosure agreement (NDA), with selected journalists way before the embargo date. We shall look at several scenarios that explain the advantages for the vendor, that is, the company that runs the press conference:

- Product reviewers typically work against a long-lead schedule. They typically define months in advance when they want to publish tests and on what product categories. An audio/video publication, for example, may want to publish the results of product tests of camcorders in January. In February, they may want to focus on TV screens, in March on DVD players, in April on MP3 players, and so on.

  Assume you are the market leader in MP3 players, but your new product will only become available in July. You would not be able to give the publication a test unit in time for their April issue. You would clearly miss out – unless you got the publication involved

---

4   Several years back, for example, one of us attended a local event in Greece that did not start until 8pm local time.

early enough to potentially even influence their schedule. If you told them, for example, in December of the previous year that they should be prepared for a major innovation in MP3 players to come in July, they may update their schedule accordingly. Your position as market leader may have enough weight to make them change their plans. It should be noted that this strategy may not work if your company is not well recognized in the industry.

- We have already seen above that we need to take into account the lead times of publications. Some parts of the lifestyle press are known for notoriously long lead times. They freeze the content of upcoming issues way in advance.

  In order to get coverage in these publications, you must share the news early, that is, way before the embargo date. If you decide to do so, you need to take two considerations into account. Firstly, you should provide the information under an NDA. Secondly, you may need to follow a special process with these publications: You may want to disclose your news to different types of publications. A single press conference may not be the most suitable approach in this case, since lead times may be significantly different. The lifestyle press may want to know the information two months in advance, but daily newspapers should only receive the information briefly before the embargo date (since they would not store the information over such a long time and thus would not cover it at all then). So, you may need to run two separate activities for the two distinct media types.

- In some cases it is common practice to give individual publications special treatment. Typical targets for such treatment are publications that are particularly important for your business. The special treatment could be an exclusive interview. It could also be early access to information (under NDA, though). You should expect special coverage from the privileged publication. Assume the following scenario: You run a press conference late in the day (maybe to be in line with a worldwide launch process). It would be too late for the daily newspapers to get the story into their morning editions. However, you disclose the information to one publication two hours earlier; this publication would then run the story exclusively in the morning. The others would only be able to follow 24 hours later.

  It should be noted that this strategy should be well thought through in advance! In some cases it is not an issue at all in the press community to take this approach. It could work, for example, if the privileged publication has a certain leadership in the media anyway that is not questioned by other publications. It could also happen, though, that while you make one friend in the media, you have the entire rest of the media landscape against you as a result of your tiered media approach.

7 *Invitation and Registration*

The invitation to a press conference is dependent on the type of event.

If the event is not by invitation only, a generic media alert should be sent out to the media. Examples for 'public' press conferences include presentations in webcasts or telephone conference-based announcements. The most common one, however, is probably a press conference at a trade show or other public event.

A media alert must contain the following information:

- What is being announced? A brief abstract of the announcement needs to be delivered – obviously without giving the content itself away. You need to make recipients of your media alert understand that you will make an earnings announcement, and not a product launch, for example.
- Who is making the announcement? The speaker should be mentioned in the media alert. If the CEO of your company, for example, is personally involved, it gives the announcement special weight.
- When will the announcement happen? The exact date and time of the announcement need to be specified. If the announcement is an international or even worldwide one, then the time zone needs to be specified.
- Where will the announcement happen? If the press conference is going to happen at a trade show, then the location of the stand or the conference room needs to be specified. If the speech is webcast or phone-based, then the logistical details need to be provided, such as call-in numbers or URL and potential logon procedures.
- Finally, it should be specified whether the presentation will be recorded and replayed. If so, the access details (URL, for example) for future access should be communicated.

If the press conference is for selected journalists by invitation only, then the existing dialogue between the PR department and the respective journalists should be used to give early notification. This early notification should basically be a heads-up or time blocker in the journalists' calendar. The details should follow later in a formal invitation letter.

The most important task of the invitation letter is to explain why a journalist would want to attend the event. Again, an abstract of the announcement should be given and it should be explained who the journalist will be able to meet at the event.

Transferable and non-transferable invitations

Also, it should be explained whether the invitation is transferable. Since you may want to have certain individuals at the event, such as editors-in-chief or product reviewers – depending on the content of your announcement – you may not want to allow the invitation to be transferred to another individual.

You may argue that non-transferable invitations make no sense for press conferences. You should be delighted that a representative from a publication shows up at all. In the majority of the cases this is indeed a reasonable approach, especially for those press conferences that are only of a very tactical nature – like a normal NPI (new product introduction[1]).

However, you may also want to run special events from time to time that address very senior editors only. Your intention may be to focus on strategic content and you may want to run the event like a forum rather than a regular press conference. At these events, relationship building is one of the main objectives. You want your own senior staff to spend time and exchange opinions with equally senior editors or journalists.

Allowing the journalists to pass the invitation on to junior staff members would contradict the objective of the event. Not only would your own executives be disappointed (at least), but the journalists would also not benefit from the event. But potentially most damaging is the fact that the participating senior journalists would question why they are attending with so many junior people being around who are not able to contribute to the event. If you want to run a similar event again, those senior journalists may not want to come again, since they would actually feel misled.

Invitation

The invitation to a press conference should contain the same information as a media alert (see above):

1. What is being announced?
2. Who is making the announcement?
3. When will the announcement/press conference happen?
4. Where will the announcement/press conference happen?

In addition, it should contain logistical details:

1. Agenda
2. Interview opportunities
3. Contact details (typically the PR manager)
4. Request to respond within a given deadline
5. Travel details
6. Dress code (if needed).

The invitation can be sent out either in a traditional letter or via e-mail – depending on the journalist's preferred method of communication.

Joint press conferences

Special attention needs to be paid to the invitation process for press conferences that are held jointly by several companies or organizations. These press conferences typically address topics

---

1   A product launch is often referred to as a NPI (new product introduction).

such as business partnerships, upcoming acquisitions, joint ventures, industry standards and so on.

Regardless of whether one company has the lead or if all companies are equal, it is important to agree on a process to show to the press at the invitation stage that a true partnership exists between the various companies. It would not look good at all if a journalist got several invitations to the same event from multiple sources; and it would look even worse if they received different messages in the invitation (for example, different agendas).

The companies should agree on a common text that is used for the invitation.[2] The distribution lists should be cross-checked by all the PR departments involved and then it should be agreed that one PR department takes the lead, all departments send out invitations in parallel (avoiding to send more than one invitation per overlapping target), or the invitations go out from a 'neutral' PR agency working jointly for all parties involved. Any one of these options is possible. The choice of process typically depends on the nature of the announcement and the relationship between the companies or organizations involved in the press conference.

Examples:

- Several companies are members of an industry standards body. They want to make an announcement about a new standard that has been finalized. In that case, the standards body – as an independent organization – should take the lead and issue invitations to the press conference in the name of all members of the organization. In practice, the standards body may be a small institution without a PR department. In that case, you should try to pursue the idea of giving the PR job to an independent PR agency, to be guided by the standards body, rather than having one of the participating companies taking the lead, since they may all be competitors and it would simply be inappropriate to make one of them 'more equal than the others'.
- Two independent companies want to announce a joint venture. In that case, both companies should check the respective target lists and agree on an invitation text and should invite their respective media contacts in the name of both companies.
- If a company only supports another company's announcement with a customer reference, it should typically not be part of the invitation process at all since the content of the conference is addressing exclusively the media of the supported company.
- If several companies sponsor a sports event or a cultural event, the invitations to the press conference announcing the event need to be agreed upon by all parties. The target media of the involved parties do not often overlap in such a case.

FOLLOW-UP AND REGISTRATION

The PR department should personally follow up on an invitation within a few days. Journalists who confirm their participation should then get a confirmation with logistical details as quickly as possible after the discussion, either via e-mail or in a letter – whichever is the preferred method of communication of the particular journalist.

The confirmation letter should contain logistical details similar to those listed above for the media alert. If you are also responsible for the journalists' travel, you must include travel

---

2   The process should be similar to crafting a joint press release. A joint text is proposed by the lead PR team or agency, and then the text is required to be approved by all parties involved.

details. If you are asking them to make their own travel arrangements, you may want to include a map and directions with the letter.

Final registrations for large events such as international press conferences are nowadays typically done via the Internet.

Online registrations can either be done by the journalists or by the local PR manager who manages the relationship with the particular journalist. In order to reduce the journalists' workload it is recommended that all relevant information be collected and then entered on the registration website internally.

The registration website should request the following information:

• Name of the journalist
• Contact details including e-mail address and (mobile) phone number
• Name of the publication
• Name of the country of origin (needed if support for visas is required)
• Travel details (flight details, for example, so local transfers can be arranged)
• Dietary information
• Requests for 1:1 interviews
• Session requests, if the event set-up allows for personalized agendas.

The most important thing about a registration website, however, is make it as easy as possible for the journalist to register (or for the PR manager doing it on the journalist's behalf).

Upon completion, the journalist should receive a registration confirmation by e-mail. This confirmation should contain all relevant information needed in a single document.

Final follow-up

It is common practice to call the journalist up briefly before the event to ensure that no changes to their plans have occurred. The lead time would depend on the scope of the event. For international events requiring travel this may be up to a week before the event; for local events it may only be a day before the press conference.

It is recommended that you share your mobile phone number with the journalist so they can call you if last minute changes occur. The mobile phone number is also a safety net if problems arise, such as with the flight ticket or the pickup service at the airport.

Special considerations

In order to 'stimulate interest' in your announcement, you may want to add a teaser to your invitation letter. This could be particularly powerful if your press conference takes place at a public event such as a trade show. In a case like that you need to grab every opportunity to direct journalists' attention to your event, since you will most likely be competing with other press activities by other vendors, happening in parallel. Do not confuse 'teaser' with 'gift'. For example, a teaser could be anything from a bold controversial statement (if appropriate), a hint of a unique photo opportunity or a voucher for a special handout made available at the event.

If you issue invitations to an international press conference, you need to make sure you are informed about all visa requirements. You should already have considered this when you selected the venue (see also Chapter 12 on venue selection). But now, during the invitation process, you need to act accordingly and help your journalist to get his or her visa approved. In many cases an invitation letter from your company is required, issued in the country where your event is going to take place.

CHAPTER

8 *Format of a Press Event*

In this chapter we will discuss several 'ingredients' you may want to add to your press conference. We will start with a typical agenda and then have a look at the individual components in a bit more detail.

'Standard' agendas

A 'standard' press conference should provide time for a presentation and a lot of interaction. The interaction could be based on workshops, formal 1:1 interviews, social events such as a dinner, or on other formats.

Here is a typical agenda of a small local press conference launching a new product:

9:00	Registration
9:30	Press conference
10:15	Break
10:30	Product demonstrations and Q&A[1]
12:00	Lunch
13:30	Interviews
15:00	End

Another option would be:

16:00	Registration
16:30	Press conference
17:15	Break
17:30	Roundtable discussions
18:30	Cocktails
19:00	Dinner

(Although, for countries in southern Europe, this agenda would probably be moved back by two hours.)

In the above example, the press conference itself is planned to take 45 minutes. As a rule of thumb, a press conference should never last more than an hour and a half. The presentations should be as short as possible. If they are too long, then you have probably tried to squeeze too much content and too many details into them.

For larger events, the agenda can become pretty complicated with several activities going on in parallel. You typically need then to look at the agenda from two different angles. First of

---

1   Question and Answer. 'Q&A' describes an interactive session that allows journalists to put questions to the press conference spokespeople.

all, we have the agenda as seen by the organizer. This agenda would be the complete structure with all activities involved, even those running in parallel. The other way of looking at the agenda is through the eyes of a participant. This could be a spokesperson who contributes to parts of the agenda – but who also makes use of the 'free' time for other activities (either related to the event or not). This could also be a journalist who can only attend at a given time, and would need to look at a personalized agenda to see which of the parallel sessions it is possible to go to.

Figure 8.1 shows a press conference agenda as looked at by the three participants – staff, journalist and executive. In order to make it easy for one of the participants to find their way around, it is highly recommended to provide them with personalized agendas in print.

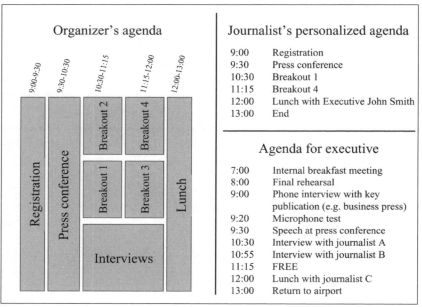

Figure 8.1   Sample press conference agenda

In this chapter we want to discuss the various parts of the press conference and the supporting breakout sessions and roundtable discussions.

The presentations in a press conference can be very different. You need to select the correct balance, depending on the content you want to disclose and depending on your objectives.

We would like to discuss five different presentation options:

1. Hosting presentation
2. Company presentation
3. Endorsement
4. Guest speaker
5. Panel discussion.

The presentations are complemented by the Q&A session that we will discuss separately later in this chapter.

Presentations

- *Hosting presentation.*The host of the press conference is not necessarily a representative from your company – even though this is typically the case. An international press conference may be hosted by the local General Manager of your company welcoming the audience in the name of the local company subsidiary. A smaller local press conference may be hosted by the main speaker him/herself.

    But, you should also consider from time to time inviting an external host for your press conference. This may be an artist or a celebrity, preferably an actor or other person who is used to speaking in public and to addressing larger audiences. It may be a radio commentator, a TV show host and so on.

- *Company presentation.*The 'company presentation' is delivered by one of your company's spokespeople. It will typically cover the main message of the event, that is, the news of the day.

    The company presentation is fully under your control. You can define exactly what is said in this presentation and what is not said.

- *Endorsement*. An endorsement can be delivered by several organizations or individuals. The most likely endorsement is a presentation from a customer who demonstrates how they have benefited from using your products, services or solutions.

    Another endorsement is from external independent sources such as industry analysts, university professors or other academic leaders, or other specialists, consultants or influencers.

    Note that hired celebrities would not be expected to deliver endorsements. It is too obvious that they were hired by your company. Their comments would not be considered to be independent. Still, they are very influential. You should just define very clearly how you want to make use of their power to influence.

    Do not consider using very influential editors or journalists to deliver endorsements. This would not be appropriate at all. Why should a journalist listen to another journalist? Would you want to listen to one of your competitors? There is only one exception to this rule: where the journalist is an icon in the industry, perhaps already retired or the head of a business publication speaking to trade press journalists. Such a person would not be competing with anybody in the audience.

    Note that you only have limited influence over what is said in the endorsement. And, most importantly, you do not want to have too much involvement in it anyway! If you try to guide the speaker too much, the presentation will come across as too cheesy. The audience will realize very quickly that the presentation is indeed controlled by your company. The speaker potentially only says what you want them to say, maybe because you are paying for the presentation. Be aware that if you are too involved, such a presentation will have the opposite effect of what you had intended.

- *Guest speaker*. It is sometimes appropriate to invite a guest speaker who does not contribute directly to the content of the press conference, but who delivers a presentation that is indirectly linked to it.

    Example:

    Your press conference is about change. You may introduce a new process that requires companies to change some of their business processes. For an event like this, you may want to introduce a retired politician who was famous for introducing change in society. We attended such an event in Germany once, where the German foreign minister who managed the change during the fall of the Berlin wall was invited after his retirement as a guest speaker. We attended another press conference once where an artist delivered a very creative presentation on colours – the event was focused on colour printing.

- *Panel discussion.* We consider a panel discussion to be very effective – if it is executed properly. If you have a good host for your event, that same person can also host the panel discussion. It becomes even more effective if the host is an external speaker, that is, not a member of your company.

  The host can liven the event up with controversial statements that challenge the speakers. But that means walking a fine line. Too aggressive, and the presenters from your company look defensive: too tame, and the speeches or responses look as though they were rehearsed. And they should not be rehearsed! Best practice is to loosely discuss a set of questions up front, but leave the order in which the questions may or may not be asked, and the context in which they are asked to the development of the panel discussion. It is obvious that the host of such an event must be very senior and very flexible to react to any developments during the discussion. This person always needs to ensure that the discussion is not 'derailed', but keeps a focus on the main messages of the press conference.

  A panel discussion can happen with members of your company, customers and industry experts. We once attended a press conference with several entrepreneurs supporting a vendor message during a panel discussion. It was so powerful to have all these different voices at the press conference that some journalists claimed afterwards that they would even have paid an entrance fee to attend the event and to listen to all the different opinions.

Q&A sessions

The initial press agendas introduced in this chapter do not provide time for question and answer (Q&A) sessions after the presentations in the press conference itself. The agenda still works, since there is a lot of time planned for interaction afterwards.

Still, it is recommended that you offer a Q&A session whenever possible. A typical scenario is a press conference in a central location with the audience coming from the same region. If they come, for example, from the same city then they may want to leave right away after the press conference itself. In that case they will not make use of interactive roundtable discussions or individual interviews. The only opportunity for them to interact with the presenters would be in a Q&A session. An agenda including a Q&A session may look like this:

9:00	Registration
9:30	Press conference
10:15	Q&A session
10:45	Break
11:00	Interviews
12:00	Lunch
13:00	End

Offering a Q&A session is also a sign of strength. You show that you are not afraid of aggressive or negative questions. You have nothing to hide; you are open to any kind of public discussion.

But you should not expect too much from a Q&A session. The nature of a Q&A session is that a question asked by a journalist is overheard by all other journalists. Thus, neither the question nor the answer to it is exclusive to the individual journalist. In fact, you may ask yourself why a journalist wants to ask a question in front of all his competitors, since he will have to share the response with everybody.

You will soon discover that the intention behind a question asked in a Q&A session is not always to get an answer to it. The intention could be very different: The journalists may want to make you aware of the fact that they are really interested in your news. You may discover in later discussions with them – that may have been stimulated by their questions – that they will try to convince you of the value of their magazines to your business. The spectrum of topics addressed by the journalists could range from simply trying to get access to exclusive information for their magazines all the way to trying to get your commitment to advertise in them.

You should take notes of all questions raised in a Q&A session. They can be very revealing. They could tell you something about how your competitors 'prepared' the journalists. They could tell you something about the attitude of the public towards your company or your products. They could also tell you something about the attitude of the individual journalist.

It should be stressed that journalists asking a question in a Q&A session are advertising themselves and their publication. One of the best examples was delivered to the public during the 'meet the press' sessions with the German football team during the 2004 European Cup in Portugal. Significant portions of these sessions were transmitted live by national TV stations. The PR manager of the team always clearly stated the journalist's name and publication before he allowed the question to be asked. This was free advertising for the publication to a large audience on nationwide TV – and it was used as advertising in a very blunt way to everybody watching.

Exclusivity – interviews and breakout sessions

By definition, a press conference is communication with a large audience. All attending journalists receive the same information, the same soundbites, the same spin on the content.

Journalists, on the other hand, are always looking for a unique piece of information that their reader, viewer or listener will receive only from them. This attitude is similar to every company's attempt to have a unique selling proposition to its customers. You want to be able to sell something that nobody else can offer. The same is true for journalists. They need to sell their magazine or promote their programme to a major TV or radio audience.

Your own goal to communicate your news to a large audience obviously conflicts with this goal of the media representatives to have exclusivity or at least parts of the story delivered in a special way.

Breakout sessions with smaller groups are a first approach to satisfying this need. When you run a large international press conference, you should select the participants in a breakout session so that there are only non-competing journalists in the same session. For example, you select journalists from different countries with a similar target audience and a similar focus of their publications to attend the same session. That way, information disclosed in the breakout session will be exclusive to the participants for their respective countries.[2]

---

2   If you run many breakout sessions at a major event, be sure that you always refer to the sessions in the same manner. Avoid even minor title changes, since they can be very confusing to the audience. Unfortunately, even at

The most common way of disclosing exclusive information is in interviews. Interviews could be set up in two different ways: they are either formally requested by a participant at the press conference, and as such are part of the formal event agenda, or they are conducted outside the formal agenda as special treatment for special publications.

Interviews 'outside the agenda' could be done with very influential publications that justify preferential treatment. Example: You introduce new products to your respective trade press at a press conference. This introduction also starts a new era for your company since it enters a new market. This would also be interesting news for the business press. Since you do not want to mix audiences at your press conference, you focus on the trade press, but you still offer selected business press journalists telephone-based interviews from the site of the event. This could, for example, happen shortly before you deliver the news during the presentation in the press conference.

Roundtable discussions

Breakout sessions allow people to delve deeper into details of selected topics of your announcement.

Roundtable discussions, though, should be as interactive as possible. Some spokespeople tend to misuse a roundtable discussion for yet another 'one-to-many' presentation. This cannot be the idea of a roundtable discussion.

It is recommended, though, that you have your company's spokesperson prepare a brief introduction to the roundtable discussion. It should last only a few minutes and it should ideally contain some controversial statements to provoke comments and to get the discussion started. The discussion should then be managed in such a way that all parties involved benefit from it. The journalists get additional background facts and opinions and your company gets an impression of what journalists are interested in and what their opinions are. In order to get to that point, though, your spokespeople also need to ask the appropriate questions from time to time, such as 'What market developments do you currently observe?' or 'What do you think about our strategy?' or 'What do you hear from your readers?'.

Do not forget that a press conference is a two-way street. Information is shared in both directions.[3]

Product demonstrations

Depending on your message and depending on your audience, it may be a good idea to allow the journalists first-hand experience of some of the content you want to communicate. There is a significant difference between talking about something and having your audience actually experience it.

The typical example is to invite a journalist to test out the new product you have just brought to market. This statement holds true for most consumer products. You will probably agree that there is a significant difference between talking about a new car and actually driving it. There is a difference between talking about a new easy-to-use computer interface and actually using it yourself. There is a significant difference between describing the taste

---

industry conferences this apparently minor requirement is not always adhered to.
3   See also the following chapter.

of a new chocolate bar and actually eating it yourself. All these examples show that allowing journalists to experience your product themselves makes a much stronger impact than just talking about it.

But again it is important not to misuse a product demonstration to deliver just another presentation which points to the new product from time to time. The key word here is 'experience'. The journalists really needs to experience themselves what you want to communicate to them. The most effective product demonstrations are not staged, but interactive – getting the journalists genuinely involved.

We know that a picture paints a thousand words. On that basis, a product experience (rather than a demonstration) says more than a thousand product pictures.

With many products the approach is more or less straightforward. If you manufacture cameras, for example, allow your journalists to take pictures and judge the quality of the images themselves. If you produce clothes, have your journalists compare fabrics. If you provide an online shopping service, have your journalists go through the ordering process themselves to realize how easy it is.

All these examples are valid for consumer products. There are obviously limitations when it comes to business solutions. For example, you cannot have a journalist 'experience' a power plant your company is manufacturing. But, you can invite a journalist who is interested in details to a guided tour through a power plant that has been built by your company. In a similar fashion, a journalist would never purchase a data centre or be able to experience the value of a data centre. But, again, you can run a demonstration that allows a journalist to visualize the advantages of your new data centre solution versus other solutions from other vendors. You can show demonstrations of computer power or storage capacity or maybe compare the size of your data centre with the size of a previous generation. There are also many opportunities for you to demonstrate commercial solutions – or even abstract concepts for that matter.

There are two important questions that you need to ask yourself before you offer product demonstrations: Are the journalists you address in your press conference interested in a product demonstration at all and, if so, what are the values of the product that are interesting to their audience(s)?

Let us take the example again of a camera manufacturer. Digital cameras have become a lifestyle device. They also represent a rapidly growing market. Thus, there is an interest in digital cameras by business, technical and lifestyle journalists. Business journalists may not be interested in learning everything about the specific technical features of your products. They are probably much more interested in the business opportunities for your company and for the market in general. Technical journalists, especially product testers and journalists who write for photo magazines, would certainly like to take pictures themselves and compare the quality of the images with those taken with other cameras. Or they want to test certain functions and features. The lifestyle press is much more interested in whether the camera fits into a woman's handbag.

This obviously means that your product demonstrations would look different depending on the audience at your press conference.

You have several options for your product demonstration:

1. You run a straightforward demonstration going through the features of the product. This would potentially be interesting for the trade press. These journalists know their industry. They would be able to translate the product features into customer benefits or to use models.

2. You run a product demonstration that is based on the journalists actually experiencing the benefits of the product first hand. In that case they should actually be given a unit, so they can test what they believe is closest to the interest of their readers.

3. The demonstration is done based on a real-life use model, that is, the product would be used just as in a case study. A computer, for example, would not just be tested against some theoretical values, but it would be used to run a registration system of a hotel or to run a grinding machine on a factory floor.

Product demonstrations should be an optional part of the programme to allow journalists who are not interested in them to either leave earlier or to do something else. You may run the demonstrations for example in parallel to 1:1 interviews. It is important to run the demonstrations with smaller groups to allow for interaction with the journalists and to allow for time to respond to specific questions of individual journalists. Demonstrations on stage in front of a large audience would be possible as well. They are, however, not as effective as those with smaller groups. You need to be careful that demonstrations on stage do not turn into 'theatre performances' that are disconnected from the audience.

The true value of a product demonstration should be to put the journalists in direct contact with the product. If they can only see the product at a distance, then they could just as well have watched the demonstration on tape – instead of coming to a press conference and spending a significant amount of time outside the office.

9 *Participants at a Press Conference*

At a 'normal' press conference there are basically three groups attending: The journalists, the spokespeople and the PR staff.

The common belief seems to be that the journalists have to receive information, the spokespeople deliver the information and the PR staff facilitate the communication. If you approach a press conference based on this assumption you probably make one of the biggest mistakes possible.

A press conference should be a dialogue, and not a monologue of a speaker. A press conference is a unique opportunity for the inviting organization or company to learn from the journalists about their opinions on current trends, market developments, competitive moves, and so on.

Thus, the PR staff should indeed facilitate the communication as a true two-way street.

In order to satisfy all participants at a press conference, it needs to be accepted that they have different agendas. First of all, it needs to be understood that a press conference is a disruption of everybody's daily work. For company executives it is often a duty they would like to avoid since they want to focus, for example, on internal company operational work. Even journalists do not attend press conferences on a daily basis. They typically need to justify to their management the dedication of hours or – if extensive travel is involved – even days to one company's press conference. And for the PR staff a press conference is probably the climax of many weeks' or months' work.

It should be noted that depending on the event, other groups of participants may be present. They can basically be identified as being a member of one of the following categories:

1. Additional audience
2. Additional presenters.

Spokespeople

An executive who appears as a company spokesperson is interested in representing the company well and in getting certain well-defined messages across to the public. At the same time, he or she is also interested in doing a good job personally, to be recognized properly and potentially rewarded for having done a good job.

We will address spokespeople in great detail in later chapters. In the context of this chapter it is important to understand the function of the spokespeople. Typically they are strong contributors to the content delivered at the press conference. They deliver the presentations and run the interviews, roundtable discussions and breakout sessions.

Since they are typically senior executives, they also have an interesting role to play at a press conference. They are typically somewhere at the top of organizational charts, that is, all other company representatives including the PR staff ultimately report to them. The way they execute their power at the event typically separates good executives from the others. A good executive focuses on his or her tasks at the event and delegates other functions to the specialists – that's what they were hired for in the first place. Other executives try to get too involved in the details of the event. In a good organization there is a fine balance between hierarchical and functional power!

Additional presenters

The simplest example of a press conference with presenters from different entities is a joint press conference of several companies. In that case all presenters are on the same level, that is, you may not need to make it too obvious that they represent different corporations. Depending on the content of the conference this may even be counter-productive.

But, even if the event is run by a single company, you may have participation from other organizations or companies. Examples are notes from guest speakers or endorsing statements from customers or business partners. It should be noted that these presenters often have their own agendas. They are interested in generating coverage for their own companies or institutions. For them, your invitation to the press conference to make endorsing statements is only the hook to present their own companies and create awareness for them. This behaviour is only natural and should not be criticized. However, you can agree on a compromise before the event and rehearse the presentations just as you rehearse the presentations of your own speakers.

Journalists

Journalists are interested only in getting a story that they can sell to their readers. Receiving a message that is not appropriate for their readers basically means that they have wasted a lot of time without being able to create any output. During that time, they may have missed an opportunity to cover another story they initially rated as a lower priority than going to your press conference.

In order to meet the journalists' needs in a proper way, we should segment them and target them very precisely by event and by message. For example, you do not want to address a journalist from a country where the delivered message is irrelevant (for example, the product is not available in that country). You also want to avoid delivering a message to the wrong type of press, for example, deliver a message intended for the business press to lifestyle media.

We can segment journalists by various parameters including:

- *Geography*: Sort the journalists by country or region. At a press conference you will need to make conscious decisions what regions to address. Decisions about who to invite are based on business criteria.
- *Type of press*: For example. business press, trade press, lifestyle press, and so on. The invited audience is defined by your news.
- *Readers*: You may have a good analysis of what publications your target audience is reading. Decision makers for buying your product may read publications other than 'the usual suspects'. Examples: Some consumer products may be bought by young mothers. But your analysis shows that the children are actually the drivers for their mothers to buy the products. In

a similar fashion, the users of business equipment in corporations are typically not the decision makers (but the IT directors). In these cases you want to focus on publications addressing the children or the IT directors, respectively.

- *Circulation*: Sort the publications by circulation and then go for high-volume publications only.
- *Publication frequency*: Publications that have a new edition published every month have a different lead time from those appearing daily or even online publications. With a given embargo date, monthlies require a longer lead time than dailies to publish simultaneously.
- *Journalist function*: for example. editor-in-chief, technology writer, product reviewer, and so on. Note that your message is not relevant for all journalists at the same time. It is most likely tailored to a specific audience.
- *Media*: TV, radio, print press, online publication. Note that different media have different requirements. For example, for TV reporters you need to be prepared for special picture opportunities, and you need to prepare your spokespeople for interviews in front of a camera.
- *Opinion*: Journalists may for example be favourable or neutral towards your company or your products. When you issue invitations to attend a press conference, you may want to focus more on neutral and positive journalists – and address negative ones more on a one-on-one basis.

Additional audiences

Sometimes it is appropriate to mix audiences. This is certainly not recommended, since different audiences typically have different needs and cannot be addressed by a single presentation. But from time to time there are good reasons to have journalists joined by other audiences such as analysts (industry analysts and/or financial analysts), customers or business partners.

It is recommended that you make the different groups recognizable, for example by colour coding the event badges. This allows you to 'package' your content to meet their respective needs. It also allows you to control access to dedicated parts of the programme that are limited to selected audiences.

PR staff

The PR staff have several functions, depending on the individuals' responsibilities at the event. They range from infrastructure tasks such as managing the event, logistics and PR agencies, via support functions such as managing rehearsals and staffing interviews, all the way to content-related tasks such as managing messaging.

Major international press conferences are typically driven by worldwide corporations or by companies operating on a region-wide basis. Journalists attending these events come from either a single continent or even from across the globe. They are typically accompanied by PR hosts coming from their country of origin. These local PR managers play an important role for the success of the event. Before the event they manage the invitation process locally. They also provide the central team with information on the invited journalists, such as their biographies, and on the publications they work for. During the event itself, they add the personal touch.

They can for example help by translating content as required, but primarily they should help to contribute local content or at least a local context to the generic information provided at the press conference.

The role of the PR hosts can be summarized in this list:

- Ensure that the trip is a positive experience for the journalists.
- Ensure that the journalists get to the venue in time and return as planned.
- Ensure that the journalists participate at the press conference and other parts of the programme (demos, breakout sessions, and so on).
- Ensure that the journalists are signed up for the 1:1 interviews they requested – and ensure that they show up for the interviews.
- Promote 1:1 meetings between assigned spokespeople and the journalists.
- Sit in 1:1 interviews as a PR representative.
- Ensure that the journalists are informed about all logistical aspects (where the press room is, where and when we meet for dinner, and so on).
- Translate for the journalists as required.
- Explain local implications of the international announcement.
- Build a close relationship with the journalists.
- Provide the central PR team with a feedback report after the event.
- Follow up with journalists as appropriate.

But, there is also a list of things a PR escort should never do:

- Be unavailable for the journalists.
- Be unavailable for the staff.
- Disappear to do e-mail, voicemail, or internal meetings, and so on.
- Disclose content distracting from the purpose of the event or even contradicting the content of the event.

10 *Agency Support*

Agency selection is a special topic. It depends significantly on the available budget and the resources you have in house.

If your company has made the strategic decision to work primarily with outsourced resources then you may not have enough staff in house to coordinate multiple agencies working on different aspects of a press conference. In that case you may prefer a major events agency that can either cover all aspects of a press agency directly – or the agency operates as a lead agency, subcontracting and managing smaller agencies specializing in individual tasks.

If, however, you have a strong in-house PR staff, then you can afford to work with multiple agencies directly and coordinate their work.

Both approaches have their advantages and disadvantages. Going with a single agency obviously makes things easier for you. The agency will look after everything from sourcing a location for the event all the way to setting everything up and execution. But this service typically has its price. Going with several complementing agencies allows you to select the best in their respective skills and should be less expensive, since you should have to pay for less overhead. But it certainly requires more investment, especially in internal company manpower.

Required skills

Let us have a look at the skills you typically do not have within your team, but you need from external sources.

LOGISTICS

Logistics includes many aspects of a press conference. It starts with the identification of the right venue (based on a proper briefing). It continues with aspects such as accommodation, travel and catering. In some cases it extends to the development of special ideas to support the conference. These could for example include sightseeing trips, the use of special locations for dinner, or the integration of local customs or specialties. In this context, logistics would also include support during the selection of give-aways or the interaction with the hotel to provide special services such as deliveries to journalists' rooms or the like.

Logistics agencies working on an international level typically work within a network of local ground agents. The complexity this causes should not be made visible to the client.

TRANSPORTATION

You could consider transportation to be just a special logistics item. For major events, however, where several tons of equipment need to be delivered to the venue, a dedicated agency with experience in special transportation may be needed. Be aware that insurance issues need to be addressed since it is often the case that you will run the press conference with expensive early production units or with prototypes of future products. In addition, you need to pay attention to import/export restrictions. From time to time these restrictions may be an important criterion when selecting a venue for your international press conference.

PRODUCTION

Venues you select for your press conferences often provide 'normal' conference facilities such as large rooms or even auditoriums – depending on what is required. But a standard room is not necessarily what you require. Your event may be themed and you may want to have a customized stage to suit the chosen theme. You may want to run the event with sophisticated audio-visual equipment and potentially you want to take advantage of lighting or pyrotechnical effects. An event agency is able to provide you with all these solutions.

It should be noted that presentation and staging technology progresses at a significant pace. What was state-of-the-art last year may not be appropriate this year. When looking at the prices for staging you are often tempted to purchase a complete set for re-use. If your company image is linked to state-of-the-art capabilities, though, you should resist that temptation. You will soon discover that the set you bought last year is of no further use.

The events agency responsible for the staging is typically also responsible for theming and/or branding of the entire event. This agency should have strong creative skills to turn your brief into something that resonates with the audience. Their proposals are an important input not only for the event theme, but also for the event logo or tagline that is used throughout the entire event – from using it on a letterhead to it being a backdrop on stage.

If your press conference happens to be linked to an appearance of your company at a trade show, you need to ensure that the look and feel of the company stand at the show is consistent with the appearance at the press conference.

TECHNICAL SUPPORT

At every press conference there is a need for technical support. Examples include support with the audio-visual (AV) equipment for presentations and managing the computers in the press room.

While the events agency is clearly in command of the AV equipment, you may need an additional agency on board to manage the press room and, if installed, hot spot facilities to provide the journalists with wireless access to the Internet.

If you represent a high tech company, you will also need technical support for demonstrating your products. This support should come from your own technical staff – unless you operate in remote places and you prefer for example the support of a local business partner.

SPECIAL SERVICES

Every press conference is different. Thus, for every press conference you may need customized services. Examples include the setting up of a satellite connection to another site or the display of surprise items (we launched a product once called Piranha and, naturally, we wanted to display these animals live during the event – and we actually did, in a large fish tank displayed in the entrance area of the conference facility). Another example is specialized agencies that manage and promote guest speakers. Through them you can book appropriate guest speakers based on a detailed briefing.

Agency selection I

The agency selection should happen in two steps. It is recommended that you initially select a pool of agencies that you move into a special status such as 'preferred vendor' or 'strategic partner agency' – or you simply qualify them for future projects as they emerge.

This pre-selection should be based on more generic criteria. It is not based on a request for a proposal for a specific press conference.

Criteria to be looked at include:

- *Skills*. Does the agency have all the skills needed by your company? Are those skills available in-house or are they subcontracted? Is the agency part of a network that could satisfy your needs?
- *Quality*. Can the agency provide references from previous clients that prove its quality of service?
- *Responsiveness*. Did the agency implement proper processes and does it have enough resources to be able to respond to your needs in a timely fashion?
- *Cost*. Does the agency offer a cost structure that is in line with your expectations?[1]
- *Financial status*. Is the agency financially stable?
- *Technology*. Does the agency provide the technology you need (equipment for events, but also for example communication technology such as an e-mail system allowing transfer of large files – if needed)?
- *Delivery/scalability*. Is the agency able to deliver press conferences at any size you may require in the future? Do they have access to all the skills needed by you, either in-house or subcontracted?

Agency selection II

The selection of the agencies for a specific project is dependent on several criteria.

Let's have a look at logistics agencies first. Here are some of the most important criteria you need to pay attention to:

- *Response to briefing*. In their proposal for an event, the agency needs to show clearly that they have understood the briefing properly. Not only should you expect that they respond factually in the right way (that is, offer all the services you requested), but they should also offer the services at the appropriate standards.

    For example, if you requested an offer for a 'small' straightforward press conference announcing just a new product, then you should not receive an offer for a beautiful resort in Hawaii – or, on a similar note, you may not want to do a briefing for editors-in-chief with a dinner at a fast food restaurant.

    Finally, you should expect attention to detail and proper consultation. It could for example easily be that you overlooked something in your briefing. In that case the agency should proactively come with a recommendation to you to address the point. An agency

---

1   A note of caution: It is common practice to judge cost by hourly rates. For a generic evaluation, this may be the only available parameter. However, at that time, you do not know what you actually get for one man hour. You should certainly re-examine this closely once you have run an event with an agency. Sometimes it is a great help to get a reference from the agency on costs of an event they have run for another client.

that only responds to the brief letter by letter misses an important point a client should expect: The logistics is outsourced since the skill to manage an event is not available in house. Therefore, the agency should step up to the plate and build on their experience and consult properly.

- *Costs.* Have a close look at the cost structure of the agency! Do they charge their own services by time or do they have a set management fee? How good are their negotiation skills with hotels and other facilities on your behalf? What mark-up do they charge for subcontracted services?

  It is important to get a complete financial picture of a project well in advance so as to be able to make any necessary corrections in time. The quote should be modular and detailed enough to understand where changes can be made and it should also be immediately obvious what consequences those changes would have. For example, you may want to save on transportation costs. But then the consequence could be that you provide minibuses instead of individual limousines or you offer tourist class flight tickets instead of business class. This may or may not be in line with your company's standards – and the expectation level of the audience.

  Finally, the agency needs to be able to stick to its initial quote. Nasty surprises after an event are unprofessional. Unfortunately, you can only rely on your experience before the event, and will only find out after an event if the costs were estimated properly or if the initial quote was too conservative. Obviously, an agency that cannot manage expenses properly should not be used again.

- *Good connections.* The logistics agency either runs the event completely without any additional support, or, especially in the case of international events, they require support from ground agencies that operate on site.

  For example, you want to work on an international level with an agency that is based in the UK or in Germany. But your business needs to run events all across Europe from time to time. In that case, your agency needs to be well connected first of all to be able to get offers from across the continent, and secondly they need to have proper local support from ground agents to run the event.

  Big event agencies tend to have subsidiaries or affiliates in all major locations across Europe or even on a global basis. This typically makes things a bit easier, but it may limit your options, that is, free selection of the best local ground agency.

- *Creativity.* Creativity should be one of the most important criteria when evaluating event or logistics agencies. For example, you may want to run your event in an unusual location that needs to be found. Or, you want to offer a special experience that is related to the message you want to deliver at the event.

  Example: Many years ago, we were involved in introducing black-and-white laser printers at an international press conference in Florence/Italy. The theme was all around black and white. An event dinner was held at a castle near Florence with Dalmatians running around in the courtyard, the tablecloths were all black and white, the waiters wore only black and white – and even the food was only in black and white. The entire event was a very memorable evening. The agency had organized the entire evening and had taken care of all the logistics around it.

You may want to go with a single agency doing the logistics and the event itself. Depending on your specific needs and the skills of the agencies involved, you may also want to have a dedicated production agency signed up to focus on items such as staging, decorating and signage. Putting aside basic requirements like budget control or proactive communication, you should pay most attention to creativity when evaluating a production agency.

If your press conference is covering a business message such as a quarterly financial results announcement or a business or strategy update, then creativity may not be the main issue. But, if you want to make an announcement for the consumer and lifestyle press addressing consumers, then you need a creative concept for your press conference. A standard press conference based on speeches from a podium followed by a Q&A session and interviews is certainly not sufficient to address the lifestyle media. To get them excited you definitely need an innovative concept. You may even specifically select an agency that has a proven record of addressing the consumer press.

Why is it so critical to have creative skills in your agency specifically for addressing the lifestyle media? There is a significant difference between addressing the specialized press (for example, IT media for computer vendors, photo media for camera manufacturers or gaming publications for software developers) and generic lifestyle media. When you address the specialized press you basically have a home game. You only compete with your direct competitors. When you address the lifestyle press you compete with vendors from very different fields for publication space. In our example, a software developer introducing a new game would compete with fashion designers, diet concepts or car manufacturers.

Another aspect is the wide portfolio of skills available from your production agency. Here are a few aspects you will want to look into:

- *Graphic design capabilities.* The production agency should be able to design an event logo, if required. This logo should be displayed wherever appropriate.
- *Production capabilities.*The agency should be able to develop complete stages as well as manage other aspects like signage, displaying exhibits and so on. Also, the agency should be able to develop visuals as needed. Displays can range from developing simple Microsoft PowerPoint slides all the way to developing video material.
- *Audio-visual equipment.* The agency must be able to support presentations with audio and video equipment as needed. This includes simple microphone support at a lectern, mobile wireless microphones for speakers, loudspeakers to suit the size of the presentation room, screens with front or rear projection, lighting and audio effects. This also includes for example speaker support such as monitors displaying scripts.

11 *Financial Aspects*

Proper budgeting for any major event is a particular skill. And, unfortunately, budgeting for press conferences is no exception.

Why is budget planning so difficult? There are two reasons for the complexity. First of all, an event has many contributors. You typically do not have a single contractor working for you, but several suppliers need to be coordinated. You need to ensure that you do not create overlaps or gaps in services from different suppliers. But proper planning or contracting the entire event to a single agency can avoid this issue.

Contracting out the event to a single agency, though, may entail a compromise on quality. A single agency may not be able to provide 'best-in-class' quality for all required tasks. Also, going to a single agency typically implies that you outsource the entire event management to that one supplier. Additional overhead fees may be the result of signing up one 'lead agency'.

A more serious issue is additional costs that are not predictable and are caused only on site. These costs could be caused by unforeseen events. Here are a few examples:

- More journalists show up at the event than registered or predicted. This may drive transportation, catering and accommodation costs up.
- A strike at the airport significantly delays participants' arrival. The resulting retiming of the agenda drives meeting room rental costs up. Any other services that are charged for by time could go up in price as well.
- Your announcement has changed during the preparation phase. You may need to postpone the event and therefore have to cover the reservation costs and cancellation fees.
- You need to redo the press kit on site since some significant part of the announcement has to be removed, added or changed.

Another source of additional costs can be on-site requests to the agencies involved for additional work that has not been part of the initial negotiations and where there has been insufficient leeway put into the plan. Since typically many employees from your company are involved in large press conferences, some of them may feel empowered to request some special services which were not included in the initial quotes from the agencies. In order to avoid this behaviour, it is recommended that you nominate certain individuals with your agencies and the staff of the venue (for example, hotel or conference centre) who are empowered to sign additional expenses against the master bill. A document with authorized signatures should be shared with all potential service providers.

Cost items

Typical cost items at a press conference include:

1. Preparation
    a. Messaging development (PR agency)
    b. Invitation process
    c. Venue selection
    d. Collateral development (PR agency).

2. Travel and transportation
    a. Journalist travel to the event (flights, for example)[1]
    b. Ground transportation (shuttle service from the airport, for example)
    c. Other transportation (bus service to dinner venue, for example)
    d. Transportation of equipment to and from the event venue
    e. Travel of invited guest speakers.

3. Accommodation
    a. Of journalists
    b. Of staff, including agency staff
    c. Of executives
    d. Of guests.

4. Catering
    a. Breakfast, lunch, dinner for all participants
    b. Coffee breaks
    c. Refreshments in rooms.

5. Conference and meeting facilities
    a. Main conference room
    b. Breakout rooms
    c. Rooms for roundtable discussions
    d. Rooms for interviews
    e. Rooms for product demonstrations
    f. Press room
    g. Office room.

6. Other
    a. Staging
    b. AV equipment
    c. Signage (design and production)
    d. Press kit including CD (development and production)
    e. On-site support staff including hostesses for large events
    f. Technical support staff

---

1   Important note: Paying for journalists' travel is a very delicate topic. There is no standard practice in who pays for the travel. Some journalists would consider it unethical to have their travel paid for; some would travel only if their expenses are paid for by the inviting entity. As a guideline you can assume the following: Lifestyle press expects you to pay. Most of the trade press would expect you to pay as well, but exceptions apply. Business publications, especially international business publications, have a tendency to make their own decisions to attend or not attend press conference, and they would then cover the expenses themselves.

Also, there is a geographical dependency. In the US, journalists would always cover the expenses themselves; in Europe there is a tendency to have the inviting entity pay. However, there seems to be a trend towards making journalists independent of vendors especially in the UK and in Sweden.

g.   Telephone costs
h.   Security staff
i.   Gifts
j.   Loan of press room equipment.

But one of the most important items is not included in the above. You should always plan for a buffer of 10–15 per cent of the overall event cost to cover unexpected costs as described above.

Budget planning

It is important to note that you may not necessarily need to plan the budget item by item, as listed above; you can also plan them by supporting contractor. We assume that you do not outsource the entire event to a single lead agency and we assume that you have distributed tasks to the various agencies involved. Furthermore, we assume that you want to execute an international press conference with participants flying in from a number of regions and countries.

Your cost items would then look like this:

• PR agency
• Logistics agency
• Production agency
• Technical support
• Direct costs
  -   Costs for invited guest speakers
  -   Travel costs for journalists
• Indirect costs
  -   Non-project costs such as travel costs for company employees (probably going against their individual expense cost locations)
  -   (Time of company employees).

In this example we have assumed that you have a certain amount of money allocated for your event. You allocate some of that money to contributing agencies for defined service level agreements or contracts.

You also pay certain tasks directly ('direct costs') from your allocated budgets. You may decide to do so since you either consider these tasks to be critical so you do not want to outsource them, or you believe you can save money managing them directly.

Finally, in order to get a complete picture of your company's spending on the event, you need to add those costs that we refer to as 'indirect costs'. These indirect costs are not necessarily paid out of the allocated budget – for example out of your event cost location – but they are real expenses your company will have to absorb (for example from travel budgets).

Budget process

Most of the resources required for a press conference are purchased as needed.

We are aware of the fact that some companies make a conscious decision to purchase a complete set of equipment to run conferences of any kind. These are stored away and used as needed. These sets are typically modular and can be put together as needed. Since these companies typically do not store the equipment in house but with an events agency, they also have the appropriate agency on standby for any upcoming event.

This approach may be viewed as an advantage. Not only since material and manpower is available right away, but also because it may be saving costs compared to starting every event from scratch. Even though there is potentially a third positive aspect to this approach – the fact that you always present your company with the same branding and the same look and feel – we would question this behaviour.

In real life it often turns out that you always run into specific requirements that are defined either by the venue or by the message and the content you want to bring across. Even a modular equipment set may not always work. And the cost saving is quickly eaten up when you take into account storage costs and shipment costs across larger distances.

But the most important factor in favour of design per event is probably the fact that you want to be consistent with your theme of the event. This is particularly true when running an event addressing the consumer via consumer and lifestyle press. You get away with the storage room based equipment for regular commercial or business updates, such as a quarterly earnings announcement, but addressing the lifestyle press requires tailored solutions. We remember a press conference where the theme was around sports – even though the content was around the introduction of consumer IT products. The stage was specially designed like a stadium with a race track leading from the audience up to the podium. Not only did this show consistency with the theme, but it also allowed for elements in the presentations that stressed certain points during the speeches, made the event less 'stiff', led to a better understanding and finally left a lasting impression – not to mention the photo opportunity for the journalists.

Our recommendation is to source not only equipment as needed per event, but also the supporting agencies. The only one agency that is obviously not selected per event is your PR agency. It is important to note that PR agency staff should focus on content and PR functions at the event and during the preparation. They should not be 'misused' for technical or logistical tasks.

Despite the fact that your PR agency is a defined item, you should separate the cost for the event out of their overall budget in order to have a realistic understanding of the overall cost for the press conference.

The remaining agency support should be selected in the light of the needs at an individual event.

This starts with the logistics agency defining a venue. Depending on your briefing, one agency may have the right venue at hand, while another agency may not be able to provide a good fit for your needs. It is recommended that you have two or three agencies from a pool of preferred agencies or pre-selected agencies pitch for the business, that is, the press conference. Selection is made based on proposal and on price.

With the other agencies, you should proceed in a similar way. From a budget point of view, you need to pay specific attention to the production agency. They are typically responsible for a significant portion of the overall budget. This should be expected, since a lot of creativity and ultimately also a lot of manpower goes into the construction of the equipment needed on site. Since it is often very difficult to estimate these costs, it is strongly recommended to get at least one or two competitive bids for this task – especially when you do your first major press conference and you have no benchmarks.

Once you have gone through all the quotes from all vendors and once you have selected the proposals you want to go with, you formally open a purchase order, or simply place the order with the selected vendors. Your simplified budget spreadsheet should look like this example now:

Project 'International Press Conference Product Introduction'		
Logistics	Venue, travel arrangements, catering, accommodation, logistics agency	$200 000
Production	Staging, AV, production agency and so on	$100 000
PR support	Content, press materials, on-site support, PR agency	$ 25 000
Technical support	On-site support services, technical support agency	$ 20 000
Guest speaker	Expenses (for example, travel, fees)	$ 5000
Staff	Expenses (for example, travel, time)	$ 10 000
Journalists	Travel – if paid for (could also be done via logistics agency)	$40 000
TOTAL		$400 000

This table should now give you a complete overview of the costs related to the event. The only cost item that is not shown specifically is the cost related to the time spent by in-house employees. In some companies this item is specifically added in order to understand the cost structure of the organization better. But this item should not really be added to the above spreadsheet, since it would not be part of the programme funding, but rather part of internal people costs.

Again, it is important to note that the above is a simplified view. There are several items that need to be clarified. To name just one, you need to specify who actually produces the press kits (potentially with a CD included). Depending on skill sets and cost structures, it may be the PR agency or the production agency, or an agency subcontracted by one of them (or potentially also a separate printing house – in which case an additional item would appear in the above spreadsheet). Regardless of how you split the responsibilities, they need to be spelled out in the briefing and they need to appear in the approved quote. Distribution of budgets needs to go with the distribution of roles and responsibilities.

To summarize, the budgeting phases in chronological order are:

1. Development of budget plan
2. Request quotes from selected suppliers
3. Pitching/negotiation/selection
4. Final quote from selected suppliers
5. Placing of purchase order
6. Optional: Down payment for venue
7. Nomination of people with on-site signature power
8. Compilation of actual costs after the event
9. Invoice
10. Payment.

Sharing best practice

In this sub-chapter, we want to discuss some special issues, you should pay attention to when planning your budget. These special issues are either known challenges or common traps:

(1)   Price/performance

The very basic question you need to ask yourself in the context of finance is whether a press conference is the right tool to get your news to the public, or whether there are more cost effective ways to deliver the message.

An international press conference, for example, has a comparatively high cost per participant, but you can only reach a comparatively small audience. Local, country-by-country press events are typically more cost effective: Less travel cost, less overhead. You should limit expensive international press conferences to the disclosure of the most important news.

(2)   Pay attention to detail

Be aware that minor exercises in the context of the entire event might have a significant impact on your budget. If you decide, for example, to outsource speech writing, this could become a non-negligible item in your cost spreadsheet. Another example would be media training specifically for the event. If you decide to run serious 1:1 training with professional coaches, you can again create a cost item that has a significant impact on your budget.

(3)   Prepayments

In order to get a confirmed reservation from a hotel or a conference centre, you may need to pay a certain amount up front – depending on the size of the event, even months in advance. Your budget, however, may be planned for by financial quarter. Familiarize yourself early enough with your company's policies. It may be that even the seasonality of your annual budget planning is already dependent on when a prepayment has to be made.

(4)   Buffers

It should be a golden rule that you do not get unexpected invoices exceeding the initial quote after the event. In order to avoid these nasty surprises, it is highly recommended to put buffers into the initial quotes. A 10 per cent buffer has proven sufficient in the quote from the logistics agency; a 5 per cent buffer should be built into the quote of the production agency. If you expect last minute changes to your content, you may also want to build a buffer into the budget for your PR agency.

Be very specific how the buffer should be used. It should be understood that this is not a carte blanche for the agency! A buffer should only be used if it is specifically released by you on site for an unexpected expense that you are willing to pay for.

Obviously, the default invoice after the event should only be against the amount without the buffer!

(5)   Journalists' expenses

Be very precise in an on-site welcome letter to the journalists about which expenses are covered by you and which ones they have to pay themselves! This is particularly important at international press conferences, since the unwritten rules are different from country to country.

In Europe, it has proven to be good practice to cover travel, accommodation and catering. Personal cost items that typically appear on a hotel bill, such as bar, mini bar, phone from hotel room, video on demand or room service should be covered by the journalists – unless specifically authorized up front.

(6)   Flights

You have several options when booking flights for journalists. A first question would be whether they fly business or economy, 'regular' air lines or low-fare air lines. This would depend on your company policy, local standard business practice – and your available budget.

For international events, you could pass funding to the local country PR managers to purchase tickets locally. But you may also decide to set up a process via your logistics agency, since they may have more negotiating power with airlines serving the main routes you need. You may get special rates for a certain volume commitment. In that case central booking via your logistics agency may be needed.

(7)   Insurance/security

Make sure you cover insurance with your suppliers. Insurance should cover accidents involving any participant at the event as well as thefts. Also, insurance agencies may require you to have security staff on site – again an extra cost item you need to consider up front.

(8)   Perception

Cost savings can have very interesting effects on your target audience. An obvious effect is that reducing costs could influence the impact of the event. For example, a press conference addressing senior high-level journalists or editors-in-chief would not be done in a low cost hotel. Your content and your audience define a certain standard level for the event. If you are not consistent with that level, you leave a bad aftertaste

But there is another effect that you need to pay attention to. Assume that you have two proposals for an event, one in Liverpool and one in Cannes at the Cote d'Azur. To your own surprise, an event in Cannes would be less expensive than running the event in Liverpool. Since your budget is tight, you decide for Cannes. Be aware that you will leave the impression then that you run a posh event in a posh place, that is, the financial situation of your company seems to be very good – or people think you're showing off. And you may leave that impression, even though you were only trying to save money.

If your content sits well with the posh location, you may want to go ahead. But if you are planning to announce, for example, a workforce reduction, then you certainly have a problem. The headlines are predictable: 'Company collapses in style'.

(9)   Good planning saves money

Bad planning or unpredictable last minute changes can have a significant impact on the cost of press conferences. For example, you may have significantly higher rates on additional rooms needed for additional participants registering only at the last minute. Or, reprinting an incorrect press kit on site typically does not simply double the cost of that item, but increases the cost beyond that because you have to work with a local print supplier, who may have significantly higher prices than your preferred vendor back at home.

(10)   Master bill

We mentioned the concept of a master bill before. You typically open a master bill with the venue where you run your event. A master bill allows you to request a special service from the hotel or the conference centre without going through a complicated process. All costs are simply added up to an amount that is picked up in the end either by yourself or an agency working on your behalf.

      With this process you need to ensure that it is not misused. Ensure that only selected people have access to the master bill. The best way of ensuring this is to have specimen signatures deposited at the venue, which should then accept orders only from approved individuals.

(11)   Currencies and VAT

When you run an international press conference, you can easily run into a scenario like this: You run PR in your company for Europe. The company is a US based international enterprise internally budgeting in US Dollars. You are based in Germany, your event agency is based in the UK, and you decide to run a press conference in Switzerland.

      In a scenario like this one you need to pay close attention to currency impacts. Your ground agency in Switzerland will quote in Swiss Francs. But you may be lucky since they may be subcontracted by your UK based events agency – which most likely will quote you in UK Pounds. At the same time, your local PR agency in Germany will quote you in Euro. Make yourself consciously aware of the different currencies, when adding the costs up. You may also want to be a bit conservative with the conversion factor into US dollars to balance out potential currency fluctuations that might happen during the course of the project.

      You also need to ensure you understand whether the quote already includes VAT or whether it still needs to be added. Make yourself aware of the latest international tax guidelines, since VAT may or may not need to be added to the bill, depending on where your supplier resides, where the service will be delivered and what kind of service is delivered.

      Just to illustrate the impact, assume that you have a budget of $100 000 for a certain activity. Assume further that you get a quote for about 100 000 Euros. You do not pay attention to the different currencies (that is, take Euros for Dollars) and you do not realize that you have to add 18 per cent VAT to the quote. The impact would be more than 40 per cent (assuming a Euro/Dollar conversion ratio of 1.2) – or more than $40 000!

(12)   Budget measurement

After the event, you need to ensure that you only accept invoices with the right amount on them. This should be more than obvious. But you should not only question invoices that are higher than the initial quotes. Even if the invoiced amount is equal to the initial quote, you may question it, since you had buffers built into the initial quotes. You now need to request a justification for having spent some or all of them.

Also, you need to plan budgets for two potential follow-ups after the event: First of all, you may want to communicate the achievements to your company's employees. If the writing is done by an agency, you need to prepare for that – unless it is already taken care of in the overall budget of another department.

And the second follow-up is the measurement of your achievements. Depending on your budget, the size of the press conference and your company's approach to media analysis, you should prepare at least for a media clipping. You may also consider a detailed media evaluation. The classical approach is to reserve up to 10 per cent of your PR programme funding for media analysis. Be aware that this value is true for your overall PR work. It should not apply to an individual event, since the leverage effect from generic analysis work done for your entity is tremendous. If you already run a media evaluation service on an ongoing basis, the additional cost of analysing your press conference should only be in the range of one to two per cent of the overall event cost. A clipping service only is obviously even less than that.

Budget optimisation

There is probably one golden rule that is valid not only for PR conferences, but for PR (and many other functions...) in general: You never have enough money.

So, what do you do when you believe you have a great plan for a press conference, but your budget does not allow you to execute it?

The issue may actually have been caused much earlier. Without going into a fundamental discussion on how to set up a PR team, here are just some basic thoughts to be considered: A PR department incurs two types of costs, people expenses and programme expenses. If you do not have sufficient programme money to execute PR programmes (incl. press conferences), then you may need to ask whether you have the proper balance between people costs and programme costs. If you conclude that you don't, you may seriously need to consider adjusting that balance to get more flexibility into the system.

Let us assume now that your programme budget is appropriate. We then need to consider trade-offs. In general, you should be guided by the question of how much to spend on message development and how much to spend on event infrastructure. If your news is 'pulled' (demanded by) by the public – typical examples include the film industry, sports, politics or crisis situations – you should focus on crafting the right message, but you can reduce spending on infrastructure. Journalists will attend your event probably at their own expense; you don't need any incentives or a fancy venue.

If you need to 'push' information out, on the other hand, you will need to find a proper balance between message development and delivery and infrastructure (venue, and so on).

Here are two examples of balancing trade-offs:

a) A beautiful expensive venue does not make up for lack of news, that is, if there is no well defined news, then you should ask yourself if you want to run a press conference in the first place, or you adjust the balance of your budget to support content development and event infrastructure.

b) You have high infrastructure expenditure, but only a small number of participants.
    In this case you spend a lot of money probably leaving a high impact on the participants,
    but the number of articles generated may be low. Such an event may be appropriate if
    you focus a lot on relationship building. In general, however, you should look at the 'cost
    per participant' value. You should put this value into context, for example, with the cost
    of advertising (keeping in mind the differences between PR and advertising, though!).

Example:

A press conference will cost you $50 000 and you have 100 journalists attending, then the
per head cost is $500/journalist. Now ask yourself whether you get the appropriate return
in coverage and improved relationships with the journalists.

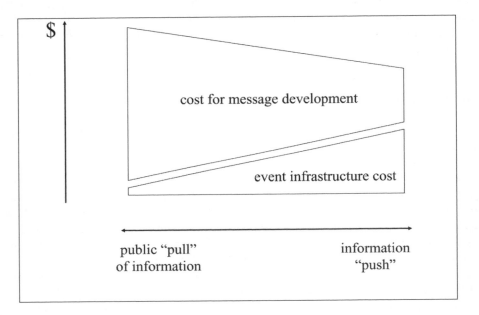

Figure 11.1   Cost balance

12 *Venue Selection*

In this chapter we want to plan for a major international press conference. We assume that we will have to host journalists from many countries, cultures and religions. Any preparation of a smaller press conference will be a subset of what is discussed in this chapter.

We will approach the selection in two steps. First, we judge the location. This will be the city or region where we want to run the event. We will look at cost levels, weather conditions and other aspects. We will then select the venue itself, that is, we will take a closer look at the conference centre or hotel.

We would like to borrow the statement 'Form follows function' from the discipline of industrial design to highlight the most important rule defined in this chapter. It is most important to remember that the selection of a venue cannot be independent of the messages of the event. In the context of this chapter, the above statement should be translated into 'Venue follows message'.

Selecting the location

In this sub-chapter we want to discuss seven criteria you should take into account when selecting the right location for your press conference. Not all of them are of equal importance. You may need to weigh the individual items in the light of your individual needs. The criteria are discussed in an arbitrary order, but the first one should be considered as one of the most important.

LINK OF LOCATION TO MESSAGE AND THEME

During the 'gold rush days' of the Internet in the late nineties, places like Finland became very fashionable. Finland was at the forefront of technology and user acceptance of new Internet-based services and mobile solutions. Obviously, a lot of Internet- and especially mobility-related press conferences were held in Helsinki in those days.

When the European Union grew to 25 member states in 2004, it became almost a fashion to embed announcements into a message addressing the accession states. As a result, many international conferences, events and press conferences were placed in countries such as Poland, the Czech Republic or Hungary. The link between location and message was only too obvious.

These examples show that the selection of the country where you want to run your press conference can already be key to supporting your message.

The location you select should support your message – or at least it should not contradict it. Also, it should provide the right style for your announcement. If you want to disclose business news, you may want to do this in one of the financial centres of the world, such as New York, London, Frankfurt or maybe Zurich. You should then identify an appropriate environment when you want to host senior business press journalists or maybe even financial analysts. If you want to introduce new fun sport utilities, then you want to find a location that is more linked to summer, sun and vacation. Southern Europe might be appropriate. A theme park may be another alternative.

You should take considerations into account like going for a rural or a city environment, or you may want to consider a modern or stylish versus a historic location. A decision for one or the other would always be dependent on your message.

Example: You want to introduce a new product with a retro look. Ideally, you find a location that is popular for its style, for example Miami in Florida being famous for Art Deco. But you may also consider temporary 'in' places like Greece in 2004, because the country hosted the Olympic Games that year, and the country is connected with energy and agility.

ATTRACTIVENESS OF LOCATION

Even though nobody would probably ever admit it, the location has to be attractive – regardless of who your audience is. You will certainly have more journalists agreeing to attend an event on a Greek island than agreeing to come to Castrop-Rauxel. However, you need to be careful. Is the invited journalist actually attending him/herself or was the invitation passed on to a junior colleague as an incentive?

We remember a press conference a few years ago for which journalists were invited to Fiuggi in Italy, a beautiful spa near Rome. The competition ran an event at Frankfurt airport in parallel, disclosing a similar message. We specifically learned from a few journalists that they knew immediately where they wanted to go when they received the two invitations almost simultaneously. The fact was that about 100 journalists attended the event in Italy, while the competition entertained a significantly smaller audience in Frankfurt.

The location should not be too common; ideally you select a place that is easy to reach, but not many people have travelled there yet. The environment should be nice and you should go at a season when the weather is suitable.

Most importantly, you should pay attention to other major events happening at the same time at your potential location. Depending on the other events, it may make the location even more attractive and you may see even more journalists accepting the invitation. On the other hand, you may have a very crowded environment and limited facilities.

The location should also offer an attractive environment for social events. The journalists should be able to enjoy their time out of the office – however, it should not be too attractive and distract from the main purpose of the trip, the press conference.

AVAILABILITY OF VENUE AND ACCOMMODATION

For a major international press conference requiring journalists to fly in and out, you may need accommodation. Potentially, some of the journalists fly in and out on the same day. But you need to be prepared to provide accommodation for those who come from far away, or you want to provide accommodation for everybody, because you are including some social activity on the agenda. Maybe you want to invite the journalists to a dinner. Maybe you have the press conference scheduled for the evening only, maybe you have additional agenda items on the following day.

Be prepared that a hotel will be unlikely to reserve all its rooms for you. Typically, a hotel will only reserve a certain fraction of their rooms for a single customer. They will reserve the remaining rooms for their ongoing business.

Since you cannot be sure whether you will get some last-minute entries or more employees from your company potentially announce their participation late in the process, you certainly want to be prepared for that. It has proven to be good practice to make some provisional reservations in a second hotel nearby, ideally within walking distance. For major events, it is even recommended to make the availability of a second hotel nearby an important criterion for the selection process.

The second requirement is the availability of a conference centre that is sized appropriately to serve your needs. You obviously need to pay attention not only to the overall capacity, but also to the breakdown of the facility. This means you need to ensure you have all the rooms you require, including the room for the press conference itself plus additional rooms for interviews, breakout sessions, press room, back office, and so on.

Finally, it is important to ensure that both hotel and conference facility are close to each other. Ideally, the conference centre is part of the hotel, or it is within walking distance. It is not recommended that you make yourself dependent on transportation in between. Events with a tight agenda can quickly get out of control, when the bus bringing the participants is stuck in traffic, for example.

Finally, you need to ensure that local transportation is available, in appropriate condition and reliable. You will need it for transportation to and from the airport, potentially for a trip to a social event and, in the worst-case scenario, for shuttling the journalists between hotel and conference centre.

The location for the social event, such as a special dinner, should be close by. Your journalists have already travelled a lot to get to your conference. The last thing they want is additional travel at the event itself. They should be able to enjoy the informal part of the day.

PRICING

During a site inspection in the venue selection process, you should not only pay attention to the venue itself and the direct cost of the venue, the transportation and the accommodation, but you should also have an eye on hidden costs.

Hotels with integrated conference centres have very different business models than for example separate conference centres. With some of them, the conference facilities are offered at a very low price, but the accommodation rates are comparatively high. Other hotels have a different model with low room rates and high prices for the conference facility. Separate conference facilities cannot do that mixed calculation, but they need to charge the service as it is ordered. Last minute changes on site can become extremely expensive, since the conference centre will charge every change separately. In a hotel with integrated conference facilities you may get that same last-minute service at much lower rates, or it may even be integrated in the overall package.

Transportation can also become a significant cost item, depending on proper planning and local prices. The shuttle service to and from the airport can be coordinated, arriving journalists can be grouped and shuttled with mini buses or travel in individual limousines. This obviously also depends on the style of the event you want to run.

Finally, you need to add up the cost of the social event (plus potentially transportation again to get to the selected locations) and any other costs related to local services. You may want to evaluate facilities and costs of typical last-minute services up front, such as copying costs. Will you, for example, be dependent on an expensive copy service in the business centre of the hotel or have access to a low-cost copy centre nearby?

TRANSPORTATION

Travel time is an important criterion for journalists. Any attendance at an event is a disruption to their day-to-day work. They may personally appreciate the change, but their management requires them to be in the office most of the time. This is particularly true today, since many publishing houses decreased staff significantly in the late 1990s and the early 2000s. For many, a journalist's job has become a bit like assembly-line work, measured by manufactured units – or written lines.

Because of this pressure, time dedicated to a single vendor – and especially a lot of time dedicated to a single vendor, with extensive travel to an international press conference – must be justifiable. In other words: time out of the office must be minimized and only those invitations will be accepted where the return on the (time) investment is expected to be reasonable. (By the way, you may want to turn this argument around as well: a journalist who accepts your invitation trusts that you will give them a good story, and is more or less required to write an article about the news and the event to justify the travel. It is just the tone of the article that still has to be determined.)

As a result, travel time must be minimized. You had better have a very good story to tell to invite a journalist to another continent, for example. The time commitment you expect from a journalist must be in line with the importance of the news you want to share.

One of the challenges, therefore, in running press conferences in Europe is to find central, but still attractive, locations that require low average travel time. Access should be easy for most if not all participants. You should try to find a location close to an international airport, if possible an airport that is itself an international hub, or has good direct connections to all the main hubs across Europe. Asking a journalist to have more than two connecting flights should be avoided (with the possible exception of transatlantic travel).

The time spent at the destination is also important. It contributes a lot to the perceived time spent on the road. It is quite interesting to consider the perceived time rather than the actual time. A one-hour flight with an additional hour on a bus is often perceived as a longer trip than a three-hour flight with just a five-minute transfer to the hotel. It is important to note that experience shows you should never be more than one hour from the airport.

Some special considerations apply here. For example, an event in Monaco could start with a helicopter transfer from Nice airport. Including the bus transfer within Monaco, this would be slightly more than an hour between landing in Nice and arriving at the hotel in Monaco. But the experience of the helicopter flight will more than compensate for the time taken and journalists will most likely appreciate the ride.

Another example is an event in Venice. Depending on where you depart from, flying into Venice may not be a short direct flight. You would then have to add a boat trip and a short drive to your hotel on the Lido. Overall the travel takes quite some time. But the cruise through the lagoon cannot be compared with a bus ride from Heathrow to the centre of London. It is hardly considered a burden!

LOCAL INFRASTRUCTURE

From time to time, the reliability of the local transportation service becomes a very important criterion. This starts with potential strikes of local air traffic control or employees of the local airline. And it continues with potential challenges from the reliability of ground transportation services.

Overall, you should examine during the preview trip whether the service personnel in the hotel and in the conference centre are reliable and properly qualified. You may want to test out some basic services in the business centre and the room service.

But more important for proper running of the press conference is a reliable power supply in the conference centre. In most regions you should not even question that. But there is a good reason why many places in Turkey or on Greek islands, for example, have a special generator installed in case of power outages. If you happen to plan a press conference in one of these regions, you may want to prepare accordingly. We have attended press conferences ourselves where the hotel generator has suddenly saved the day.

To be fair, though, we should mention that we have also had power issues in other countries. We managed a press conference in London in the late 1990s that was part of a worldwide event with parallel conferences in San Francisco and New York. About 30 minutes before the press conference started, the live satellite link with San Francisco broke down. We had to react very quickly and deliver the news with executives other than those initially planned from London and New York. The event was very successful, and nobody noticed the issue – except for the local audience in San Francisco, of course. We found out afterwards that the issue was caused by a power outage in San Francisco.

Other local aspects you need to consider include customs and visa requirements.

When you want to run an event in a remote place, you not only need to worry about the logistics of getting all your equipment to the destination, but you also need to ensure that you have covered all customs requirements. If your headquarters and your equipment are located somewhere within the European Union, then it is quite straightforward to ship equipment within the EU to any destination. You would not be too concerned about shipping, unless you want to go to remote places like Malta, requiring ferries. But as soon as you leave the EU, you need to have all your customs declarations properly taken care of – or you could end up with an audience, but no content. Be aware that the customs challenge starts with countries such as Switzerland. Even though places such as Morocco may not be ideal for an international press conference since they require too much travel for Europeans (see above), we have seen events in these places. But then you face challenges with both logistics and customs.

Finally, you need to pay attention to visa requirements for your delegates. Journalists from Russia and the CIS countries will require a visa for most European countries, for example. Journalists from Israel may not even be able to travel to certain Arab countries. These limitations need to be taken into account when choosing a location for a press conference. Also, be aware that you may need to have local help to support a journalist applying for a visa to attend the press conference. You may need an invitation letter to be issued by a local official. This invitation letter may come from the head of your local office or, if you do not have a local representative office, you may need to have a local partner or the ground agency help you with that invitation.

SECURITY

More and more, security aspects need to be considered for large international events nowadays.

You obviously face security issues at many levels. You should, for example, secure your computers in the press room from virus attacks (that is, install a firewall). But, you should also ensure that only approved people have access to your conference area. You can address this with a proper badge system (see Chapter 21), but also with security staff that you may need to recruit locally. Ensure that those services are available, either from the hotel and/or the conference centre, or from an agency.

But security aspects also need to be taken into account on a different level. If in doubt, check the local political stability at your potential destination and potential threats of any other nature (local riots, terror threats, and so on). But also check for potential natural threats such as severe storms (for example, Florida during the hurricane season may not be a good idea). Yes, you are right, we are getting a bit carried away here. You cannot seriously predict any potential issue of this nature, but you can minimize the risk.

You can, for example, know about matters such as a high number of pickpockets in the area and you can warn or protect your audience accordingly (or not go to that location in the first place). But you cannot predict earthquakes, for example. Nor can it be expected that you predict the impact of global politics on a local environment. In this context we remember a press conference planned for early 2003, which was all of a sudden overshadowed by the beginning of the war in Iraq – which then made half the audience reconsider their travel and not show up at the event.

Selecting the venue

Until now we have examined the environment of our potential press conference venue. We will now explore details of the venue.

We touched on some basics already in the above sub-chapter. For example, we would like all facilities within close vicinity, and they should also all be close to the airport – certainly no more than one hour's drive from there. This does not only allow for short transfer times, but as a result it also allows more flexibility in the agenda and potentially you would even be independent of shuttle services. People could walk between the hotel and conference facility.

APPROPRIATE STYLE

The venue needs to match the level of the announcement. It needs to link to the message and the theme of the press conference.

A few positive examples:

A museum or a gallery might be the right venue for an announcement that is related to the fine arts, perhaps one focusing on technology supporting fine arts. You may want to consider Antwerp for a topic embedded into a theme around diamonds or 'brilliant' solutions. And a race track would be good for anything related to speed and performance. We saw another example earlier – due to the acceptance of mobile solutions in Finland, Helsinki is a good location for announcing news around mobile and wireless solutions. Or you may consider a sports stadium as a venue to host a press conference on certain consumer products or if the theme of the announcement is around agility or flexibility or competition.

You also need to consider whether to go for a modern facility or a historic building. This choice may support your message (or be counter-productive) and can have a strong impact on logistics. One example for logistical challenges was a press conference we did early in the 1990s at a museum in Brussels, which was set in a historic building with castle-like walls. It was the early days of the Internet, and we wanted to present online access to the web during one of the presentations. We only learned during the set-up that we had to install Internet access into the building ourselves. Today it would be an easy task – you would probably even consider wireless access. In those days it was a major project, and the structure of the building did not really help.

An example for a facility supporting the news would be a modern 'in' or 'hip' place to introduce the latest electronic gadget. You would certainly not want to do this in a natural history museum with a dinosaur as a backdrop. We can already see the headline of a cynic journalist who is not too convinced by your message: 'Just as dinosaurs did not survive, this product will not make it either'.

In the same way, you should compare rural venues with venues in a city. You certainly do not want to introduce high tech on a farm, or new equipment for outdoor activities in an opera house – unless you can craft a strong message that allows you to be controversial with venue and message.

We recommend that during a site inspection, you listen to your 'gut feeling', that is, you also pay strong attention to your first impression. Not only is it often a correct judgment, but your journalists may also have a similar first impression when they see the venue.

Finally, we should address the term 'style' once again. Your brand values and perception may require you to deliver a certain standard. If your company is proud of being a young informal start-up, then you should certainly not plan for a black tie event in the city's most formal venue. If you are a serious formal company, then you may not want to invite people to a shabby place with fast food, especially since the audience was probably expecting a formal seated dinner and a proper stylish facility for the press conference.

Be aware of the fact that a conference venue does not always have to be a hotel. There are much more attractive facilities available. We have already mentioned museums or sports arenas. We can extend this list to venues such as galleries, theatres, cinemas, concert halls, TV studios, factories, castles or palaces. In summer, you may even consider large tents.

LOCAL STAFF

One way of rating the reputation of a company is rating the employees of the company. At a press conference, all representatives of your company are subject to this measurement. Unfortunately, your audience may not always be able to differentiate between employees of your company and supporting staff. You therefore need to ensure that all supporting staff treat your journalists just as you would yourself.

Hotel staff and employees at the conference centre should be supportive not only to you, but also to your guests. You need to pay attention to aspects such as friendliness, helpfulness, reliability, flexibility and efficiency. The language capabilities of those employees who interact with your journalists should be adequate. And, most importantly, you should have a sufficient number of people supporting you at your venue.

CONFERENCE FACILITIES

In this section we want to discuss all your conference room requirements. Be prepared, this section will be very intensive. We will discuss a lot of details that you should keep in mind when going on your preview trip. In Appendix A we provide a checklist you may want to copy before going on that trip.

Depending on the size of your event, you will require the following rooms and allocated space:

Presentation room   Ideally this room is sized slightly bigger than actually needed. You need to plan for some space not only for the stage and potential backlit projection, but also for the AV crew. You also need to consider additional participants registering very late or, for example, local journalists appearing without having registered. A room sized about 10 per cent larger than initially planned always gives you some last-minute flexibility. A warning, though: do not oversize the room too much! If only a fraction of the room is used and the rest is empty, you could leave the impression that you planned for a larger audience, but people did not show up, that is, there was no interest in the message. Journalists will most certainly pick this up!

Breakout rooms   You may want to run special interest groups or roundtable discussions after the press conference on special topics and/or with special subsets of your audience. If possible, try to avoid using the large room where you have the press conference. It would not be set up properly and the smaller audience would feel lost in the large environment. In a perfect venue you have smaller breakout rooms nearby.

Interview facilities   We have attended press conferences where the main press conference room was refurbished over lunch and used for the interviews afterwards. If you want to do this, you should make this a comfortable environment with tables set up for the executives and flexible walls set up between the tables to reduce the noise level from neighbouring tables.

But you may also want to set up dedicated rooms for the interviews. One option could be to use the sitting rooms or office areas in your executives' hotel suites (if available); another could be to book separate little rooms for the interviews. The set-up would be dependent on the number of interviews that would run in parallel and also the level of the executives available for the interviews. Your CEO, for example, should be given a separate room. Product managers may want to share a room (but conduct the interviews at separate tables).

Room for technical demonstrations (demo room)   You may want to run technical demonstrations of your product. Depending on the space needed, these demos could be done at the back of the actual press conference room, in a dedicated room, in the hall or in a corridor. During the site visit, make sure that the necessary infrastructure is available. You may need daylight for the demonstrations (instead of electric light in a basement room, for example), or you may need a significant number of power outlets. If you want to bring in large items (for example, cars), you need to ensure that they fit through the doors.

If you have your products installed on a demonstration truck (that may tour in the region afterwards), you may want to have that truck driven up to your conference centre or the hotel you are using. In that case ensure that you have enough space for the truck and permission to set it up at the chosen site.

Press room   The size of the press room depends on the number of journalists attending the press conference. Experience shows that you should ensure sufficient space to be able to set the room up to facilitate workspaces for about 20 per cent of the audience. The room should be easily accessible and located so that it cannot be accessed by other hotel guests (if you run the press conference in a hotel).

Back office   The back office is for your staff. It needs to be marked clearly as an internal room for staff only. In a perfect venue, such a room is available close to the other rooms, but more or less out of sight of the journalists. The ideal would be a room at the end of a corridor, or a room on a different floor, but easily reachable. It should have telephone access as well as

Internet access. If appropriate, it can be used as a store room as well. If not, you need a separate store room.

Store room A store room would be required for anything the journalists are not supposed to see. If you have a big exhibition, you may need to store boxes that contained the exhibits. Or you may have other material stored there that you only want to make available later during the press conference.

Rehearsal environment Under normal circumstances you can use the conference room and the breakout rooms for the rehearsals. But, depending on timing, they may still be under construction at the time when you need to do your dry runs. In that case you would need a room where you can simulate the actual presentation rooms. Depending on the technology used, you should be able to display the slides used during the presentations either with a digital projector or with an overhead projector (which is actually not very common nowadays).

Space for welcome desk Somewhere in the hotel lobby or the entrance area of the conference centre you should be able to set up the welcome desk. Some hotels do not appreciate such a set-up, so you should get their approval up front to avoid wrong expectations.

Space for interview registration desk The 'counter to register for interviews' needs to be close to the main press conference room. You can expect journalists to become interested in talking to certain executives after they have seen them in the press conference. They will probably leave the press conference wanting to book an interview with them. They should be able to do so right away.

Now that we understand what spaces we will need, we define our basic requirements:

- *Closed environment, no access to public*. You want to avoid that any hotel guest having access to the environment that you use for your press conference. We have seen several hotels that offer a perfect infrastructure. Their conference centre is for example in a separate building or on a separate floor (mezzanine or basement, for example). Access to the area is possible only via a single entrance. You can place security at the entrance to allow access only for people wearing the appropriate badges.

- *All facilities are close to each other*. Close vicinity would make it easy not only for the organizers, but also for the participants. Nobody would be required to walk long distances.

- *All facilities are on the same floor*. Experience has shown that events become significantly more difficult to manage, once you have them distributed across multiple floors. We attended an event once that was partly on the first floor and partly on the top floor of a hotel. This is certainly not a preferred set-up since felt as though the event was mainly dependent on the speed of the elevators. Unfortunately, even sophisticated conference centres sometimes require you to use facilities on multiple floors.

- *Access to bring in large demonstration equipment, if required*. We have already discussed the potential need for a demo room. In some cases you certainly want to bring big equipment into the press conference room. Just assume you run PR for a Formula 1 team and you want to introduce the new car for the upcoming season. You certainly want that car to be on stage. So, the facility should allow for bringing the car in.

- *All interview facilities can be managed from a single interview desk*. Do only allow registration for interviews in a single location to avoid double bookings (or ensure a process that allows immediate updates, for example, with a central database).

- *Environment for photo opportunities*. The options to fulfil this need are endless and depend strongly on the nature of your announcement and on your creativity. It could be the Formula 1 car on stage, it could be a celebrity, it could be special exhibits, it could be special performances, and so on. It could also be special actions like signing a contract, new partners shaking hands or handing over a large cheque.

Inside the rooms, we need to pay attention to these requirements:

- Basic demands
  - Height of rooms
    - It must be sufficient for stage
    - It must allow for use of cameras from the back of the room
    - It must allow for good air quality
  - Visibility for audience
    - No pillars in the room
    - Lighting (dimming, partial on/off)
    - Window blinds to darken the room if needed
  - Air conditioning
    - Effectiveness
    - Noise level
  - Room size
    - Sufficient for expected audience
    - Sufficient space for a stage
    - Space for video equipment
    - Space for back projection
    - Space for TV media
    - Space for AV centre
- Technical details
  - Lighting
    - Lights can be dimmed
    - Integrated spot lights
    - Curtains can be closed if required
  - Power
    - Power outlets
    - Power adaptors
    - Power backup generator, if required
  - Projection screen
  - Integrated audio system
  - TV

- Data projector
- Overhead projector
- Flipcharts
- Internet access
- Furniture
  - Chairs
  - Desks
  - Podium
- Environment
  - Temperature
  - View from window
  - Noise level
- Security
  - Access control
  - Theft
  - Fire control
  - Any other.

When going on a preview trip, you should also evaluate two supporting facilities.

Ideally, you will have at your service a business centre in either the hotel or the conference centre. The business centre should support printing capabilities, quick access to a computer with standard software such as the Microsoft Office Suite installed. Most importantly, MS Word and PowerPoint should be available. You should also have Internet access and a fax facility.

Secondly, you ideally have a copy shop close by. Pricing should be reasonable, and it should ideally be open around the clock to allow for potential last-minute printing of handouts. Depending on your needs, it should offer colour printing, binding, specific formats, and so on.

ACCOMMODATION

When you evaluate the journalists' accommodation, do not just request to see a typical or average room, but the lowest-quality room in the hotel. Do not just see a single one, but try to see different ones at different quality levels.

You may in fact want to reserve rooms at different levels anyway. You should treat your journalists all in the same way, that is, their rooms should all be of the same quality. But you may want to reserve some rooms that can be used as meeting rooms, or you may need larger rooms for your high-level executives who require not just a bedroom, but also need an office, for internal meetings or for telephone conferences, for example. If appropriate, they can also run their 1:1 interviews with the press in these offices.

But there are some additional aspects you should pay attention to. If your company delivers a consumer product that could also be available in the hotel rooms, you may want to ensure that the hotel is not equipped with your competitors' products. This could be drinks from competitors in the mini bar or the TV in the rooms being from a competitor.

3 *Content and Speaker Support*

13 *Content - From Hell to Heaven*

We call this chapter 'From Hell to Heaven' since we want to demonstrate how we can develop something we call the deadly sins of PR into something we may want to consider the 10 commandments of PR – hopefully bringing you closer to heaven.

Deadly sins

The deadly sins can be described as follows:

1. You deliver boring content.
2. You hide the news.
3. You deliver too complex messages.
4. You break your content into too many separate announcements.
5. You go off message.
6. You deliver a sales pitch or an internal presentation.
7. You deliver an 'inside-out' presentation.
8. You deliver a presentation that is not aligned with other speeches.
9. You believe that every journalist has the same needs.
10. You bend the truth.

We will discuss all ten items separately in detail and then convert them into commandments.

YOU DELIVER BORING CONTENT

Journalists think in headlines. Delivering boring content means that you do not deliver or at least propose a headline to the audience. The reporters do not understand why the content you deliver should be relevant to their audience.

A typical scenario that leads to boring content at a press conference is the desperate attempt of an organization to run a press conference simply to raise people's awareness of them, but not because they have breaking news to share. In that case the initial objective for running the event was wrong.

Another typical scenario leading to boring content is not to adapt the presentation to the audience. An engineer who developed a new product would certainly like to talk about all the new features of the product in detail. If they were allowed to do so, they would probably prefer to do a presentation that is close to delivery of a scientific paper. While scientists may be delighted by this approach, journalists would not. Again, journalists need to get the content into a brief headline with only a very small number of words. A boring presentation would not only make them lose interest; they would no longer be able to do their own job afterwards, that is, write a proper article about the press conference.

So, is the simple answer to make a presentation exciting?

Yes, but there are several angles to that.

Firstly, as a presenter you want to deliver an exciting, memorable presentation anyway – regardless of who your audience is. In this case, however, 'exciting' means more than just that. You want the presentation to be exciting since you want the journalist be left with the impression that you are absolutely convinced of what you are saying. You are credible, you are believable. Also, an exciting press presentation needs to be clearly structured. You clearly highlight your main message, and you do not shy away from repeating it several times.

The old approach of first telling journalists what you want to tell them, then telling them and finally telling them what you have told them, is still valid.

You may argue that such an approach sounds boring to you. It may sound boring to you; you are the specialist on the topic and you know it inside out. You do not need to hear things three times. Well, that is true, but the presentation has not been designed to fulfil your own needs, but to deliver the content to an audience that may be hearing about the topic for the very first time. They will appreciate your efforts to package the content in a way that they understand. And they will especially appreciate the fact that you provide clear guidance on a potential headline.

YOU HIDE THE NEWS

Journalists expect news from your presentation. When there is no news, then there was no reason to hold a press conference or to request an interview. Often , however, there is no lack of news in a press conference, but it is hidden by mistake so that the press audience does not recognize it.

When journalists do not find any news in a presentation, they can react in several ways – and none of them is appreciated by you.

The least damaging reaction would be not to write anything about your event, and be very disappointed to have wasted time at your event. In that case the journalist would probably think twice about coming to one of your events in the future.

A more aggressive reaction would be to suspect a reason for not delivering the expected news. The journalist may assume that you do not share important information because you consciously want to hide something. In this case the journalist may try to dig for a negative story or may even write something speculative immediately.

An example may be that you did not talk about a new technology that was supposed to be covered in detail at the press conference. The journalist may then conclude that it is delayed or that your company has encountered technical difficulties. Another example may be that you did not address your company's cooperation with one of your strategic partners, as expected by the journalist. Would that indicate that the partnership has been terminated or is at least threatened?

None of these reactions would be in your own or your company's interest. Important to note is that the journalist's reaction is caused by two things: the expectation (or the expectation that you created) and the fact that you did not deliver any news. If you had delivered any news, then you would have been able to address expectations right away. But no news would stimulate doubts of your company's abilities immediately. Most importantly you would lose control over what the journalist would write or do.

But how can you actually hide the news?

There are several typical mistakes made by spokespeople. Two of the most common ones will be discussed separately in the two following sub-chapters: hiding the news in complexity and hiding the news by splitting it into too small portions.

Other mistakes include:

- Lack of emphasis on the news of the day – you mention the breaking news in a side comment only.
- Insufficient visual support – while a lot of details are shown on your slides, the main message is not visible.
- Different speakers emphasize different highlights during the event – presentations and main messages are not coordinated.
- You are not consistent in what you communicate in your presentation and during interviews.

It becomes obvious from the above that getting a clear message across does not only depend on delivering a focused presentation. It also depends on good coordination across the entire event. Any lack of focus would lead to a distraction from the main message(s).

We can recommend two straightforward best practices that could help avoid the main messages being hidden:

1. Always close your presentation with a summary slide where you reiterate your main messages and articulate the news of the day again.
2. During the rehearsals, invite colleagues who are not familiar with the content. If they re able to summarize the news after the presentation then there's a good chance that you are delivering it appropriately. If they are not able to do so, then you should reconsider.

YOU DELIVER TOO COMPLEX MESSAGES

Presentations to the press are not to be confused with presentations to an academic audience!

Your goal cannot be to cover all aspects of the topic you are addressing. The art in a press presentation is the art of 'reducing to the maximum'.

We shall look at a simple example. Let us assume we want to run a press conference to introduce a new product to the market. The product is not unique. Similar products exist in the market already. You only have a single unique selling point. This situation is probably very familiar to you if you manage PR for commodity products.

In this situation you want to focus almost exclusively on this one unique differentiator. Do not get distracted by other features of your product, regardless of how tempting that may be. Imagine your product is slightly less expensive than competitive products in the marketplace. This may be interesting news for the press, but it may distract them from the one main point you want to get across. Thus, you should avoid stressing that price point too much. Otherwise you may see headlines like 'Company X challenges its competition on price'. What you had been hoping for, though, was something like 'Customers will benefit from new feature from Company X'.

The above example should be very obvious. In real life, the situation may not be as obvious. It may be a challenge to identify a potential trap that makes you deliver a too complex message.

There are several indications that you should reconsider your presentation. They include:

- Your presentation is too long. Remember that a press conference should be as short as possible.
- You make use of too many slides. Fewer slides typically translates to more focus.
- You talk too much about features of a new product rather than benefits for the customer. In this case, you run the risk of delivering a 'scientific' presentation that is not suitable for the press.

YOU BREAK YOUR CONTENT INTO TOO MANY SEPARATE ANNOUNCEMENTS

PR strategies sometimes follow a 'rolling thunder' approach. The idea of this approach is to create coverage over a longer period of time. The approach is very valuable under certain conditions. In other cases, however, it is inappropriate.

In a rolling thunder campaign you 'slice' your message into many smaller parts and get them distributed to the press over a longer period. The threat in this approach is that you might slice the information into portions so small that they no longer really contain news value. Thus, you run the risk that your information will be ignored by the media. In other words, the system backfires on you and you achieve the opposite of what you planned initially.

A press conference as part of such a misused rolling thunder campaign runs the risk of not providing sufficient news to justify either your investment or the journalists' investment in attending. Sometimes even a stand-alone press conference does not provide sufficient content.

But even when you run a press conference with sufficient news value, you can run the risk of hiding that news in an inappropriate event structure. For example, you may decide to split the content across too many speakers at your event. You parade a large number of spokespeople on stage, all of them delivering only a fraction of the news. And then you forget to bring that person on who puts the jigsaw pieces together to deliver that powerful message. In that case you pass the baton on to the journalists to put the picture together – and it is not a given that they will all get the same image…

The individual speaker at such an event may not be the culprit. The issue was caused by poor structure.

In 2002 Hewlett-Packard made an announcement that even outside the company was later referred to as the *Big Bang* announcement. Tens of products were bundled into a single announcement positioning the company in the consumer market. The results were fabulous, both in PR as well as in business. The key to the success was to make an impact by addressing the entire product portfolio in one go – rather than announcing product after product separately.

We may want to summarize this sub-chapter by noting that the whole is often greater than the sum of the parts. It should be considered to be the role of the PR department or the press office to advise the organization on packaging the news appropriately for the announcement – without necessarily owning the content itself.

YOU GO OFF MESSAGE

The previous sub-chapter addressed more the delivery tactics rather than the presentation of an individual spokesperson. In this sub-chapter, we have quite the opposite. We address a mistake that is made by an individual speaker at a press conference or during an interview with a reporter.

Before we run a press conference we define the messages we want to deliver (see for example Chapter 4 on the PR plan). Any speaker involved is then expected to deliver exactly those messages. The speaker should not distract from them, should not dilute them and should not introduce different messages during the speech.

Sometimes you need to show quite some discipline not to wander off track, especially when reacting to questions during a Q&A session or during an interview. If you have decided to focus on your company's business in Europe, you should not distract people with US business results. If you decide to focus on the pricing of a new product, you do not want to lead the discussion with the product portfolio you offer or the rich feature set in your product.

Less is more! Focus is the key.

Going off the defined messages could have serious consequences in what journalists hear and in what they will write afterwards. Going off message can easily spoil the results of the entire press conference.

Sometimes it is extremely tempting to respond to a journalist's question with an answer that would be factually correct, but off message. In that case, it is very appropriate to use the question as a prompt only to repeat your main messages. It is certainly more appropriate not to answer a question directly than to give an answer that would derail the train or open a can of worms or simply give the story a different headline. Politicians understand this very well.

YOU DELIVER A SALES PITCH OR AN INTERNAL PRESENTATION

One of the most common mistakes of a spokesperson is not to pay attention to who the audience is during a press conference. Executives with a strong sales background especially run the risk of going into their comfort zone and delivering a sales presentation rather than a press presentation. They try to sell the journalist your story or your product.

The least that can happen is that the journalists are annoyed. The worst that can happen is that the journalists simply leave the press conference. The outcome depends on the degree to which the presentation has missed the audience. But the journalists' reactions also depend on cultural aspects of the country in which the presentation has been held. A more aggressive 'sales flavoured' presentation is more acceptable in some countries than in others.

In some cases you may also get away with the approach if you show enthusiasm for your company, your message or your product. You show that you are convinced of your product, that you are carried away. In that case the journalists may approve your approach.

A cheesy sales presentation, though, will hardly be accepted by journalists. They will not tolerate you trying to sell them your product.

You need to keep in mind that the simple fact that reporters are going to write about your products does not make them potential customers.[1] In many cases this is obvious. If you happen to sell power plants, then you would not expect a journalist to buy one. But you may be much more tempted to take the sales approach if you happen to sell commodity consumer products.

When rehearsing your presentation you need to pay attention to the wording you use. You can certainly use terms like 'you will like this feature'. But you should avoid terms like 'you should certainly get one of these'.

---

1 In fact, more or less the opposite is true. The journalists are not expected to buy, but you expect them to help you sell. So, you need to 'sell' the message to the journalists to have them help you 'sell' it further to your actual target customer. Note that 'selling to sell' is not the same as 'selling' itself!

YOU DELIVER AN 'INSIDE-OUT' PRESENTATION

What actually is an 'inside-out' presentation? The simple answer is that speakers delivering such a presentation define themselves or their company as the centre of the world.

On the other hand, it is quite obvious that the centre of all activities should be your customer.

Therefore, 'inside-out' presentations can be very revealing to a press audience. They can indicate that your company is focusing more on internal company challenges than on responding to customer needs. You can consider 'inside-out' presentations to address topics that are relevant only to internal company communication. These presentations tend to be independent of market dynamics, that is, you may come across as not being connected to your customers and as not understanding the market, the industry and/or your competition.

Here are a few examples that indicate that it is very likely that you are about to deliver an 'inside-out' presentation. For all these examples, there are proposals on how to avoid the issues:

- You cover topics that do not contain benefits to your customer. You may stress company re-organizations that have no impact on what the customer gets.
- You focus too much on company achievements rather than communicating the benefits to the customer. A typical symptom is that you start every other sentence with 'we do this' or 'we do that'. With this approach you also run the risk of coming across as arrogant, that is, you do not seem to pay attention to what your competition does at the same time.
- You use internal company acronyms or abbreviations that are not relevant to an external audience. By doing so you will clearly leave the impression that you are too internally focused. You must certainly avoid that.
- An indication of taking a company-centric presentation is to refer to customer references or customer case studies as customer wins. Yes, it is understood that the referenced deal was a win for your company. But at a press conference it may be much more important to refer to it as an example of what customers can achieve in cooperation with your company, rather than what your company is capable of doing. Exceptions apply here, though. For presentations to the business press and/or financial analysts you may still refer to wins.
- Your presentation starts with your company's activities (R&D, product development, and so on). The customer benefits only appear as an afterthought on one of the final slides you present. In this case, although you may take a chronologically correct approach, you position your customer as an afterthought.
- Your presentation is only one of many presentations from your company at the press conference. In this case, you may make the internal complexity of your company too visible to the public. This approach certainly runs the risk of being too internally focused.
- You only refer to internal findings rather than to independent research.

All these examples are indications only. They do not prove that you are making an 'inside-out' presentation, but they should make you re-think. You may indeed be on a wrong path.

YOU DELIVER A PRESENTATION THAT IS NOT ALIGNED WITH OTHER SPEECHES

Journalists will always pay specific attention to potential contradictions of speakers or to presentations that reveal that there was no coordination or no consistency. Examples of non-alignment are endless. It is important to note that they typically make excellent headlines like 'Company XYZ paralysed by bad management' or 'Power battle at company XYZ' or 'Confusing strategy'.

There are several potential sources for lack of alignment. We shall go through them in turn. It is important to note up front that there are two levels of misalignment. The first and most severe one is obviously that the content of presentations is indeed not coordinated. In this case two speakers have two different opinions on a certain subject. It is obvious that in this case a press conference was premature. The content and the message had not been well prepared. You had really set yourself up for failure. We do not want to address this issue here; it should have been addressed in the initial planning phase (see for example Chapter 2 on the PR plan). In the second case the content of presentations is consistent, but it is delivered in a way that is misleading, confusing or distracting. This is the kind of misalignment we want to address here.

Probably the most common cause of misalignments is that more than one party is involved in delivering the content of a press conference. Two companies doing a joint announcement may want to say the same, but different individual agendas caused the content to be delivered in different 'flavours'. For example, the companies may want to put a focus on their respective contributions to the joint project. The story may then come across in such a way that each company positions the other one as the junior partner in the project. This is a classic scenario. It allows the press to play off one company against the other. Both are immediately in a defensive mode that creates scope for additional errors, for example during a Q&A session. This is a scenario you certainly do not want to be in.

Another scenario is that two speakers from the same organization deliver content that is not synchronized. In this case you may reveal internal communication issues or different interests of different departments. An example may be that you launch new products that you want to sell through the distribution channel as well as directly via the Internet. The respective presentation, however, is done by the manager of the online sales team, who will focus on the direct sales route, potentially not putting the right emphasis on the channel activities.

A third scenario we want to address is based on the need to align with other communications from your company either in the past or in parallel to other audiences. A journalist may (and most likely *will*) remember what you presented at a previous press event. Make sure that you are consistent with that earlier presentation made by either you or a colleague! A prerequisite is obviously to keep a record of what was presented to the public or to maintain a repository of all communications to the public (press, analysts, business partners, customers, and so on). It is probably needless to say that your company still has the freedom to make strategy changes that lead to inconsistencies. This is absolutely fine and the result of a conscious decision. It is easy to defend such an inconsistency. However, it would be embarrassing if a reporter made you aware of such an inconsistency that may not actually exist, but is simply the result of a misunderstanding (due to a confusing or misleading presentation) – or it is the result of an unconscious strategy change, or a change that was at least never properly documented.

Good preparation avoids you ending up in an embarrassing discussion with a journalist, trying to explain misalignments.

An obvious good practice is to have all presenters at a press conference do at least one rehearsal together in front of an internal sounding board to test the delivery of the message. Another useful tip is to repeat certain key visuals in multiple presentations. All speakers can then position their respective presentations within the same framework. This approach does not rule out inconsistencies, but it can be a tremendous help both to the speakers and to the audience.

YOU BELIEVE THAT EVERY JOURNALIST HAS THE SAME NEEDS

A popular saying is that everything will look like a nail when your only tool is a hammer. As a presenter, however, you should be more flexible. We saw in item 6 above that different audiences require different presentations. A customer would expect a different presentation from you than a journalist, for example.

We now go one step further. The question now is whether all journalists are the same. And the answer is obviously no. Different groups of journalists require different presentations – they may even need very different communication tools. A press conference itself, for example, may not be the right way of communicating to certain journalists: journalists writing for online publications may not want to spend hours or even days attending press conferences, since their lead times are typically minutes. They typically prefer a media alert via e-mail or a phone interview.

Your presentation at a press conference will also differ quite significantly depending on the audience. If you try to give the same presentation to a trade journalist, a business press journalist and a lifestyle journalist, you most likely will make at least two of the three very unhappy.

The key to success is to understand what drives particular journalists. Just as the driver for everything you are doing should be your customer, so journalists are led by their customers, that is, the readers of their magazine or the audience watching or listening to their programme.

A trade press reporter is probably very interested in technical details of your new product. A lifestyle journalist may be *personally* interested as well. However, he knows that his customer will be interested in other aspects. He is certainly much more interested in the social risk of purchasing your product. He will ask questions like 'Is it fashionable?' or 'Is it cool?' or 'Who else has it?' He will most certainly not ask questions like 'How does it work?'.

So, if you for example want to promote a new car to lifestyle journalists at a press conference, you want to stress the fact that a certain celebrity owns it, or you may want to focus on design features or some new gadgets. Promoting the same car to a journalist writing for a car magazine would require you to take a very different approach. You may want to focus on that new engine feature, that enhanced suspension or that new safety technology. In other words, your presentation may be completely different, depending on who you talk to.

In real life, you may even make the selection of the speaker dependent on the target audience. A marketing manager may be the right person to address the lifestyle press, whereas an R&D manager may be the right spokesperson to address the technical press. Along the same lines, a sales or business manager may be the right speaker to address the business press.

Once it is understood that different journalists require different presentations, it is much easier to deliver a presentation that is really valuable to them.

We would like to add one more aspect to the need to tailor presentations to the needs of the journalists in the audience of your press conference: at an international press conference there is a need to pay attention to aspects such as language barriers or cultural influences.

If you anticipate that your audience may have diffculty following your presentation because of language barriers, you should be prepared to speak at a lower speed, be more articulated and use simpler language. Cultural influences (or legal requirements) may force you to adapt to local standards – depending on local customs. For example, you may or may not want to be aggressive towards your competition. Or you need to comply with local demands such as measuring in local units or pricing in local currency.

YOU BEND THE TRUTH

This item may be stating the obvious, but spokespeople too often escape from aggressive questions by using lies.

There is a significant grey area between the plain truth and a blunt lie. Where do we cross the border? According to some, not putting an incorrect assumption right is already equal to a lie. Or, remaining silent on a specific topic is also a lie.

We do not want to end up in an academic philosophical discussion. Using some common sense and considering the potential consequences of some behaviours will generally answer the question of what to do and what not to do.

We will look at two examples:

In the first one, we assume that your company needs to downsize. You need to make the standard announcement that your company wants to focus on its core competencies in the future. You list the areas that your company wants to focus on in the future, but you do not spell out where you will disinvest. You should not consider this approach to be a lie. It is questionable, however, whether it will give you the headlines that you are hoping for. You should still be prepared to see something like 'Company XYZ drops support for ...' rather than 'Company XYZ increases investment in ...'. Most importantly, though, you need to be prepared to address a journalist's question about whether you do intend to drop support of that service or product of yours. Answering this question correctly may be painful, but you should always keep in mind that answering it incorrectly may come back to haunt you very soon.

In the second example you are challenged with a question from a reporter on some internal company data. Since you believe that the reporter will not be able to verify your answer anyway, you just make something up. This approach is probably the worst thing that you can do, for several reasons. First of all, you need to be aware of the fact that a lot of internal company information will at some point in time become public – directly or indirectly.[2] But secondly, you may be contradicted very quickly by another spokesperson from your company making your lie obvious. In this case you have a serious crisis PR project ahead of you.

Most lies are actually not told in prepared presentations, but they are used as an escape route to a challenging question during a Q&A session or in a 1:1 interview. You need to remember that not knowing an answer almost always leaves you with the option to take a question offline (and then take advice before you finally answer it) or to simply admit that you do not know the answer, but promise to get back to the reporter within a given deadline. This approach not only allows you to draft a proper response, but it also gives the PR manager the opportunity to stay in contact with the reporter.

The 10 commandments

Journalists will attend your press conference because they expect interesting content they can share with their readers, listeners or viewers. Newsworthy content is the most important item

---

2   Directly: You announce your financial results – and they contradict an earlier statement from you. Not only could you run into legal issues here, but you could also have reduced investors' trust in your company significantly. Indirectly: Market share data from industry analysts contradict your earlier claims. You have undermined your trustworthiness significantly.

Refer also to the book *How Companies Lie* by A. Larry Elliot and Richard J. Schroth (Nicholas Brealey Publishing, 2002, ISBN 1 8578 8322 5).

at a press conference – despite the fact that, according to research, people remember more the presenter and the way the content is delivered than the content itself.

You can focus the audience of a press conference on the content by following a few little guidelines. In the light of what we have learned in this chapter so far, we will refer to them as the 10 commandments:

1.   Only call for a press conference when you have exciting news to break.
2.   Keep a focus on the news.
3.   Keep it simple. Do not distract the audience with a complex message.
4.   Deliver a complete story.
5.   Always stay 'on message'.
6.   Tailor your presentation to the need of the journalists.
7.   Be as objective as possible.
8.   Align all outbound messages and presentations.
9.   Understand the needs of your specific target audience.
10. Always speak the truth.

Other dependencies

We have now learned some basic guidelines you should follow when you are acting as a press spokesperson. These guidelines allow you to shape your content so that it is attractive to a press audience.

But we have also learned already that the delivery of your content depends on your target audience. Different sets of journalists may have different interests and you may have to address them in very different ways. But there are in fact several additional dependencies you should keep in mind when speaking to the press.

At the very beginning of this book we referred to the fact that a press conference is somewhat special, since the actual target audience of the event – the customers – are not even participating. Since there is obviously a wide spectrum of customers out there, you need to define very early in the process who you want to reach. Very obviously, this drives the selection of the media to be invited to the event, it defines the content and the message, but it also has a significant impact on your presentation.

You would present differently to a commercial trade press targeting commercial customers for B2B business than you would to the lifestyle press addressing specific consumer groups. The values these audiences hold could be very different. Assume that your company is in the IT industry addressing commercial customers and consumers. You may find that the consumers are always interested in getting access to the latest and greatest once it becomes available. You commercial customers may behave exactly the opposite way. They are interested in getting a proper return on their investment, that is, they expect you to support products for a long time, rather than your company bringing out a new generation every few months. You obviously must take these differences into account when preparing your presentation.

In order to focus on the right message and the appropriate way of delivering it, you typically ask questions like: 'Who is the customer who actually makes the purchase decision?' This question is very valid in both the consumer and the commercial businesses. Questions like this one drive which press you target at your press conference, the messages, the tone of your presentation and often even the speakers selected to present at the event.

It is obvious that different customers are driven by different topics.

In the commercial business, you want to deliver a presentation to the press addressing CEOs, for example, that is different from the one to the press addressing functional managers. Their interests could be significantly different from each other, and this needs to be reflected by your presentation to the respective press audience.

With consumers, you want to segment in a similar way. You can segment them by gender, by age, by income or any other attribute. However, you may also seriously consider segmenting them by the type of product you want to offer to them. A presentation for a new tooth brush should be considerably different from a presentation on the latest high-priced sports car, for example. The social and financial risks involved in a purchase are significantly different for these two products. So, the presentations would not only be different because of the products being different, but also because you want to tailor your presentation to the expectation your audience will have of your products.

The 'social risk/financial risk grid' (see Figure 13.1) is actually a very good way of characterizing different presentation tactics depending on the quadrant in this grid that you cover with your products.

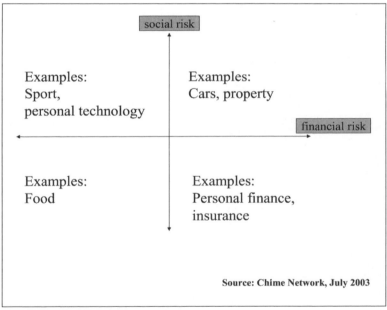

Figure 13.1   Social risk/financial risk grid

When your products are positioned in the lower right quadrant, then you will most likely take a much more facts-based approach to your presentation compared to representing products positioned in the upper left quadrant. When you sell personal finance solutions, you want to be more conservative and to position your company as a reliable partner who provides a safe solution.

When you promote a sports event, however, you want to be emotional; you want to create an exciting atmosphere during your press conference. You probably want to have journalists experience your products or services during the event rather than just talking about them.

Being in two different quadrants would not only influence the style of the event, the venue, the decor and so on, but also the presentations delivered at the event.

14 *Preparation of Spokespeople*

Spokespeople know their content. This is the basis for all further discussion in this chapter.

Spokespeople know their content. This is a prerequisite for all PR work, but it is not sufficient for achieving good PR results. Several studies evaluating the impact of speakers have consistently revealed that the vast majority of what people remember of a presentation is not linked to the content, but to *how* the content was delivered and the personal appearance of the speaker including aspects such as body language, tone of voice, haircut and clothes.

In order to achieve the optimum result, a spokesperson needs to go through proper training, potentially individual coaching, and finally specific preparation for the particular upcoming press conference.

Long-term preparation

Presenters at press conferences should develop their skills consistently over a long time period. Executives are most likely to have reasonable presentation skills already, which they have developed in internal company presentations and on other occasions. Companies should consciously invest in developing speaking skills with talented individuals who are on a development path into positions that will require them to speak to the public. This training should run parallel to the development of functional skills.

Presenting to the media requires skills over and above those needed for internal meetings. These additional skills may be grouped into two blocks:

- Personal skills
- Content related and PR skills.

In order to develop personal skills, it is strongly recommended to coach executives individually – in an ideal situation with the help of an external trainer. This training needs to focus on items including:

- Body language
- Interaction with the audience
- Use of the language (mother tongue or foreign language)
- Timing.

It is recommended that appropriate time be dedicated to this training. The actual amount of time is dependent on the individual's experience and needs. Initially, several hours per month in 1:1 sessions between executive and personal trainer are recommended. With increased knowledge, generic training may no longer be needed, but refresher sessions may be useful. They should be tailored to specific situations and actual presentations.

Content related and PR skills include:

- Interview tactics
- Articulation of messages
- Focus on main messages
- Customization for audience
- Media role and agenda
- Reporters techniques.

These skills should be addressed in PR or media training offered by some institutions, agencies and individual trainers. They can also be offered by the internal PR department or the PR manager directly. However, it is recommended that an external consultant be brought on board to get an independent opinion. In strongly hierarchical companies it would make particular sense to have external coaches deliver this training. It would be easier for them to articulate the personal challenges a spokesperson faces, than it would be for an employee to raise such concerns with somebody who is potentially his or her manager.

Event-specific preparation

It is the responsibility of the PR department to support spokespeople before, at and after press conferences.

Before a press conference, several tasks have to be fulfilled.

After it has been agreed to do a press conference, the objectives have to be defined very clearly. These objectives will drive all further decisions: content, message, selection of spokespeople, location, and so on.

Once the speakers have been selected, their time has to be secured and a proper first briefing has to be done.

The initial briefing should address basic topics such as:

- Situation analysis
- Objectives
- Preliminary agenda
- Definition of the speakers' roles.

It is preferable to have all speakers receive the initial briefing in a single meeting. That way you can reduce the risk of potential misunderstandings, you can support cooperation and you set expectations of all participants right from the beginning.

The goal of this first briefing is to get buy-in from all the speakers. An additional, much more detailed, briefing has to happen later on, at which time, it is strongly recommended that an enhanced briefing document be put together that contains the following items:

- Situation analysis and event context
- Objectives
- 'Three main messages'
- Rehearsal schedule (location, time, participants)
- Complete final agenda

- • Press conference
- • Interviews
- • Breakout sessions
- • Hospitality programme
- Content summary of all sessions
- Personal schedule
- Target audience incl. biography of attending journalists and their profile
- Survival guide incl. Q&A document
- Other logistical details:
  - • Dress code[1]
  - • List with names and mobile phone numbers of staff (PR team and event team) and other speakers
  - • Venue description, potentially incl. map
  - • Transportation and accommodation details (airport pickup service, for example)
  - • Security details, badges, and so on
  - • Meals.

Dry runs and rehearsals

Presentations at press conferences have a significant impact on a company's reputation. It is therefore strongly recommended that those presentations be rehearsed in at least two stages.

The first stage should happen in the office, based on a draft version of the presentation that is already close to final. The presenter should be comfortable with the content and the flow and the PR manager should feel comfortable with the clarity of the message. If time allows, it is good practice to test the presentation with a person who is not familiar with the specific content, but who has a basic understanding of the context.[2] Feedback from that person will reveal whether the main points of the presentation have been understood.

If several presentations are to be given at the press conference, it is important to ensure consistency across all presentations. This consistency is needed not only in the content, but also in the style (which may be governed by company guidelines). The style of the presentation is driven not only by the template of the slides that may be used, but also by the tone (aggressive, factual, humorous, ...), wording, images used, and so on.

One important aspect you need to pay attention to at international press conferences or local events with international guest speakers is the use of language. You typically have presentations given in a language that is not necessarily the mother tongue of the majority of the audience. In that case you need to ensure that a native English speaker slows down and articulates well. He or she should avoid slang. He or she should also avoid examples, sayings or comparisons that cannot be translated.

Finally, it is important to ensure consistency with the content of previous press conferences and with content delivered by other parts of the company. Also, consistency with company communications to other audiences (customers, partners, analysts, and so on) needs to be

---

1   It is not only recommended to pay attention to the fact that all company representatives at the event comply with a defined dress code (business casual, for example), but speakers should also pay attention to tactical aspects. If a TV interview is planned, for example, you should avoid red clothes, since the colour red is not well displayed by TV systems.

2   Even though this may not be politically correct, this test is often referred to as the 'housewife test'.

guaranteed. It would be most disturbing for customers to see a different story in a direct mailing piece from your company, for example, from one that they read in the press.

A complete 'dress rehearsal' should be held on site with all speakers. This final test should be done assuming the audience is in the room. The speakers should not only make themselves familiar with the AV equipment and the venue, but they should also test on-stage processes that may be considered of minor importance – but are in fact significant.

The processes include opening and closing procedures, changing slides, triggering special effects (light changes or starting a film on screen, for example), an agreement on who introduces whom, how to walk on and off stage, how to hand over from one presenter to the next, and so on. Again, these processes may be considered to be of minor importance. However, they often make all the difference. Just imagine, a presenter is not introduced because it was never discussed how that would be done.

One important aspect you need to pay attention to is timing of the presentations. A typical mistake is to overrun the planned time significantly. This would not only potentially bore the audience, but also risk disrupting the timing of subsequent events. As a general rule, you should assume that the real presentations take slightly longer than the rehearsals. The additional time is typically absorbed by additional opening or closing comments or by interaction with the audience that was not anticipated.[3]

Presentation support at the event

Presenters typically have very different habits.

Some like a fully scripted presentation. Some like bullet points only. Some internalize their presentation completely and some do not like any notes at all. We'll go through some of the techniques a bit more in detail in the following two Chapters (15 and 16).

You have several options to support a speaker on site. They include scrolling the script on a monitor or projecting it on a display.

In addition, you may need to be prepared to monitor the time during the presentation and provide the presenter with feedback, using signals (invisible to the audience) that have been agreed earlier. You may, for example, slow the presenter down or speed him or her up. You may also give signals on how much time he or she has left to finish the presentation.

Support during interviews

Interviews should always be conducted with a PR manager present. The PR manager should: act as the facilitator of the interview or the conversation; introduce journalist and executive to each other and set expectations as appropriate. This would include giving the timelines of the interview ('we have 30 minutes') and then acting as the timekeeper. This may also include telling the journalist the topics the executive can cover and – if appropriate – explaining what topics cannot be discussed during the interview.[4]

---

3   Even though there may be no question asked, a good speaker would for example react to obvious disbelief on people's faces.
4   This could be topics that are not relevant to the announcement of the day, topics that should be referred to another spokesperson, or topics the spokesperson cannot comment on due to company policies.

Sometimes you may be uncertain how to introduce people to each other. In general it is appropriate to introduce your executive to the journalist first and then the journalist to the executive. If you are inviting a translator to the interview you may want to introduce him or her as well and explain the process of translating the journalist's questions and the spokesperson's answers if appropriate. It may be interesting to look into the etiquette of introductions when people meet each other for the first time. It varies greatly, depending on regional cultures and individual countries' customs. In some cases women need to be introduced first, in some cases the younger person has to be introduced to the older one and in some cases the order of introduction depends on the status of the people.

The PR manager should document the questions and the answers given (for later evaluation), step in if the conversation starts to de-rail (per earlier agreement with the executive) and afterwards follow up unanswered questions either with other spokespeople at the press conference, or later with specialists in the office.

15 *Speech Writing*

Before we go into the topic of this chapter, we will discuss what *not* to do.

First of all, we will – at least initially – *not* discuss spokespeople's behaviour in this chapter. Even though the behaviour on stage and the message delivered need to be closely matched, we will focus in this chapter on the content itself and the 'packaging' of the message. Only at the end of this chapter will we discuss in some detail behaviour on stage and tactics to deliver the speech in a presentation.

When we look into development of the speech itself, we again want to stress first what *not* to do. It is unfortunately common practice to start development of a presentation by collecting inputs from earlier presentations held internally within the company. The first draft of the speech is then a Microsoft PowerPoint slide set that is full of internal language – and it absolutely ignores the target audience.

When you want to develop a speech for the media you should start from a very different angle. The first questions you need to answer are what the objective of the event is and what your main messages will be. It is a basic in PR that you need to focus your content on a maximum of three messages. They need to be carefully selected and the speech writing must then focus entirely on getting these three messages across.

Internal presentations should only deliver content. These presentations cannot be the core of the speech. In a typical scenario the internal presentations contain far too many details for a speech to the press. The art of writing a press presentation is to introduce a very effective filter that only allows content to pass through that is contributing to the main messages. All energy in speech writing for the press is on focus, focus, focus.

Speakers with a scientific background in particular tend to believe that more details help to make things more understandable. In reality the opposite is true. Journalists are not interested in writing scientific papers, but punchy articles that make their readers buy their magazines. A consumer, for example, is unlikely to be interested in the detailed chemical components of a tooth paste, but wants to know if the paste cleans the teeth and potentially if it is healthy. In general, you should always think in terms of benefits for the customers, rather than in terms of product features – unless you are, exceptionally, pitching a story to a scientific publication.

Even though we want to exclude the speaker from this part of the planning process it is obvious that a speech needs to be tailored to an individual. All people are different. All spokespeople are different. One person prefers to integrate personal anecdotes into the presentation. Another person prefers to be much more facts-based. One person has a technical background and feels comfortable with product details. Another person has a sales background and prefers to cover business and economic content.

Together with the marketing department you craft the three main messages. They should be sustainable and most importantly they should be consistent. In fact, they need to be consistent across all speeches at the press conference. But they also need to be consistent with messages from other departments in your company and they need to be consistent with earlier messages from your organization. Journalists should not all of a sudden listen to a message that is contradicting everything they have heard from your organization up to now.

But you also need to be consistent with those messages you share with other audiences such as business partners, analysts and customers. This does not mean, however, that you have identical messages for all these audiences. This does mean that all those messages do not contradict each other! In fact, they need to complement each other and address the needs of the respective audiences.

We will look at an example. You may introduce a new range of products that should allow your company to go after a new market segment that you were not able to target before. The growth potential for your company is tremendous.

How do you deliver this message to your target audiences? Well, it is obvious that the financial analysts will be interested in the growth potential and your strategy – and your capability – to achieve aggressive goals. Industry analysts will be more interested in the value you plan to deliver to customers, unless they focus exclusively on market share analysis. The two presentations for these two audiences will be very different. They will complement each other, but they will not contradict each other. Depending on your strategy, the three main messages for the press may again be different from what the industry analysts or the financial analysts have heard. You may want to focus on benefits for customers, certain product features, price structures, superior performance or technology, ease of use, special solutions for special customer segments or your go-to-market model.

It is important to note that the key messages do not only depend on your company's position in the market and on business and marketing goals. The key messages also depend on your press audience. You would obviously deliver a different message to the business press from the one you would deliver to lifestyle media.

Now, let us assume we know our target audience and we have defined our three main messages. We would then collect all facts that would support the selected messages. After we have done that we need to find a way to tell a story with a logical and natural flow.

Here is an example. The scenario is a product launch.

You may want to start your presentation with the market development driving your product development and your go-to-market strategy. You could then lead into your business partnerships and finally into announcing your new products. The advantage of this story would be that you start with the market rather than with your own company. It would be an 'outside-in' approach. The disadvantage would be that you would position your company as reactive rather than proactively delivering against market needs.

A different way of telling the story is by starting with your company's objectives and its strategy. You would then lead into tactics and execution. You could do a brief update of what you have accomplished so far and then introduce the next step, that is, execute the product introduction of the day. This story would centre clearly on your company rather than on your customer. It is an 'inside-out' approach. You may get away with this story if you intend to deliver it to analysts or to the business press. It would certainly not resonate with the lifestyle press, to pick a contrasting example.

A third way of doing this presentation would be to focus on the customer, rather than your own company or an anonymous market. You may want to describe a typical challenge your customers are facing today. Current products in the market cannot address this challenge, but your new solution can. Note that you now truly put the customer at the centre. You position your company as customer focused and committed and you can still lead, later in the speech, to a higher level and embed your announcement of the day into your strategy. Also note that you address the customer challenge with a solution, not just with a product.

The above is just an example. With every message, you have many options to deliver your story to the press. What you should remember is that you need to tell a story that flows from beginning to end. There should be no disruption in the story – unless you want to use this presentation tool consciously to create attention. But when you do so, be sure that you do not leave any loose ends.

The backbone of your presentation now exists. The messages are defined and the flow is defined. The next step is to add meat to the story. From the collection of facts you amassed up earlier you now need to sort out those that support your story.

Once you have selected the facts that should contribute to your story, you need to embed them into the presentation. When doing so, you should pay attention to the following criteria. You will note that some of these criteria are valid for almost every speech, but some of them are specific to presentations to media representatives:

1. Continue to pay attention to keeping your message simple. Don't end up in too much complexity. Remember, you are not delivering a lecture to university students, but a speech to journalists who think in headlines. They are mostly interested in your main messages, ideally in a single one that will make it into the headline.
2. Do integrate so-called quotable quotes. These are carefully crafted quotes that you build into your presentation. They must be presented in such a way that it is crystal clear to the audience that these quotes contain your main points. Stress them clearly, speak them slowly. You may want to repeat them, so you give the journalists a chance to note them down word by word.
3. Be controversial! Journalists appreciate controversial statements. You could even build them into your quotable quotes. Controversial statements could be going against a common belief in the industry or they could be unexpected results from your research.
4. Continue to take into account your specific target audience. Different press audiences require different content. Do not bore the business press with product details, do not bore the trade press with too much strategy, do not bore the lifestyle press with product features.
5. Keep the presentation short and exciting. Our experience is that this harmless looking demand is one of the most challenging ones for most speakers. They will have to learn that things that are exciting to them may not be exciting to the journalists – and vice versa. The role of the PR manager is to be the advocate of the audience when the speech is written. The PR manager must veto a speech that does not meet the needs of the attending journalists.
6. Pay attention to the context of the speech. Will it be the lead presentation or a supporting presentation at the actual press conference? Will it be a short introduction to a breakout session? Will it be a dinner speech? All these speeches would obviously be different. This is true not only for the length of the respective presentations, but also for the content and the style.
7. Keep the presentation lively. Integrate examples that the audience can relate to. Always

remember that the presenter is the specialist. The journalists in the audience may not be as familiar with the content as the spokesperson. They need examples, references, customer case studies and use models that they can relate to.

8. Remember the good old approach to structuring the presentation in three parts: First tell the audience what you want to tell them, then tell them and, finally, tell them what you have told them. In other words: Start with a clear agenda and close with a summary or a list of take-aways.

We now finally have our presentation complete.

But is it really complete? Can we send a spokesperson to the podium now?

Not really. There are still a few more steps to be taken. In particular, we need to tailor the presentation to a specific spokesperson, we need to develop slides if appropriate and we need to craft an internal Q&A document[1] for the executive to prepare him or her for anticipated challenging questions. Also, the Q&A document should contain background facts that could be built into answers to questions coming from the journalists. It may also contain drawer statements[2] on anticipated questions related to known concerns or issues.

So, if you think in terms of documents, you may want to think of three documents that make a presentation pack:

1. The script of the presentation
2. A slide set (a PowerPoint document, for example)
3. A Q&A document.

If you want to roll the event out to other geographical zones, you may want to share these documents with your colleagues for appropriate localization, as needed. Note that the presentation does not need to be fully scripted. Depending on the speaker's preferences, you may only provide him or her with bullet points rather than with full text. These can obviously be integrated into the PowerPoint presentation (into the speaker notes).

The Q&A document

We want to address the Q&A document here right away. We have already clarified the difference between an internal Q&A document and an external Q&A which you share with the press, by inserting it directly into the press kits for example. Let's have a closer look at the internal Q&A and how to create it.

As a PR manager you prepare Q&A documents.[3] We believe there are a few points to pay attention to when writing an internal Q&A. The document is based on your professional intuition, that is, your experience as a PR professional. It enables you to predict the journalists' questions related to the announcement you prepare. Also knowing the audience of the journalists you can expect certain types of questions. For example, if you know that

---

1   Be very careful not to confuse an internal Q&A document with an external one. The internal one prepares a speaker for challenging questions. The external one is a tool to be shared with journalists anticipating their most burning questions.

2   Drawer statement' is a technical term in PR. It refers to a prepared answer to an anticipated (challenging) question.

3   Sometimes this document is also referred to as the 'Talking Points' document, since it is used to prepare spokespeople for their presentations and the interviews with the journalists.

none of business press, but only trade press have confirmed their attendance, then you can predict the questions accordingly and prepare for answers that may be more focused on the product or service you are announcing. If, on the other hand, you know that many business journalists are attending the event, you may need to prepare more figures and numbers for them. Journalists may already ask questions when confirming their attendance to the event. These initial questions already give you a good indication of what is on their mind. So if you or your PR agency talks to the journalists on the phone to receive their final confirmation, the discussion may trigger additional ideas for you on what else to include in internal Q&A.

Another aspect you need to look into is the nature of the announcement itself. Background information related to a product launch, for example, or to the company business, should be represented properly in the Q&A document.

And last but not least – it is important to sit down with your spokesperson to identify the topics and areas where they need more supporting materials to be included in the Q&A document. For example, you need to add more detailed information on the company you are acquiring or more background information on the products in the company portfolio. This may include pricing, technical features and competitive data.

Flow of presentations

Under normal circumstances, several speakers are involved in the presentations at a press conference. In order to make the session livelier it is not recommended to have all the presenting done by a single person. Also, you typically want to position a person for a certain topic. For example, at a product launch, you may have one presenter focus on business aspects and strategic trends in the market while a second presenter focuses more on the product aspects.

Unfortunately, in real life you may face the opposite challenge. In larger corporations you typically have many entities involved in contributing content to a press conference. They all have specialists who can cover their respective contributions in great detail – and they have an interest in presenting to represent their entity properly at the press conference. They may be driven by internal company performance measurement schemes. With this approach you run the risk of displaying the internal complexity of your company to the outside world. The individual internal entities may not have any meaning to the press and their respective contributions may not contribute to the event's main messages, but only dilute the content.

This results in a significant challenge for the PR manager, whose task is to find a balance between positioning spokespeople by topic on the one hand and parading dozens of executives on stage on the other hand. Experience shows that for a 1 to 1.5 hour press conference you should consider having three to four executives present. One executive may take the strategic business approach, one takes a technical approach and a third one may deliver a customer reference story. You may also have a guest speaker invited who takes an external view on the market, your company's position or certain technological aspects.

It is important in the context of speech development to have a clear understanding of what content and what message is covered in what presentation. There should be no redundancies, nor any gaps. Also, there needs to be a logical flow across the presentations. The audience needs to be able to follow the session across different speakers. It is proven good practice to create 'link patterns' across the presentations. This could be a visual that re-appears in every speaker's presentation. This visual could function like a map explaining to the audience where you are at a given point in time. You could also specifically refer back to key points from a previous speaker to link the new content to what has been said in a previous speech.

Typical mistakes

We all learn from mistakes. And we should not be afraid to make them.[4] In this sub-chapter we would like to discuss a few mistakes that are typical for inexperienced spokespeople who develop their own presentations.

- The presentation does not focus on three clearly identified messages. The speaker tries to cover all different aspects of the topic, shying away from consciously cutting content. Product managers, for example, tend to cover all features of their product rather than focusing on those two or three unique selling points or those aspects where your product has a competitive advantage. The audience is then challenged to make its own decisions to separate important from unimportant content. The result would be that you could see almost anything in articles afterwards. There was no guidance. Your intended message would be there only by accident.
- Do not learn the speech by heart or read a fully scripted text from a piece of paper or a teleprompter. Unless you are a very experienced speaker, you will come across as very stiff. You will not be able to connect with your audience.
- Do avoid abbreviations, especially when they are not commonly known.
- Every larger company tends to develop something like an internal language. Avoid those internal terms.
- Do not use complex language. Especially when you present at an international press conference, you need to respect the fact that most of the people in the audience are not native English speakers.
- Even experienced speakers sometimes have a tendency to begin every second sentence with a phrase like 'I guess', 'I assume' or 'I think'. The impression such a speaker leaves is obvious: He does not know, he is only assuming. Using these phrases, though, may only have become a bad habit at some point in time, and may have nothing to do with being insecure. They should be avoided just like the use of the phrase 'I would say', because a speaker is not pretending to say, but he actually does say.
- Avoid the use of too many slides. Slides are only supporting your presentation; they are not your presentation. You are not supposed to read slides. Remember that more than one slide per minute is a movie, not a presentation.
- Speak to the audience, not to the projection screen. Insecure speakers tend to use slides as their 'safety belt'. They tend to have all their text on the slides and then read from the slides. Since those slides are displayed on the screen behind them, they tend to turn their back to the audience most of the time to read from the screen.
- Tailor the wording to the audience! Inexperienced speakers sometimes address journalists with notes like 'you will like our product' or 'you should buy one of our products'. In other words, they address journalists as they would address potential customers. For journalists this sounds very disturbing. They are not there to buy a product. They are there to report on it, but they are not the target audience for the product – although there are obviously exceptions apply.

---

4   But there should be no excuse for making the same mistake twice.

- Try to avoid building projected slides or uncovering only gradually revealing an overhead projection slide. This looks a bit like trying to educate and does not necessarily go down well with many journalists. Experience shows that it is better to reveal the complete slide in one go and then walk the audience through it.
- Time management is a hassle for many speakers. A typical tendency is to underestimate the required time. A dry run is done speaking too fast and potential interaction with the audience is not built in.

On-site speaker support

- *Microphone*. There are different types of microphones that can be used for speeches. You may want to use those fixed to the podium or lectern. They can be recommended only to speakers who tend not to walk around on stage. Wireless handheld microphones are not recommended at all. They do not allow a speaker to use both hands during a presentation for gestures and limit the conscious use of body language. Wireless phones attached to the clothes of a speaker are probably the most common devices today and can also be recommended. They give the speaker sufficient flexibility to walk around on stage. Also, the speaker still has both hands free to point, use a cueing device for the slide projection or hold a script in one hand.

  It is important is to test out the use of the microphone. A final rehearsal should be done with all final equipment, pretending the audience is actually in the room. The volume should be checked for the right level and for consistency. Finally, it should be standard practice to put new batteries into the wireless microphones right before the event. You certainly want to avoid nasty surprises during the event itself
- *Teleprompter*. A teleprompter is a device for experienced speakers only! The incorrect use of a teleprompter can make the speaker look boring and emotionless.

  A teleprompter projects a written script for the speaker. It is invisible to the audience. The speed at which the text is moved on is either driven by the presentation speed of the speaker or it is the other way around, that is, it drives the speed of the presentation. It basically makes the speaker a remotely controlled robot. A teleprompter may be a useful tool for other occasions. It can certainly not be recommended to be used at press conferences. It kills connection and interaction with the audience, and any spontaneity. We would even argue that it is a dangerous tool since it makes a speaker dependent on it.
- *Slide projection*. Visuals are a very useful tool – if used in the correct way. They should support a speech. They should not replace it. Speakers often use it like a script, just reading all their text from the very busy slides.

  Slides should contain as little text as possible. They should just stress the main messages. Also, the number of slides used throughout the presentation should be as low as possible. The number of slides should be limited to only one slide per three to five minutes of speech.

  Images can be used on slides, but they should not dominate. They should certainly not distract from the speaker and the content. You should always remember that most of what the audience will remember from a presentation is not content related, but linked to the speaker's appearance, his voice, his clothes, his gestures. Slides can support the audience to remember the content but, if incorrectly used, they can achieve quite the opposite.
- *Monitor support*. Speakers typically stand on a stage, while the slides are projected on a screen behind them. Inexperienced speakers tend to turn around to the slides too often

and then talk to the screen. It is actually a natural behaviour to turn around from time to time to ensure that your speech is in sync with the slides being projected. But it is extremely distracting to the audience if done too often.

You can reduce this behaviour by placing a small monitor in front of the speaker on the ground. The monitor is linked to the projection system and shows the same display as on the screen. It should be placed so that the spokesperson can see what is on the screen without too much movement of the head. This little tool helps a speaker tremendously to focus on the audience and react to feedback from the audience in a much better way.[5]

- Cueing device to forward slides or to trigger film or other effects. The speaker should be able to focus on the speech, without having to worry about technology issues such as changing slides in line with the progress of the speech.

In an ideal world, the supporting AV staff will have been able to rehearse with the speaker so they would be able to forward the slides as the speech progresses. The speaker should not be involved at all. In order to give the speaker some control over the speed, they may want to use a cueing tool. It is basically a simple remote control which, while not addressing the system directly, sends a signal to a technical person managing the system and moving on to the next slide.

Directly changing slides, in a PowerPoint slideshow for example, would be possible as well, but you may want to avoid doing that as a speaker. You may want to use a direct remote control in more informal presentations. But you should certainly avoid them at major events with large audiences, since it takes away control from supporting staff; if there are problems, they will be unable to provide the appropriate help.

- *Timekeeping*. You should introduce some kind of time management. Real presentations tend to be slightly longer than dry runs. Since a press conference often runs to a tight agenda anyway, you should avoid delays.
- A simple method is to nominate one person at the back of the room who gives small signals to the speaker about the time remaining. These signals would be invisible to the audience. Having a clock on the lectern is not recommended. It can be very distracting. If you are using a very sophisticated system, you may also be able to provide information on the monitor referred to above. – Or, you simply have a little lamp on the lectern that will be controlled by the supporting staff. It can be turned on when only five minutes of presentation time is left, and it could start flashing when only one minute is left.
- Large screen behind the audience (not recommended). We have attended several press conferences, mainly in the US, where the speaker was supported by a large screen placed behind the audience. Similar to a teleprompter it displays the script to the speaker.

We strongly recommend that you do not make use of this technique. At every event where it was used, the audience discovered the display and from then on focused more on the text at the back than on the speaker in front of them. It is extremely distracting both for the audience and the speaker.

- Last, but not least: Have a glass of fresh water available for the speaker at the lectern.

---

5   We have seen monitor support with up to three monitors helping the speaker. One monitor would show the current slide displayed simultaneously on the large screen. The second one would display the next slide, in order to lead properly into the upcoming topic and to allow for a smooth transition. And a third monitor would display speaker notes or a script, depending on what the speaker would feel comfortable with.

Personalization of the presentation

Any presentation must be tailored to the respective spokesperson who is intended to deliver it. We believe it is impossible to have a speaker deliver a story that is not personalized to that individual. In order to make the presentation lively the speaker must feel comfortable with it. Any discomfort will be visible.

Spokespeople typically have different skill sets. Some are very good in 1:1 interviews. Some are very good in front of larger audiences. Some speakers feel more comfortable with business messages. Others prefer to talk about technical topics.

What is most important in a speech is that the speaker brings the content across in a convincing way. The style of the presentation needs to fit the style of the presenter. Speakers should never artificially change their style to match that of a written presentation. They should rather adapt the speech to their own presentation style – without changing the content and the main messages.

16 *Tips for Spokespeople*

The following tips are useful guidelines for inexperienced spokespeople who have never attended a press conference before. As the PR manager you should share these tips with them before the event.

It is needless to say that these tips do not replace proper PR or media training. But they could be considered a refresher for the spokesperson. PR or media training should still be a pre-requisite for any speaker at a press conference.

In this chapter we will address press conferences as well as industry analyst events. The reason is that they are often considered to be identical. However, there are subtle differences. Analysts and journalists have different skills and different requirements. Thus, spokespeople need to provide different content – or at least the same content needs to be packaged in a different way. And you may use different tactics to deliver the messages. Spokespeople need to be aware of these differences, especially when you have decided to mix the audience, that is, journalists and analysts are invited to the same event.

But both events have one important aspect in common. You want to be open with the audience. Or, rather, you want to create the perception that your company is open with the public. We do not want to say that you should only pretend to be open. But you should keep in mind that even if your company follows a strict open door policy, there are still topics that you cannot or are not allowed to talk about in public. For example, you do not want your competitors to read in tomorrow's newspaper everything about your company's future products or certain strategic or competitive moves. In some cases you are also restricted by external limitations. If your company is listed at the stock exchange, for example, you need to comply with certain blackout periods or silent periods before the regular (typically quarterly) earnings announcements.

It is important in this context to deliver content at a press conference in an open manner and to create a general atmosphere of openness. Still, certain content may not be disclosed. Even though these two demands seem to be contradicting, they can be managed very well: with good content preparation and with well-trained spokespeople. When you are well prepared, then you have a drawer statement for all anticipated questions that lead into topics you want to avoid discussing. And your speaker then applies what was learned in the PR training; to stay on message while not coming across as closed or trying to hide something the journalist might now try to hunt for.

'DOs' and 'DON'Ts' at international press conferences

In this sub-chapter you can see a 'superset' of guidelines that may be relevant at a press conference. At some point during the training of a spokesperson these topics should be discussed in detail. You should not need to discuss all of these during the preparation of a specific event. However, during a final briefing, you should be able to share some 'refresher' or reminder with them. You will find these quick references in the following lists.

PREPARATION

DO:

1. Be prepared: Read your pre-briefing material before the event.
2. Be consistent with what has been said in earlier analyst briefings.
3. Be familiar with what is said in the keynotes and integrate your own messages accordingly. Be consistent!
4. Be familiar with what your colleagues discuss in other presentations or sessions and be consistent.
5. Be prepared to respond to criticism.
6. Spend time with the journalists. Do not spend it on company internal meetings.
7. Know your target audience! Industry analysts want facts. Journalists want headlines.
8. Know the people you'll meet in 1:1 meetings; their profiles are in the material you should have received prior to the event.
9. Be on time. Start an agenda item on time and – even more importantly – finish an agenda item on time as well. The agenda at a press conference is very busy and therefore very vulnerable.
10. Be aware of blackout periods or quiet periods! Note that no statements can be made about the business performance of the recent quarter during the month before public announcement of the financial results.[1]
11. Bring some business cards along to the event.

CONTENT

DO:

1. Provide facts, examples and (customer or partner references). Customer references are especially appreciated.
2. Provide analysts or journalists with company information of interest to their coverage areas. Do not bore them with what may be interesting to you, but not to them.
3. Be as candid as possible. If you don't believe in something 100 per cent, or fear something may be incorrect, don't say it.
4. Stay facts-based when comparing your company with the competition. Do not jump into marketing lingo! This will not be appreciated.
5. Be extremely careful when discussing your competition; avoid condemning statements by using generic overviews. You may be held responsible for all your statements. If you say enough positive things about your organization, the journalist will be able to draw his/her own conclusions about your competitors.

DON'T:

1. Reference other analyst firms' studies, work, stats or opinions during briefings with analysts.

---

1   This requirement is valid for publicly listed companies in order to comply with Securities and Exchange Commission regulations regarding material containing non-public information.

2. Quote another analyst to an analyst.
3. Try to fool an analyst or a journalist. If you don't know an answer, acknowledge that you do not have the answer at present. Either follow up yourself later (and ensure you really do so) or – if not your area of expertise – pass the action item on to a member of the analyst/press relationship team so a colleague can follow up later.
4. Argue based on opinions. Stay facts-based!
5. Aassume the analyst/journalist knows everything about your company.
6. Make product or financial projections for the next quarter or year unless they have been stated publicly prior to the meeting. Mistakes can come back to haunt you.

TACTICS

DO:

1. Ask for their feedback in 1:1 meetings or breakout sessions. Make the sessions interactive.
2. Frequently ask for feedback to be certain the analyst/journalist understands. Ask questions such as 'Do you see what we mean?' 'Does this make sense?' and 'Does this reflect what you're hearing from others?' (especially with analysts).
3. Remember the names of the analysts/journalists and firms/publications and use them during the 1:1 as appropriate. Also, acknowledge the value the analyst is providing to you, if appropriate.
4. Request that the analyst ask any questions that come up during your comments. It is appropriate to say that you view the interview as a valuable learning opportunity – especially when with industry analysts.
5. Speak slowly, particularly if the analyst is taking notes and/or is not a native English speaker.[2]
6. Sell to analysts or the press, don't do a marketing presentation. Analysts in particular do not like that at all. They prefer facts!
7. Take notes; this may encourage the analyst/journalist to do so as well, but don't attempt to read the analyst's/journalist's notes and don't point to a note an analyst/journalist has made to correct it. If you think something has been noted erroneously, reiterate it in an effort to make a point.

DON'T:

1. Expect every analyst/journalist to be well prepared. As in any organization there are stars and there are those who just do enough to get by. Use the opportunity to educate an unprepared analyst/journalist; have some titbits of extra information to give the well-informed analyst/journalist.
2. Be afraid to say you can't answer a question. It's appropriate to say you would prefer not to answer a question because it is proprietary or might prematurely disclose future plans that you are not at liberty to discuss. Under no circumstance should you say 'No Comment.' This response is reserved for high-level politicians and is often taken negatively.
3. Talk about internal company topics with colleagues in areas where you can be overheard. Try to avoid internal meetings altogether.
4. Listen to your voicemail in areas where you can be overheard.

---

2   This is assuming that the presentation is done in English – a reasonable assumption in today's international business world.

5. Leave confidential material in areas where it can be accessed by unauthorized people.[3]
6. Compare the current press conference with previous events.

FOLLOW-UP

DO:

1. Take notes of questions that were left unanswered after a 1:1. Pass the note on to a member of the analyst/press relationship team for future follow-up.
2. Try to identify areas of interest for future follow-ups in order to allow your company to stay in contact with the analyst/journalist.
3. Leave contact details (ideally your mobile phone number) with the analyst/press relationship team, if you have to leave the environment for a while.
4. Keep the analyst/press team informed about follow-up activities such as future contacts with the analysts/journalists. This helps to prepare for future activities.
5. Follow up with analysts you have met at the event, if at all possible. Give them a phone call, provide additional information, request second opinions, and so on.

Tips for a successful press conference

1. Be prepared! Always reserve time for rehearsals and/or dry runs!
2. Read your briefing material!
3. Be on time!
4. No voicemail or internal meetings in public areas!
5. Do not leave confidential documents unattended!
6. Do not compare the current event with earlier press conferences!
7. Be aware of company policies (for example, NDA policy, blackout period, and so on)!
8. Note: Even the content of informal chats can result in coverage!
9. Always meet commitments to journalists (follow-up call, for example)!
10. Report any action item for follow-ups to your favourite PR manager!
11. Never forget: You are an ambassador for your company!

Tips for a successful press interview

1. Know your three key messages!
2. Prepare examples (for example, a customer reference demonstrating the use of your company's innovative technology or showcase, how your product or service improves people's lives)!
3. Know the journalist (name/publication/key interests)!
4. Be consistent!
5. Be honest!
6. Think headlines!
7. Make the interview interactive!

---

3   By the way, it is not even recommended to throw confidential material is publicly available waste baskets. This may sound neurotic, but there have indeed been cases where journalists have gained access to internal company information by looking in waste baskets at a press conference venue.

8. Think visually – consider photo opportunities!
9. Never speak 'off the record'!
10. Do not argue based on opinions! Stay facts based!
11. Avoid internal company acronyms and abbreviations!
12. Make a summary – do not expect the reporter to do so!
13. Do not judge a journalist by age or appearance!
14. Take notes and report back to your favourite PR manager!

Another way of preparing for a press interview is the following summary.

Quick guide for interviews

The following textbox has proven to be a useful Quick Reference Guide for executives, telling them what to do and what to avoid during interviews. It covers basics that should be self-explanatory.

Prepare effectively!
Have three key messages!
Illustrate with examples!
Stay good natured!
Avoid jargon, acronyms and internal speech!
Know the company disclosure policies!

Do	Don't
– be confident!	– debate!
– be clear!	– defend!
– take control!	– discuss!
– be punctual!	– keep journalist waiting!
– know journalist and publication!	– ask for copy of publication/article!
– be prepared!	– ask to see an article before publication!

You may want to tailor this reference card to your specific needs. A good practice is to make it available on a little card, ideally in credit card size, for easy storage.

Tips for successful interviews – reporters' techniques

Naturally, both parties – interviewer and spokespeople – have their respective agendas. We have already talked about tips for spokespeople to make interviews successful. Let's have a look now at reporters' techniques and how they may influence the outcome of the conversation.

It is important to remember that everything you say is on the record and may end up in print. This makes it important to answer the reporter's question directly but always bring the discussion back to the key messages.

The 'traps' journalists may want to use include:

- False questions. A false question is asked to test your spokesperson's knowledge, to make the spokesperson underestimate the reporter or simply to 'fish' for an interesting statement. Such a question may be 'Why did you drop to 30 per cent market share?' – knowing that your company actually has a higher market share. If your spokesperson knows, he will simply correct the assumption that is embedded in the question. If he does not know, he may make up a story – and this can end his corporate career immediately – or he admits that he cannot answer this question and refers the reporter to a colleague who can address it.

- Using negative words. A negative question is asked to see your spokesperson's reaction. The journalist's intention is to have his wording used in the spokesperson's reply. The result will typically make a snappy headline. An example is the question 'Why did your company not achieve its business results?' An answer like 'We did not achieve our results because...' would be the ideal single sentence taken out of context and broadcast on TV. It would certainly make your company look bad.

    Your spokesperson's reply should obviously make your company look good, even though the topic may be challenging. He should therefore use his own wording on the topic, rather than just repeating the journalist's phrase. In the above example, a better answer may be 'We are growing at the rate of the market – but we still have ambitious goals to grow even faster.'

- Silence (to encourage a spokesperson to speak more on a certain topic). Silence can be a very powerful weapon for a journalist. Imagine, a spokesperson has responded to a question and, instead of asking the next question, the reporter only looks at the speaker in silence. It is a very natural behaviour of most people to start talking again to avoid the silence. For a journalist it is very interesting to see what is said in such a situation. The interesting thing is that the pressure to ramble on is more or less self-inflicted by the speaker, who often then says things that would have been better left unspoken.[4]

- Reporters may pretend that they know something, for example using information from earlier leaks. In this case it is best not to confirm or deny the leak but to ask PR people to deal with such a request.

- Asking a question starting with 'Somebody said...' This actually means nothing. The statement does not reveal the source nor does it reveal the degree of truth in the statement to follow. This statement is just a trick to challenge a speaker. It is used to articulate a speculation and to see how a speaker responds. Sometimes reporters go as far as even mentioning a vague source like 'your PR department said' or 'one of your managers said'. Again, a response like 'Well, then it must be right, they should know' would be a wrong response. It is better not to confirm nor deny and refer them back to their original source – that was most likely made up in the first place.

- Asking questions out of context. This technique is mainly used to confuse a speaker. Any journalist who begins to realize that a speaker is only delivering a message he has learnt by heart earlier, will then attempt to break into that prepared speech by suddenly referring to completely unrelated topics. The journalist may also decide to quickly jump back and

---

4   Using silence as a weapon can be a very powerful tool in a phone-based interview.

forth between two unrelated topics. Untrained speakers can easily be distracted and get caught off guard.

Keeping in mind those basic 'traps' it is important to pay attention when you are forced to use a reporter's words (negative words) or when the journalist asks you hypothetical questions. These 'what if' questions only lead to speculation and move you off message.

So additional 'dos' and 'don'ts' will be:

- Don't use negative words (reporters' words) – do start with positive phrases
- Don't distribute negative stories
- Don't try to remember or answer all the questions – do select the question you like best
- Don't answer hypothetical questions
- Do correct a false question
- Don't confirm someone else's statement
- Don't be forced to choose from a limited number of answers like 'yes' or 'no'[5]
- Do be careful
- Don't keep talking just to fill in the silence – do use the silence to bridge to your key messages
- Don't try to answer questions outside your expertise.

Tips for an industry analyst briefing

Industry analyst briefings are somewhat similar to press conferences. Specific differences will be discussed in Appendix D. In the context of providing tips to spokespeople, however, we provide a list of recommendations in this chapter. Note that some of the items are relevant only for 1:1 briefings rather than classroom briefings to larger audiences. As in earlier lists in this chapter, the list will consist of things to do and things to avoid:

DO:

1. Know the analyst's area of coverage.
2. Provide materials in advance of briefing.
3. Provide facts, examples, references to sway analyst opinions.
4. Acknowledge the value the analyst has provided in earlier business intelligence projects.
5. Respond in a timely manner to incoming requests.
6. Respect the analyst's time by briefing only when necessary.
7. Provide analysts with information of interest to their coverage areas.
8. Invite their feedback.
9. Respect the analyst's time by making briefing appointments in advance, not at the last minute.
10. Brief analysts in advance of the press, partners, and so on. This gives them a lead time to form an opinion and consult journalists and others afterwards.

---

5   An interesting example is a question like this one: 'Can you confirm that your company will not make that stupid mistake again? Yes or no?' – Either answer is obviously wrong, since they would both admit that your company had made that 'stupid mistake' at some point in time. An appropriate reply therefore should not address the question itself, but it needs to correct the assumption that is embedded in the question.

11. Remember the names of the analysts and firms and use them during the briefing.
12. Request that the analyst asks any questions that come up during your comments. It is appropriate to say that you view the interview as a valuable learning opportunity.
13. Be prepared to respond to criticism. Stabilize the situation by noting positive steps that have been taken to address any problems. If appropriate, acknowledge that addressing the problem is a top priority. A company as large and as important as yours is apt to have its detractors.
14. Speak slowly, particularly if the analyst is taking notes. Always keep answers short; most questions can be answered in a minute or so. Frequently ask for feedback to be certain the analyst understands. Ask questions such as 'Do you see what we mean?' 'Does this make sense?' and 'Does this reflect what you're hearing from others?'.
15. Take notes; this may encourage the analyst to do so as well, but don't attempt to read the analyst's notes and don't point to a note an analyst has made to correct it. If you think something has been noted erroneously, reiterate it in an effort to make a point.
16. Be as candid as possible. If you don't believe in something 100 per cent, or fear something may be incorrect, don't say it.
17. Be extremely careful when discussing your competition; avoid condemning statements by using generic overviews. You may be held responsible for all your statements. If you say enough positive things about your organization, the analyst will be able to draw his/her own conclusions about your competitors.
18. Follow up as promised to the analyst.

DON'T:

1. Try to fool an analyst.
2. Reference other analyst firms' studies, work, statistics or opinions during briefings.
3. Argue with analysts based on opinions (you won't always see eye to eye relative to the facts).
4. Assume the analyst knows everything about your company.
5. Quote an analyst to another analyst.
6. Don't expect every analyst to be well prepared. As in any organization there are stars and there are those who just do enough to get by. Use the opportunity to educate an unprepared analyst; have some titbits of extra information to give the well-informed analyst.
7. Don't be afraid to say you can't answer a question. It's appropriate to say you would prefer not to answer a question because it is proprietary or might prematurely disclose future plans that you are not at liberty to discuss. Under no circumstance should you say 'No Comment.' This response is reserved for high-level politicians and is often taken negatively.
8. Don't make product or financial projections for the next quarter or year unless they have been stated publicly prior to the meeting. Mistakes can come back to haunt you.
9. Try not to cite a competitor by name. Remember, the briefing is about your company. If asked to compare your programme or product to that of a competitor, make clear you have no direct knowledge of their programme or product.

4 *At the Event*

CHAPTER 17

The Atmosphere at a Press Conference

Before we drill down into the set-up and the logistical details of a press conference we would like to discuss the environment of a press conference itself in a more generic manner. You may consider this chapter to be an introduction to the following chapters that will address on-site aspects of a press conference. In other words, we have completed the planning task and will start to execute the press conference itself now.

At the very beginning of this book we discussed the differences between a press conference and a generic industry conference. We now want to come back to that aspect and add one more topic to the discussion.

An industry conference is typically managed by an organization that is not necessarily in the limelight itself. Often they are associations of vendors, a marketing organization, an analyst firm or a trade show company. Typically, they are profit organizations that charge a significant fee to participants. In return, they provide content, knowledgeable speakers and a certain infrastructure.

As the organizer of a press conference, however, you go beyond being just an organizer of a conference. We would actually compare your duties to those of a good host.

Imagine, you invite good friends to an evening together at your house. The perfect host would know his friends very well. He would know their interests and opinions. He would know their preferred food and their favourite type of wine or beer. If you take your duties as a host seriously, you will create the right atmosphere for a good evening together.

The same is true for a press conference. You organize an event that all participants will hopefully appreciate. You create an atmosphere that allows all participants to benefit.

However, you should not go too far with the above comparison. Your evening at home is (hopefully) strictly a private event. But at a press conference all participants have a clear business objective.

We now come to a point that is often misunderstood, especially by executives who do not have too much experience with the press yet. It is important not to mix up the atmosphere of a press conference with the comfort zone of an individual participant. A spokesperson should not take it personally if asked a tough question by a journalist, and should not blame challenging or even aggressive questions on a bad atmosphere at a press conference.

Yes, it is true that challenging questions may move speakers out of their comfort zone. But the journalist is only doing what journalists are supposed to do. They are only doing their job, which is to question the news they are given; to look behind the curtain, so to speak. But, just as it is the journa;ist's job to ask questions, it is the job of the spokesperson to give answers according to the defined message. And, if confronted with a question that cannot be answered for legal reasons or because of corporate policies, the speaker must not answer it. In that case it was the journalist's job to ask, but it is the speaker's job (not) to answer.

Not being able to satisfy all the needs of a journalist does not mean that you have contributed to a bad atmosphere. Very often it is quite to the contrary. A good journalist asks specific questions as tests only, to check for consistency, and accepts it if a speaker does not answer for acceptable reasons.

Heated debates during an interview should not stop the interviewer and the interviewee having a glass of beer together in the evening (still being on the record, though!).

The atmosphere you create at a press conference is not measured by the fact that everybody is nice to everybody else, but a certain set-up that is consistent across the entire event and allows all participants to get the maximum out of the time spent at the press conference.

A few examples will illustrate the point we want to bring across.

Press conferences need to be tailored to the audience addressed. Your content, your agenda, your message, your set-up would look different, depending on whether you are addressing lifestyle journalists or the business press. Events for the lifestyle press are typically more focused on experience. You may even say they are more fun oriented. In comparison, it is probably fair to say that events with the business press are more conservative.

If you tried to run a lifestyle press conference for business press journalists, they would probably compare your event with a kindergarten. If you tried to run a business press event for lifestyle journalists, they would probably be bored to death. This means that you need to create an atmosphere that is appropriate for the particular audience you want to address.

But the atmosphere needs to match not only the target audience, but also your message, your company values and other parameters. Style, tone and manner need to be consistent across all ingredients of the press conference.

Here are a few examples of what might look inconsistent:

- Moderate presentations would not go along with aggressive visuals in the decoration or the signage.
- If your company is known for its openness, it would be inappropriate to be very protective at the event. For example, in this case it would be questionable consciously not to give journalists access to certain speakers. It could leave the impression you have something to hide.
- The style of the event is inconsistent in itself. For example, you fly journalists First Class to a luxurious location and a smart limousine between airport and conference centre. But, on site, you only offer unacceptable accommodation and hardly any infrastructure. An approach like this is only confusing. You leave the impression you have tried, but failed miserably.
- The right atmosphere is particularly important at reactive press conferences due to public pressures, that is, in crisis communication. Assume that your company is accused of something and decides to address the public in a press conference to prove that all accusations are invalid, or to comment on an accident. It would be counterproductive if you created an atmosphere of arrogance. It would be much more appropriate to show that you care and to provide facts.[1]

For a change, let us illustrate, with an example, how proper set-ups can contribute to creating the right atmosphere:

Assume you want to run a press conference that is focused more on relationship building and exchanging thoughts and ideas – rather than just introducing a new product, for example.

---

1   There are numerous examples of speakers who did not do their companies a favour with their appearance at such an occasion. One of the best examples was probably the CEO of the Deutsche Bank, who referred to the money lost in a deal as 'peanuts'. It was perceived as very arrogant. Waving an obvious problem away is not always the best strategy.

At such an event, it may not be appropriate to set up a classroom style seating arrangement. We managed such an event in 2003. We decided to put armchairs and sofas in the room, together with little tables where you could have a drink. The seating arrangement was very informal. This little trick contributed significantly to bringing all participants into the right mood. The event immediately lost stiffness. The gap between presenters and audience was reduced. Everybody felt encouraged to get involved in discussions immediately. Presentations became very interactive, all participants opened up very quickly. Very fruitful discussions for everybody were the result.

But it is obvious that armchairs and sofas do not make the difference between a successful and an unsuccessful event. They make an important contribution to the atmosphere, though, just like many other factors.

One of the most important factors at any event is the human factor, though. The behaviour of your company's representatives is the factor that typically makes the difference. Because of this, all your company's employees present at the event need to be briefed properly – even though they may not have an active role as a spokesperson at the event. They need to understand that they represent your company, regardless of what their actual role is. They need to think 'journalist first' all the time. It would not be appropriate at all, for example, to 'misuse' a press conference to have internal company meetings with colleagues who may be based in a different office. It would be more appropriate to spend the time with the journalists.

It is strongly recommended to do a briefing with all company representatives on site before your audience arrives. Dedicate time to go through the agenda and explain to every individual what is expected of him or her. They must clearly understand where they are supposed to be when. Also, everyone should be able to respond to any logistical question from a journalist without re-directing them to another person. For example, they must know where and when the lunch break is, where and when the breakout sessions start, and when to meet in the hotel lobby to be shuttled to the dinner. They must know where to register for interviews and, if necessary, they should be able to introduce executives to the journalists. However, it is important in this context to reiterate that only empowered speakers are allowed to speak to journalists about content.

Open and helpful employees are probably the best reference for your company at a press conference. They are the most important factor in creating the right atmosphere.[2]

---

2   In this context it is important to remember that journalists will hardly distinguish between company employees and staff working for supporting vendors such as your PR agency. Do always make sure that your PR agency staff understand that they need to behave as if they were employees of your company. The impression they will leave with journalists clearly reflects on your own company's image.

18 *Event Branding*

Your press conference should become a memorable event. There is a very obvious reason for that: you want the journalists to remember your messages and write about them as you planned. Ideally, you see headlines after the event that you had put down in your objectives before the event.

But there is a second reason for you wanting the journalists to remember your event and the messages delivered at it: You should have a strong interest in making the event have a long-lasting effect. Ideally, you have positioned your company as a leading thinker. You want journalists to recognize you as industry leaders whose opinion is relevant in the market.

In other words: You should be aware that you can achieve much more at a press conference than just delivering a certain piece of news on a certain date. You can leave a strong impression with journalists so that they also want to hear your opinion on any development in the industry in the future. If, for example, a competitor of yours makes an announcement at some time, the journalist would come back to you for a comment. Not only does this approach position you automatically as a leader, but it also gives you additional coverage and will allow you to have a free ride even on competitors' PR activities.

You could also say that the journalists trust you. They are willing to listen to you. And they will come back to one of your events in the future without questioning whether they want to invest the time.

The most important aspect is obviously to have a strong content at your press conference that has justified a journalist's time investment. On top of a strong message, there are many tools to make a press conference a memorable occasion. They include innovative presentation formats, special locations, and so on. You may call this the marketing hype. But you should understand that all vendors make use of this 'weapon'. So, even though you may want to avoid it, you can't. It is part of the overall experience. Journalists are only human, and they are receptive to these influences, whether or not they want to be.

A relatively straightforward tool is to theme or brand the event. Branding would involve several topics including:

- Logo
- Tag line
- Consistent look and feel.

A prerequisite for event-specific branding is a company policy that allows branding in the first place. This is not a given! Many companies are very specific about branding guidelines. They may, for example, allow only the company branding itself, but no sub-branding – for either product ranges or events.

A second prerequisite is a precise messaging framework. The message needs to be very well defined to allow for the development of a logo and a tag line, for example. Basically, a messaging hierarchy needs to be developed with only a single message at the top. This one single take-away can then be transferred into a tag line and into a logo.

But branding does not only require a logo and a tag line. It is as important to provide the journalists with a consistent look and feel at the entire event. Here it is important to note that this includes the complete process visible to the journalists from the very first invitation to potential follow-ups after the event.

Layouts of documents or signage, font styles used, the use of words and images, and so on, must be consistent to provide a consistent look and feel. And, of course, consistency needs to be provided across all aspects of the event. For example, the selection of the location needs to take into account the defined branding or theme. The presentation style needs to match the theme. For example, you may not necessarily want to introduce new cool toys for kids with managers in white shirts, ties and black suits.

Here are some examples of where to make use of an event logo:

- Letterhead of any event communication, incl. invitation letter.
- Table cards, 'with compliments' cards, and so on
- Press kit folder
- CD labels
- Badges
- Websites
- Event signage
- Presentation slides
- Backdrop on stage
- Agenda
- Registration desk
- Gift.

Example:

In the mid-1990s, Hewlett-Packard introduced a new microprocessor called the PA-8000. This new processor was one of the most powerful chips of its time. It was decided to use a panther as the symbol for the power and theme all activity around the introduction with a special logo of the panther.

Not only were PR activities branded with the panther, but other marketing communication functions (advertising, direct mailing, and so on) also made use of the panther.

All paper items weres branded with the panther; even video material had an animated panther walk across the scene. At some press conferences in Europe, the event itself was even themed accordingly. At an event in Zürich, Switzerland, for example, the venue was even transformed into a jungle. And during a break, actors with body painting played animals mingling with the audience. Soft toy animals were given away. And exotic fruit drinks were served.

The effect was so significant that many people still remember the 'panther introduction' today, about ten years later.

Example:

In spring 2005, Hewlett-Packard in the UK launched the so-called 'Smile' campaign. This campaign can be considered an integrated marketing campaign spanning across PR and other communication disciplines from advertising to in-store communication. Interestingly enough it was developed out of the PR department and then adopted across the entire consumer go-to-market organization.

All outbound facing activities in spring 2005 were themed around the Smile theme. PR activities embedded the smile message, which for example included some research results addressing the effect of smiling on people's mood. NCH, the children's charity, was sponsored as part of the project. Sports teams supported and promoted the campaign. Media partners were brought on board. And ultimately, the British public was invited to contribute to a photo gallery to exhibit people's smiles. In August 2005, the gallery became the world's largest photo gallery, according to the Guinness Book of Records, with over 33 000 smiles.

This campaign is a good example for considering branding or theming not only for a single press conference or a PR campaign, but for an entire campaign involving more than just the PR department. Journalists (and consumers) would be able to make a connection between the different deliverables from the campaign – from branding at a press conference to advertising to channel partner communication to in-store communication. The impact of such an integrated campaign is more than the sum of its individual components.

19 *Decoration*

We talked earlier about branding and theming an event. This can indeed be a very powerful tool to create a consistent experience for all participants.

You can support the selected theme with appropriate decoration of the conference room, the breakout rooms and any other facility used during the press conference. Even the corridors and the dinner venue can be decorated.

You need to ensure that all decoration is in line with the entire look and feel of the event. You should select exhibits that match not only the content and the theme of the event, but also the overall style in which the event is executed.

Appropriate decoration can intensify the experience and can help carry the news across to the audience. In particular, it can leave an impression that cannot really be quantified, but addresses the audience on a subconscious level.

The most common decoration is placement of your company logo all over the event. For a very simple reason it certainly makes sense to have the logo on the lectern and/or the backdrop of the stage during the press conference: note that the main speaker at a press conference is always a good photo opportunity for the press. It would be very nice to 'plant' your company logo into the picture that gets printed afterwards with the article.[1]

Photo opportunities

In general, you need to think of decoration in the context of photo opportunities – especially since decoration is not just the placement of company logos or posters on the walls. You can indeed do much more than that.

The options for good decoration are probably endless. In the following paragraphs we will discuss a few examples. Hopefully these examples will stimulate your own ideas for one of your own press conferences in the future.

- As already mentioned, the placement of posters may be a good idea. Although you need to select the posters carefully, they can generally, show almost anything, as long as the content is in line with your event's objective. If you run a business-oriented event addressing your go-to-market strategy, you may want to show examples of your latest or upcoming advertising campaign. You may also display your product range, technical highlights or reference quotes from customers, business partners or industry watchers – if appropriate for the event.

---

[1]   If timing allows, you should consider 'simulating' your speaker's presentation and take a professional high-resolution picture of your speaker on the podium prior to the event. You can place a hardcopy of this photo into the press kit or maybe even onto the event CD. Since you are in control you can select the angle and the speaker's facial expression and pose to your advantage. If you hand out the press kit only after the presentations are done, the photos may well be perceived as live photos from the press conference itself. (Just ensure that your speaker wears the same clothes on the photo as during his live speech.)

- You may want to display your products behind glass, as in a museum. If you are celebrating an anniversary such as ten years in business or 100 years of manufacturing cars, you may want to exhibit some of your products including the very first you ever brought to market. You may also do something like having the very first computer you ever produced on display right next to the latest one you are announcing at the current event.

- If you work with celebrities promoting your products, you may want to exhibit a picture gallery of those celebrities showing how they use your product. If you work for a company in the automotive industry, for example, you may want to show celebrities in cars from your company.

- You may want to show industry awards you have achieved, such as product awards or awards positioning your company appropriately around the theme of the press conference.

- If you represent an international company and you manage an international press conference, you should consider having displays from across the region that you are addressing.

- You may want to show how your products are actually used by your customers. Assume your company sells typical commercial products such as manufacturing devices (grinding machines, drilling machines, and so on). You may want to show the machines actually being used on the factory floor of blue chip companies – or you show samples of products that have been produced with the help of your machines.

- If your company is involved in sponsorships, you may want to make use of them at your press conference. The exhibits may be the sports car you sponsor, or a ball with the autographs of all players from the team you support. If you sponsor the fine arts, you may get an exhibit on loan from the gallery or museum you sponsor.

Regardless of what you display, you must document on plaques or signs what people are actually looking at. The best display does not support your message if it is not explained.

20 *Registration Desk*

The registration process contributes significantly to journalists' first impressions. The support they receive during the registration can have a significant influence on their mood throughout the entire event.

Put yourself in the shoes of journalists who have been invited to attend your press conference. They probably have with them your invitation letter and potentially some initial briefing you provided. When they arrive at the address you you have given, they will first of all be looking for a sign that tells them they are indeed in the right place.

Typically they will find themselves in the lobby of a hotel looking for a registration or hospitality desk. Even though your event may be in a different part of the hotel or maybe an adjacent conference centre, you should have a welcome desk in the location that was indicated in the invitation letter. In this case, you should have such a facility in the lobby of the hotel.

It is important that signage clearly indicates your presence on site. The desk should be visible from a distance. Your company logo or an event logo should be clearly visible and identical to what the journalist has seen in the invitation letter.

The desk should be staffed well in advance of the announced start time. Exact timing is dependent on the type of the event. If the press conference is a local event with participants being just from the same city, you may need to have the desk staffed an hour before the event. If the event is an international press conference with participants travelling quite a distance, typically by plane, then you want to have the desk staffed significantly earlier – depending on the scope of the event, up to a day earlier.

In the case of an international press conference, you actually need to consider additional aspects such as a pickup service at the airport if you have prior notice of the journalists' flight details. In that case the journalists will have made first contact with your staff at the airport, from where you will have arranged ground transportation to the event venue. In that case, your staff at the airport should again make use of signage which is in line with the signage the journalists have seen earlier, in the invitation letter. Once an initial contact is made and the journalists are on their way to the event venue, it is good practice to inform the staff at the registration desk by phone that they should prepare to welcome and register those individuals.

There are several important aspects you need to pay attention to when setting up a registration desk. Probably the most important one is to be well prepared. Especially after a long journey the last thing journalists want is to spend unnecessary time registering.[1] They want to have a clear understanding of what is coming next. Either they have arrived early and are invited to a coffee or a welcome reception to bridge the time until the press conference starts, or they should go immediately to the conference room; or they should pick up their room key first at the hotel reception to make themselves comfortable – all this depends on the timing and flow of your event.

---

1   Every frequent traveller knows the situation arriving at a hotel late in the day. The last thing you want is to fill in lengthy registration forms. All you are interested in is a key to a room. The situation here is very similar.

In order to speed up registration it is even recommended that you combine hotel registration with conference registration. In other words: You should arrange with the hotel that they will provide the journalists with both a room key and the conference materials in one single process. The journalists would not even have to go to the hotel reception desk. Note, though, that there are limitations to this process in some countries due to legal aspects of the registration, that is, if personal data (passport details, for example) need to be submitted to the authorities.

Conference registration

The registration itself should be comparatively straightforward – especially when you are well prepared. Since you should know who registered for the event, you should have prepared an information pack for the journalists up front. Collating it only when the journalists arrive is definitely not a good idea.

The initial pack should contain all basic materials, such as the agenda (potentially a personalized agenda – if appropriate, you should confirm interviews based on earlier requests from the journalist), a badge and maybe a map of the venue. Also, it should contain on-site contact details of people who can assist with potential questions or issues. It may also contain the press kit[2] (if timing is appropriate) and maybe a gift.

You may also want to quickly go over certain logistical aspects with the journalists, such as notifying them of any changes that have occurred since they received their invitation or their confirmation of registration – or you want to double-check that their departure plans have not changed since you last exchanged information. Travel plans are obviously particularly important for you in case you are responsible for their travel. For example, you may need to shuttle them back to the airport after the event – in time to catch their plane.

In some cases it is also appropriate to have the journalist sign an NDA immediately upon registration. This, however, should not come as a surprise! He or she should have registered for the event with the right expectations having been set up front.

Registration desk set up

The staff at the registration desk may be PR managers from your company. You may also delegate this task to an agency. You need to decide who actually welcomes the journalists, depending on the nature of the event. If you have a close relationship yourself with the journalists you expect to attend, it will be very appropriate if you run the registration desk yourself – or you are at least in the area to greet the arriving journalists.[3] If you are meeting the journalists personally for the first time (maybe you are hosting an international press conference and you do not have the relationships yourself with the local journalists), then you may run the desk with agency staff.

As mentioned before, the desk must be clearly visible and branded with your company logo or event signage.

---

2   See also Chapter 23 on the press kit.
3   Just put yourself in the shoes of the journalists again. If you are there when they arrive, you add a very personal note to the situation. You show that you care. The journalists have access to a familiar person, a 'go to person', they trust. It may not always be comparable to two old friends meeting but, if possible and if appropriate according to local custom, you should work on creating this kind of relationship.

It is strongly recommended that you have the welcome packs ready and sorted in alphabetical order, so it is quick and easy to find a pack for an arriving journalist.

Very importantly, the desk staff need to be able to get hold of other staff very quickly. Depending on the size of the event, the staff may be connected through walkie-talkies or simply via mobile phones. This will make it easy to get help quickly if the journalist has questions the desk staff cannot answer directly.

Message board

The registration desk is also the ideal location for a message board. The message board allows the organizers and participants to post information for other participants. If, for example, participants want to arrange meetings with each other, they can leave messages for each other on the board. It also gives the organizers an opportunity to share last-minute changes with the journalists. You can also pass on information coming in from outside, for example asking a journalist to return a call that was received by the organizers of the event.

At major international press conferences, the message board can also be used to post the logistics of the return travel. It is common practice at events we manage to post the departure details on the board together with re-confirmation of the flights for every single participant.

21 *Badges*

In his book on manners, Asserate Asfa-Wossen[1] describes how much he dislikes badges being worn at events. He is convinced that he has had the best conversations with people who tried to avoid wearing badges – just like himself – and to whom he had to formally introduce himself. According to him, badges are a distraction. You focus more on trying to read a person's badge than on the person himself.

Unfortunately, Mr Asfa-Wossen did not provide an alternative to badges for conferences. So, it is strongly recommended that you have participants of your press conference wear badges at all times.[2] This is especially true when you operate in an open environment, that is, where anybody has access to the conference facilities. In fact this is the case for most press conferences, since you typically do not have exclusive access to a hotel or a conference centre or any other public building where you may run your event.

Badges should be handed out during registration of the journalists. Staff and spokespeople should already be wearing them during the on-site preparation and set-up phase.

Badges fulfil several needs:

- You will always be reminded of the name of the person you are talking to. You can address the person by name – something that always adds a personal note to a conversation or a press interview.
- You may want to separate your participants making use of colour coding. For example, you have a mixed audience with journalists and industry analysts at your event. There is a special programme planned for analysts only. You can easily control access to their dedicated sessions if you have badged people properly.
- At larger press conferences you may want to break the audience into smaller groups to attend, for example, breakout sessions or product demonstrations in groups that allow for interaction or for a good view of the demonstrations. Another example would be a factory visit where you may want to rotate the audience in small groups at several stations where they are shown separate aspects of the manufacturing process. In order to make it easy for the journalists to remember what group they are in, you may want to have the group name or number on the badges.
- They are a security item, since people without badges would not be allowed access to the conference room. Badges allow you, for example, to control access to the venue during the set-up phase, when you do not want to have journalists around who have arrived early. Security guards should control access not only during the conference itself, but also during installation and de-rigging times.

---

1   Asserate Asfa-Wossen: *Manieren* (Eichborn-Verlag), in German – see also appendix on references.
2   Badges may not be needed at smaller events with fewer than, say, a dozen journalists. People probably know each other anyway, or there is sufficient time to introduce yourself personally to everyone before the event and familiarize yourself with the participants.

- They allow you to restrict access to certain locations or at certain times to a limited number of people only. For example, you may want to allow your staff access to store rooms, but not a journalist. Also, you may want to allow certain contractors access only for setting up staging or de-rigging, but they should not have access to the conference itself. All these limitations can be managed with colour coding of the badges.

The content on badges should be comparatively straightforward. First of all, it should not be forgotten that a badge is an item that allows branding with either the event logo or with your company logo – whatever is appropriate. Also, if there is a tag line going along with your event, you should consider adding it to the badge, unless this is distracting.

For a journalist it should contain his or her name – correctly spelled, which is often a challenge at international events. It should also contain the name of the publication he or she writes for (or the note 'freelance'), and if appropriate, the country the journalist originates from.

For spokespeople, the badge should contain the person's name, the company name and, if appropriate, their country of origin.

For staff, it should contain the name and the generic comment 'staff' (colour coding is another option).

As already mentioned above, colour coding of the badges is highly recommended in general. This could be done through colourful lanyards or through coloured text on the badge itself.

It is important to have a font size on the badge which is big enough to enable reading from a distance of 2–3 metres/yards. Otherwise the badges do not really fulfil their tasks. Badges could be handwritten on prepared templates, but it is recommended that you print them properly for advance registration. For journalists who do not register before the event, though, you should still have a facility in place to get badges printed on site. This is also needed for journalists who lose their badges or leave them in their hotel room.[3]

Figure 21.1   Event badge (example)

---

3   If the distance between conference centre and hotel is significant, you cannot simply ask the journalist to go back to his room and pick up his badge; you should be able to print a new badge upon request.

Finally, let us give you some hints to make badges a really useful tool:

Some time ago, it was fashionable to use self-adhesive badges that stick to your clothes. We would recommend not using those; they look cheap and the badges tend to crumble and come off far too often – and, in any case, people do not really want to stick something like this to expensive clothes.

It was common practice for a long time to make use of badges in little plastic holders that you can clip to the pocket of a shirt or a suit. Again, they cannot really be recommended since it may be impossible to clip them to women's dresses, for example.

The best option seems to be badges that are worn on lanyards around the neck. These badges are not only easy to wear, but you can for example use the lanyard for colour coding. Just be aware of the fact that badges worn around the neck have a tendency to turn around from time to time. Thus, it is recommended that you also print on the back of the badge so that the desired information is visible at any time – so you do not have to face the embarrassment of asking someone to turn their badge round, potentially because you have forgotten their name.

But the back of the badge can also be used for other purposes. For example, useful information for the owner of the badge can be printed there. We have seen beautiful examples of having a short version of the agenda on the back of a badge or a map of the venue, in case it is complex and you easily get lost. Also, important contact details may be noted on the back of the badge. For the journalists, you may want to offer an emergency telephone number giving them access to central on-site support. This central support could be a person from your logistics agency coordinating all services, maybe located at the reception desk or at a hospitality desk. That person should be able to initiate services like travel arrangements, interaction with the hotel, or technical support. For badges of staff members or company executives, you may want to have contact details of the most important players on the back, such as mobile phone numbers of the PR department team leader, the PR agency, the production agency, and so on.

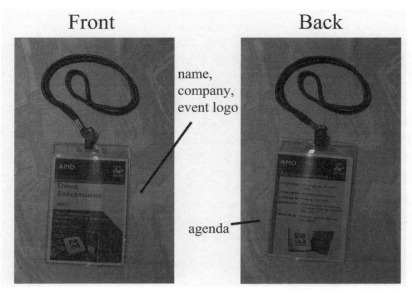

Figure 21.2   Event badge (example)

Finally a comment addressing the 'hunter-gatherers': Some people collect nice badges. They display them like trophies on the wall by their desk. This may be another reason for you to brand your event badges and make them look really beautiful.

22 *Press Room*

Journalists attend a press conference because they expect to receive information they can share with their readers. It is mandatory to provide a facility at the press conference venue that allows journalists to connect with their offices and to pass the received information on to their offices immediately after the actual press conference is over.

This 'press room' is a dedicated room for journalists where they have access to all facilities they require to format the information for their respective needs and to send the information back to their offices. The press room is particularly important for journalists who work to short deadlines, for example daily newspapers and especially online publications, where articles can be placed at any time and minutes often count.

A press room must have certain facilities:

- Computers with access to the Internet and equipped with standard word processing software (typically Microsoft Word or the entire Microsoft office suite).
- Free phone lines to allow for access to the Internet for journalists who prefer to use their own laptops.
- Phone lines.

Apart from these basics, it is strongly recommended that you provide some additional equipment in the press room, including:

- Copier.
- Printer (you can either equip selected or all computers with a printing device, or – preferably – you provide a network printer for the entire set-up). By the way, the network printer(s) should be set up as the default printing devices on the computers.
- Document shredder.

The size of the press room is dependent on the size of the press conference. It is recommended that you have seats available so about 20 per cent of the participants can access the Internet or use phones simultaneously. The size of the room and the set-up should allow the individual journalist to have some privacy when using the computers. In particular, anybody entering the room should not be able to view the content on a monitor.

The number of seats can be reduced when providing a wireless LAN capability at the conference venue. The installation of wireless LAN has become more and more popular especially at major events. This feature is often already built into the conference facility or the hotel and allows journalists to access the Internet with their laptops typically from anywhere in the building. You should make wireless access cards available on loan and respective technical support, if required. A note of caution on wireless LAN capabilities, though: it is strongly recommended that you do not have it functional during the main press conference, since it tends to distract the audience. The journalists should not browse the Internet during the presentations. You want to have the journalists' full attention during the presentations, so you should start the wireless LAN only after the session is over.

A press room should be open throughout the entire duration of the press conference. If the conference starts at 9 am and interviews last until the late afternoon, it should be opened immediately after the press conference (not in parallel with the press conference, since the journalists should be attending the conference at that time) and be available until the last journalist has left the event. If the event is an international event where several journalists stay overnight and only return on the following day, it should be available until roughly midnight. Experience has shown that it is indeed in use until very late at night. By the way, it helps tremendously to have refreshments available in the room at all times.

Since not all journalists can be expected to be computer experts, it is important to have on-site technical support available at any time – for the press room itself and also for the wireless LAN capability you may have installed. You either have a person available right in the room, or you advertise a telephone number to call if issues need to be resolved. The support engineer on duty should then be available within minutes.

There are some additional considerations when setting up a press room.

You have several advertising opportunities in the press room. The screen saver and the mouse pad can be prepared to represent your company and/or event logo – depending on what is appropriate.

If you have an online press kit, then the default URL of the Internet browser should be set to that website. Otherwise, you may want it to point to your company's home page.

Side note: You should pay attention to the fact that the press room was set up for journalists. Your staff should not use it as an extension to your office, and your executives and your spokespeople should not use it to connect online to their e-mail accounts or block the PCs for other purposes. Not only would that be counterproductive but they could also disclose internal information to the press representatives. Phone calls can be overheard and the content on screen can be visible to others.

CHAPTER

23 *Press Kit*

The term 'press kit' (or press pack) defines all material that is made available to the journalists at the press conference.

Often the documents are not collated, but the individual items are handed out separately, or they are made available in separate piles. Since there is a high likelihood that some journalists may overlook some important documents, distribution via 'self-service' is definitely not recommended. Also, handing out documents separately should be avoided.

It is best practice to compile all documents before the event into a single package and make that package available as one piece – the 'press kit'.

We shall now look at three aspects of the press kit more in detail:

1. Preparation
2. Content
3. Timing of delivery
4. Method of delivery.

Preparation

Typically, several individuals and organizations in your company contribute to the development of a press kit. There is obviously you as the PR manager and there may be your supporting PR agency. Your product managers and your marketing organization may also provide significant content. Your marketing manager, for example, should deliver the messaging framework and your product management should provide product features – and ideally also customer benefits for selected target audiences, that is, targeted customer segments.

You need to define roles and responsibilities during the content development very clearly. Otherwise you may for example see a message that is not in line with other activities from your company or you may select the wrong features and benefits for the audience that you selected – maybe a certain vertical market, maybe a special consumer segment. (Note that – for a defined product – the benefits for different markets may be very different.)

The role of PR should be to coordinate all efforts and to 'package' the message in a proper way for the press. In particular, PR should ensure that all documents developed for the press kit are consistent. This can be a difficult task, since content can come from very different sources in very different styles. A market analysis from your intelligence department may contain good facts, but it may come in very dry spreadsheets. Also, the content provided by your R&D department for the technology backgrounder may be very good for scientists, but it will be your responsibility to take the content and make it readable for journalists.

Depending on the size of your company, you should define a shared repository during the content collection phase for all inputs for the press kit. This could be a folder for hardcopy contributions or – preferably – a shared electronic repository such as a shared drive, a Lotus Notes environment, an internal website structure or any other shared tool.

The tool itself or the defined processes describing how to use the tool should ensure that it is made impossible for a document to be developed in parallel by two or more members of the team. Clear version control of documents is a prerequisite for successful work.

Definition of the rules is up to every team. It could involve a folder structure, file name structures or declaration of version numbers in the files themselves, in Microsoft Word documents, for example.

Content

The content of the press kit depends on the objective and type of the planned press conference. Some documents are fundamental and should be available at any event. They include:

* Agenda
* Press release
* Photos and biographies of the speakers

Other basic documents include:

* Additional photo material
  * Examples: Company logo, company CEO, company building, products, high-resolution photos of key images from the presentation slides, environmental photo shots of your products[1]
* Backgrounders and white papers
  * Examples: Company backgrounder, technology white paper, market backgrounder, product line-up, by-liners
* Customer references and third-party endorsements
  * Examples: Customer case studies, quotes from business partners
* Presentation material[2]

---

1 An environmental shot of a product could be a workstation computer as it is used in a CAD department of a company. It could also be a consumer using the products, such as a child playing with a toy, a housewife using a kitchen implement or a street scene with pedestrians using mobile phones.

2 Presentation material typically undergoes many revisions and draft versions before finalized. You are often still making changes during the very last rehearsal the night before the press conference. At that time the handouts have typically been printed already. You then need to decide whether you want to reprint the handouts or leave the slide version in the press kit unchanged.

I strongly recommend a reprint if ever possible. There are several reasons for going that extra mile. It may cost you some extra time and money, but it is certainly worth it. If, for example, you remove or add slides to the presentation, then the journalists will be confused comparing their handouts with what they see on the screen. This will not only increase the noise level in the audience because the journalists will turn pages over looking for the missing slide. It will also confuse many journalists who are used to scribbling notes on the handouts that will be the basis for the articles they will write afterwards.

A more serious issue is caused when you enhance slides. You may have discovered a mistake on a slide or something that can be misunderstood. In that case you must change the handouts, since a difference between the handouts and the presented slides will actually highlight the issue to the audience. Now they will certainly pick up on it...

But the biggest problem is probably caused when you change something in the strategic slides. If you are not consistent across handouts and presentation slides, you will almost certainly leave the impression that you have only just made that strategy up; that it is not really a sustainable strategy of your company; that you will probably show yet another one at a future event. In other words, your commitment to the strategy is questionable.

- • Example: Microsoft PowerPoint slides
- • Q&A document[3]
  - • Example: Most commonly asked questions about the new product – and the respective answers.

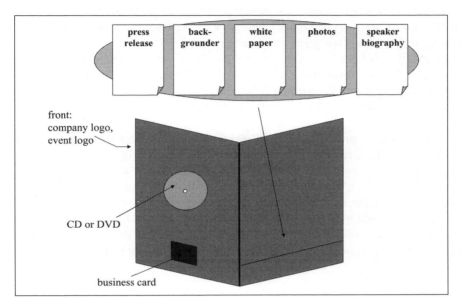

Figure 23.1   Press kit content

Even though they may not be part of a generic press release, it should be mentioned in this context that you may also want to have special materials available for specific media.

This could be a so-called opinion piece written by one of your executives. In such a document, a representative from your company could express his opinions about trends in the industry and position your company accordingly.

You may also want to have film/video material available for TV stations or online media.

If your press conference happens to be at an industry event such as a trade show, you may want to describe your presence at the show in a separate document. This document could include a description of your stand and also other activities of your company such as presentations (outside the press conference itself), exhibits on business partner stands, and so on.

Timing of delivery

The press kit should be made available to the journalists neither too early nor too late.

If you deliver the content too early, then the journalists could try to file their story straight away – not even bothering to wait for the upcoming press conference itself. Also, they may no

---

Because these last minute changes are common, you should check early in the process if you have a 24-hour printing service close to your venue or if you have in-house printing capabilities in a hotel business centre or maybe in your office close by.

3   Be very careful not to confuse an internal Q&A document with an external one. The internal one prepares a speaker for challenging questions. The external one is a tool to be shared with journalists anticipating their most burning questions.

longer see a need to go the conference at all, since by then the news will be old. Note that in the age of online news services every minute counts.

If you deliver the content too late, you will not only have unsatisfied journalists, but you may also see less coverage as a result. It should be a golden rule that at least the press release and the presentation slides are available during the main presentation(s) to allow the journalists to take notes on the hardcopies. A more detailed press kit can then still be made available when they leave the press conference room.

Best practice, however, is to make the complete press kit available either upon registration (if not time critical) or upon entering the press conference room. And, by the way, do not forget those journalists who registered for the event, but did not show up due to unforeseen changes in their diaries. You should follow up with them and send them the press kit straight after the event.

Until now we have only spoken about a press conference with a homogeneous audience, where all journalists are treated the same way and they all get the press kit at the same time. Take into account, though, that this is not always the case. You may encounter situations where you have a mixed audience with, for example, trade press and daily newspapers. In that case you may want to consider making the press kit available to the dailies the night before, since they could then publish on the following day – in line with your embargo dates. It would not be acceptable, though, to see the news in the next day's early morning editions, while your press conference is only later in the day. So, you want to be very careful managing these exceptions.

Method of delivery

Basically, there are three different options available today to deliver the press kit:

1. Hardcopy
2. Electronic
3. Online.

A mix of the three options is also possible – and sometimes strongly recommended.

HARDCOPY

Handing out the press kit in a nice folder on paper is probably the most conservative way of delivering the material. This option has a significant advantage: Your journalists have a copy in front of them during the presentations, so they can take notes and scribble down comments during the presentations. (By the way, since journalists always want to be able to take notes during presentations, you should never darken the room to a level where taking notes is impossible.) These notes will also help the journalist to get actively involved in any Q&A sessions after the press conference or they will stimulate questions for any 1:1 interviews.

Disadvantages of hardcopy press kits are that they are no longer necessarily appropriate support for journalists, since they went electronic themselves some time ago. A paper copy of a document does not allow for 'cutting-and-pasting' important text passages. Images need to be scanned in rather than making direct use of a high-resolution .jpeg or .tif file, for example.

ELECTRONIC

To some degree it is state-of-the-art today to make press kits available in an electronic format. This could be on a CD or a DVD. The material could also be on a USB memory stick (which itself could then be a nice gift, by the way).

A word of caution up front: Making documents available electronically contains a serious risk that you should be aware of. Your documents may contain information that is not intended for the press. Two examples:

1. The 'notes' section in Microsoft PowerPoint may contain internal company text, especially if the slide has been used for other purposes before. Ensure that all notes pages are either erased or only contain information you consciously want to share.
2. Microsoft Word tends to store older revisions of documents even though they are not necessarily directly visible. Smart journalists, however, know the tricks to get access to those hidden treasures. Analysing older versions could give them a hint of where you felt uncomfortable when crafting your message. Obviously, this is not really what you want to share with the public. A simple way to avoid this issue is to cut-and-paste the final version of the document (the press release, for example) into a virgin Word file.

But there are more challenges with electronic press kits. If you do not make the information easily accessible, then journalists may not take the time to search for the information they are looking for and they give up. Two rules should always be followed:

- Provide a good content list. Ideally this is in hardcopy and comes with the electronic media. The content list could be on the cover of the CD displayed in the jewel case.
- Make files easy to find. A very sophisticated solution would be a graphical user interface (GUI) that starts automatically when the CD is inserted in your computer. Development of such a customized interface may not be in your budget, though. In that case, you need to make sure that the naming of the files is as self-explanatory as possible.

We would like to elaborate a bit on file naming. What a user would see on the CD or the memory stick is a collection of files – if there are many of them, they are hopefully stored in a proper folder structure. The order in which they appear in the directory depends on the setting of the journalist's computer. You can assume that the majority of users sort files by name. A typical directory could therefore look like this:

JMiller.doc
John.jpg
Mainpressrelease-final.doc
Speaker1.jpg
Supermanwp.doc
Tom.doc

This list is not very self-explanatory. The following list contains the same files, but named differently. We assume it is obvious that this CD is easier to use than the one above:

_Press_Release.doc
John_Miller_bio.doc
John_Miller_photo.jpg
Tom_Smith_bio.doc
Tom_Smith_photo.jpg
White_Paper_Technology.doc

In this example, you should pay particular attention to the name of the technology white paper. In the first version the name of the file contains 'Superman', the internal codename of the technology. You may not actually want to share that name, and unless it is explained in the event, it is meaningless to the journalists anyway.

One important advantage of an electronic press kit is to allow journalists to simply 'cut-and-paste' important text portions from your documents into their articles. Because of this, you should always consider having document formats that allow for cutting and pasting. A Microsoft Word document is ideal, since the format is readable by almost everybody. An Adobe .pdf document would not allow for cutting and pasting that easily.[4]

ONLINE

Over the past few years, the use of online press kits has become more and more popular. The idea of directing a journalist to a website has a certain attraction to the organizers of a press conference:

- You can make last-minute changes without print re-runs, CD-reproductions or – in a worst case scenario – a distribution of 'corrections'.
- You can make the press kit available to everybody, even to journalists who do not attend the press conference. Just send them the URL.
- You can hyperlink to other relevant material available on the Internet.
- You can update the press kit with additional material as it becomes available – for example, you can make pictures available from the conference almost in real time.

Despite all these advantages, it should be noted, though, that there are also a lot of disadvantages that go along with the use of an online press kit. These disadvantages include:

- An online press kit is anonymous. It takes away one important part of PR: the R – Relationship. So, if you want to use an online press kit, you must at least have a contact person set up with all contact details documented. So, if issues come up, the journalist would know where to go to for help.
- You have changed the process of information transfer significantly. In the old paradigm it was your responsibility in PR to make information actively available to the journalists. With the emergence of online press kits you transfer the active role to the journalists. It has now become their problem to collect information as needed.[5]
- When using an online press kit, you must advertise its existence very strongly. We have often seen that with the availability of an online press kit no paper material has been

---

4   A .pdf document, however, does not contain information from older revisions. Thus, it is certainly safer than a Word document.
5   In the German language the difference is nicely described by the two words 'Bringschuld' (obligation to be performed at creditor's habitual residence) and 'Holschuld' (debt to be collected from the debtor at his residence).

handed out at all. This is fundamentally wrong! Not only do you no longer make copies of the presentations available for taking notes during the sessions (see above), but also you do not even hand out leaflets with the URL of the online press kit. You should note that a short reference on a slide during a presentation will not be sufficient to advertise the press kit.

- The online press kit will typically be removed from the website at some point in time – depending on the policies of your company. Be aware that as soon as you do that you basically destroy the 'archive' of the journalist. He will probably store a hardcopy or an electronic copy for as long as he thinks he will need it, but he is at your mercy with the availability of the online press kit – unless he goes through the painful exercise of downloading everything for potential future use, which is very unlikely.

- An online press kit is based on the assumption that all journalists have access to the Internet. Nowadays this is probably a reasonably fair assumption. Still, you need to ask yourself whether your entire audience has reasonable access. Maybe in some regions journalists still have access through slow modems only or they have to share access with their colleagues. In some countries, access can still be slow – and downloading a 5 Megabyte presentation, for example, can be a very time consuming and expensive exercise.

Having listed all of the above, it looks as though we are not friends of online press kits. They are actually an appropriate tool, but given all these limitations we would strongly recommend that you make use of them only in combination with other deliverables.

DELIVERY MIX

It may have become obvious that the different ways of delivering a press kit fulfil different objectives.

The hardcopy version is a good basis for the journalists to take notes on site. It is also a good tool for getting easy access to information without requiring a computer or online access.

The electronic version allows you to make material available that cannot be shared on paper, such as mpeg video files. It can also be much more complete than a paper copy without weighing too much.

An online version can be updated with new information at any point in time.

It has been shown to be good practice always to make a paper version of the basic materials available at press conferences. They include the agenda, the presentations and the press release. All these documents should typically be stored in a folder. A strong recommendation, by the way, is to include in the folder the business card of the PR manager responsible for the event, so the journalists know who to turn to if any questions are left open at the end of the event or if any other follow-ups need to happen.

If appropriate, a CD or a memory stick should be included in the folder. It can contain the hardcopy material in electronic format plus any additional information you want to share with the journalists. As mentioned before, it is essential to provide a good content list in hardcopy.

If an online press kit is made available, it should ideally only be in addition to the press kit we have just described. In that case the URL should be clearly advertised in the folder you hand out on site. The advertisement should also explain why you may want to visit the site (for example, it contains additional picture material that is neither in the hardcopies nor on the accompanying CD).

It is important to note that the online press kit should be embedded in your company's 'online press room'. This will make it part of your PR archive and it will automatically also become visible to journalists who do not attend the event itself.

Special considerations

So far, all discussions in this paragraph have been fairly straightforward. However, it should be noted that one approach does not meet all needs – and sometimes you need to be very inventive with the press kit to create a lasting impression.

We want to discuss four special considerations:

- Consumer press kits
- Joint releases of multiple organizations
- Non-disclosure agreements
- At a trade show.

CONSUMER PRESS KITS

The press kits we have described so far were very factual. Press kits for the consumer press, however, should go beyond just providing facts and figures. Here you may want to cross the border from pure education to include a dose of entertainment as well. Your press kit can easily become a piece of 'edutainment'.

This can already show in the format used. You may not want to use a standard A4 size (or US letter) format, but maybe a very different one. If it fits with your message, you may want to print out on large format endless paper. It would then be similar to what messengers used in Ancient Rome or in the Middle Ages. You may also use different materials such as canvas to print on.

Finally, you can prepare the content in a way that is different from a potentially dry format driven by company guidelines.

Examples:

- A press kit announcing a new surfboard may be written on card shaped like a board.
- A press kit announcing a new fashion collection may be printed on fabric.
- A press kit announcing new photographic solutions may be done based on photos rather than regular paper.

If you want to address the younger generation with a typical consumer product, then you should also consider adapting the content and texts accordingly. You certainly want to use a language that resonates with the audience. As an example, you may also want to re-write the biographies of your executives. It may, for example, be more important for this audience to stress the hobbies of an executive than his achievements as a business manager.

JOINT RELEASES OF MULTIPLE ORGANIZATIONS

When companies partner up to do joint announcements, you typically run into conflicts with the formats for press materials defined by the individual partners. In that case you either agree on a compromise or one company takes the lead.

The press kits of joint announcements must be reviewed and approved by all participating partners. It is important that the joint message and the chosen format are in the interest of all partners. You need to keep in mind that the respective partners may have different agendas at the joint press conference and it needs to be agreed up front how to address them in a consistent way.

It should be no surprise that journalists will try to find weak points in the announced partnership – and an inconsistent press kit would be an ideal starting point for them.

NON-DISCLOSURE AGREEMENTS

Sometimes, the content of a press conference or parts thereof are subject to a non-disclosure agreement (NDA), that is, the press embargo date of the news is only in the future. We covered NDAs in Chapter 6 on the embargo date but it is appropriate to refer to them briefly in the context of press kits because it may be a prerequisite for journalists to sign an NDA before they receive information on the announcement.

If we indeed hand out press kits as the journalists enter the press conference room (or they find the kits on the chairs in the room), then the journalists must have signed the NDA beforehand. It is best to get this done immediately upon arrival or registration for the event.

AT A TRADE SHOW

If you happen to run a press conference at a trade show (or any other industry event), you have a unique opportunity to share your news with a wide range of journalists. Even journalists who do not attend your event may be interested in getting access at least to your press kit.

You typically find a dedicated place in the press room of the trade show, where you can promote your press kits. You should confirm the availability of such a space. And you should print an appropriate quantity of your press kit.

24 *Interviews*

Interviews are the spice in press conferences. They are a unique opportunity for the journalist to get exclusive information and for company spokespeople to focus content on the needs of an individual journalist and to initiate a dialogue with the journalist.

Press conferences that do not allow time for interviews miss an important point. Without interviews all journalists have received identical information. They would not have received exclusive information. They would not have received a unique selling proposition for their publication based on information they can offer to the public.

Because interviews are so important, several prerequisites must be fulfilled by the organizers of a press conference. We will discuss these tasks one after the other.

1. A sufficient number of interview partners need to be available at the event. At major international press conferences typically about 100 or more journalists participate. Let's assume that all journalists request an interview. Let's also assume that an interview takes about 15 minutes and let us assume that 2 hours on the agenda are reserved for interviews. Simple mathematics shows that in such a scenario more than 10 spokespeople must be available for interviews to allow for a sufficient number of interview slots at the event.

2. The spokespeople can meet all demands at the press conference. When you put your team of speakers together for a press conference, you need to consider two aspects. The first one is to address the 'pull' from the journalists, that is, the request for information of the attending journalists. Your spokespeople will have to address all possible questions related to the content, but they will also have to be able to communicate properly. This means you will have to anticipate most of the questions to select the appropriate set of spokespeople to cover all potential content areas. In addition you may need to cover communication-related aspects such as addressing the journalists in different languages, if needed. The second aspect you need to consider when selecting spokespeople is the 'push' from your company, that is, it is linked to the content you want to disclose and focus on at the event. For example, you may need several speakers to cover technical aspects (of a new product, for example) and others to cover business aspects.

3. Prior to the event, journalists need to know which executives will be available for interviews. The level of executives speaking at a press conference defines how important an announcement is for the company. It is obvious that the appearance of your CEO would attract more journalists to the event than running the event with lower level executives only. However, this may not necessarily mean that the CEO is available for every journalist for 1:1 interviews. For interview purposes you need to be precise who can be booked for by whom for a 1:1.

Journalists must have the opportunity before the press conference to register for interviews.

During the registration for the press conference the journalists must be able to register for interviews either using the registration website or by filing the request with the PR manager who issued the invitation. Once the request is entered and confirmed, the journalist needs to get feedback. If an interview timeslot with the requested executive is no longer available, then an alternative executive should be offered.

Registration for interviews

Before the event you have to develop an interview schedule. This schedule is basically a straightforward spreadsheet defining available interview timeslots with your executives. It should also contain a definition of topics the respective executive can address and the target audience the executive should address. This interview schedule is an internal document that is used to fix, to document and to confirm interview requests.

Here is an example:

Executive	Topics	Audience	11:00-11:20	11:20-11:40	11:40-12:00
Mr Jones	Company strategy	Business press	Slot 1	Slot 2	Slot 3
Mr Schneider	Product details	Trade press – German only	Slot 4	Slot 5	Slot 6
Mr Baker	Business update	Trade press	Slot 7	Slot 8	Slot 9

To continue with this example, suppose a journalist requests an interview with Mr Jones. You will then check whether the journalist meets the criteria defined for Mr Jones' audience, that is, if he is a business press journalist. If not, you will either decline the request or propose another speaker.

If he does, you would use your internal criteria to approve or to decline the request. These internal criteria would be used if more requests for interviews come in than there are slots available. You may want to make slots available on a first-come-first-served basis, but you may also prioritize journalists by business criteria. For example, you run a special campaign in a certain country and you want to support it with PR activities in that country. Then an interview with a journalist from that country would be preferred over others.

Once the interviews are confirmed, you need to develop schedules for executives and for journalists. The schedule for your executive should contain some briefing document on the journalists he or she is going to meet. The briefing document should contain information on the magazine the journalist represents, such as the type of readership, circulation, and so on. It should also contain information on the journalist, such as: the last contact with your company; attitude; interest; whether currently writing an article.

At the event itself, you need to be flexible to address last minute changes. It is a common scenario that journalists change their minds after having attended the press conference. They may no longer need to talk to the executive they had registered for initially. If such a change happens, you should check why the journalists have changed their minds, since there are reasons that are positive for you, and there are those that have negative implications. The journalists may have received all the information they need during the presentations and be pleased with it. On the other hand, they may have discovered that they want to talk to another executive since there are angles to the story that they were not aware of before your press conference. The worst case scenario for you is that a journalist realizes that the story is not really relevant for their publication at all. In that case you have probably made a significant mistake inviting that person in the first place. You have probably not paid attention to the areas of interest of the journalist, the magazine and its readers.

Interview desk

It is good practice to offer an interview desk at a press conference since changes happen all the time at press conferences.

The interview desk is a place where a journalist can request, change or cancel an interview with an available executive. Ideally, he can see at any point in time which interview slots are still available or whether a certain executive is still available or already fully booked.

The interview table should be in a central place that can easily be accessed by all participants. It should be staffed from the moment when the press conference is over and the participants leave the presentation room.

It has proved to be good practice to have the person running the interview desk work with a spreadsheet or with dedicated software which displays the slots in a way similar to the above table (excluding the columns on 'topics' and 'audience'). Ideally that information is passed to a large screen that is visible from a distance. The content in our simple example could look like this:

Executive	11:00-11:20	11:20-11:40	11:40-12:00
Mr Jones			
Mr Schneider		1:1 available	1:1 available
Mr Baker		1:1 available	

Note that at larger press conferences this table would be more complex.

Three recommendations:

1. In order to make it easier for the journalist to select the right interview partner, you may want to put not just the name on the board, but also the job title of the executive. This is particularly true if the person in question was not one of the speakers at the press conference and is not be known by the journalists.
2. It is also helpful to have small piles of hardcopies of the biographies of the executives available at the interview desk. Again, it helps the journalists to identify the right person to interview.
3. You should not display the names of the journalists who have the interview on the board. Some journalists do not appreciate it if their competitors can see easily who they have an interview with. You should just 'remove' the taken interview slots from the table (perhaps by using black as in the above example).

Logistics

Ideally you have small interview rooms available for your executives. At big events with too many journalists and too many executives this may not be feasible. In that case you should set up a larger room with several little tables.

You need to pay specific attention to the noise level in the room. The participants in the interview should not be distracted by what is going on around them. Mobile walls usually do the trick. Not only do they provide some privacy, but they also absorb noise sufficiently.

Every table should be equipped with at least three chairs, since you will need one for the executive, one for the journalist and one for a PR host. You should be prepared, however, for several journalists wanting to interview an executive jointly in one session. This is particularly common when language barriers need to be overcome. These logistical aspects are sometimes more demanding than the request for an exclusive interview. In that case the support of a PR host translating for the executive (and also for journalists) is often enough appreciated.

Finally, some basic recommendations:

- It is useful to have a sign on the table with the name of the executive, since the journalist may not know him or her by sight.
- You should have paper and pen available, since the journalist may want to take notes, or the executive may do some sketches for better explanation.
- You should have some water and glasses available. They should be renewed after every interview.
- You need to pay attention to the timing. An interview should not take longer than planned, since the next interview with the same executive may be scheduled right afterwards – and since the last thing you want is delays in the agenda.

TV interviews

We have already seen above that we need to pay attention to the noise level in the area where interviews are conducted. This is particularly important if a journalist tapes the interview for future evaluation. This is even more important for journalists who tape the interview for radio broadcasts.

In addition, TV journalists require an environment that is also visually attractive as well. They are always looking for a background and an environment that match the style of the programme in which they intend to show the interview (or parts thereof).

At press conferences after sports events it has become a common practice to do interviews in front of a backdrop displaying the sponsors of the event or of the teams. At a corporate event, you may not want to copy that practice directly, but you may want to have a backdrop prepared with an appropriate image on it. Your spokesperson can then be filmed in front of it responding to questions from the journalist.[1]

It should be reiterated in this context that spokespeople typically require special training if they want to handle TV interviews.

---

1   By the way, if you position two of these backdrops appropriately, you can easily simulate a little TV studio with the journalist and your executive being placed on chairs in front of it.

25 *The Appropriate Give Away*

The idea of a 'give-away' is often only considered as an afterthought when planning press conferences. In other cases it is outsourced to an agency or an administrative assistant looks after it.

The typical result is that the give-away is completely disconnected from the rest of the event and most likely has no link to the message delivered to the press.

We have seen other cases where hours are spent in meetings discussing what give-away would be appropriate at an upcoming press conference. The search for the appropriate give-away all of a sudden becomes more important than the message at the press conference.

Neither paying too little nor paying too much attention to give-aways is actually appropriate. Paying too little attention could result in confused journalists who do not understand why they were given this funny item. And paying too much attention could result in the present getting more attention than the message (from the organizers as well as from the participants).

A proper give-away should meet certain criteria. They include:

1. Support of the message
2. Usefulness
3. Practicability
4. Uniqueness
5. Ethics.

Before we go through these criteria in detail, we should try to answer the basic question of why we want to provide a little gift to the journalists in the first place. What is our objective?

If you believe that the whole intention is bribing members of the press – or at least giving them a gentle reminder to write something nice about your company or its products, then you should stop reading here. This cannot be the goal. It is not only unethical, but it is amazing that people may believe that they can buy a journalist with a $10 or $20 item anyway.

The goal is rather to support your event message – just like you support it with the decoration of the venue or the signage at the event. The difference, though, is that the gift provides you with an opportunity to address the journalist personally – and he or she can keep it to be reminded, hopefully for a long time afterwards, of the great event – and the message you delivered.

Support of the message

The most important aspect of the give-away is to support the content of the press conference. If your message is around a low-cost consumer item, you should consider providing the reporter with a sample of your product. This is probably the most logical gift – especially if you are convinced that you are delivering a product that the reporters will enjoy and ideally even benefit from in their daily life. It is probably fair to say that the consumer lifestyle press almost expects a product sample for testing.

If your message is about a service or an expensive commercial or industrial product, you may need to look for another option.

An option could be a part of your product prepared as a paperweight. If the product is attractive enough, journalists would certainly consider using it on their desks in the office.

Examples of attractive parts could be components from racing cars or computer processors moulded in plexiglass. If your product is endorsed by a celebrity you may also consider autographed items that hint at your message.

Generic items like a bottle of champagne or a cuddly toy should not be considered, unless you happen to sell the champagne or manufacture the toy. There are obvious exceptions, though: The Shell company, for example, may consider giving away cuddly tigers ('tiger in the tank'). Other generic toys such as music CDs should also not be considered since there is a high likelihood that your journalist's taste in music is not the same as yours; unless you have found an attractive CD which is typical of the region where you are running your event.

Products with a local flavour should always be considered. They are a nice souvenir, especially from places that are considered exotic for the majority of the audience. This could be art such as local music (Tchaikovsky in Russia, Riverdance in Ireland, country and western music in the USA, and so on) or replicas of famous masterpieces (Michelangelo's David in Florence, ancient Greek statue in Athens, da Vinci's Mona Lisa in Paris), local food (cheese in Switzerland, olive oil in Greece, anything in France), local clothes (tie with local motif, local hat or cap), or others.

Usefulness

When you are in a location that your journalist has probably not been to before, you may consider making a travel guide or at least a map of the environment available – especially when your agenda allows for some leisure time.

Another very useful item is a briefcase, a bag or a rucksack that allows the journalist to take all the documentation home. At major industry events it has almost become a standard to give such an item away to store the conference proceedings, agenda and other items. At press conferences it is very appropriate to make the press kit available in such a bag. If the briefcase or bag is branded with your company logo, you will also have some free advertising. But do not make the branding too cheesy, or nobody will be willing to actually use the bag.

One more example of a useful item: very often, press kits are made available nowadays on electronic media. One example is the material to be stored on a USB memory stick. If the memory size is attractive for the journalists, they will certainly continue to use the stick after they have erased or – better – downloaded your material to their hard disks. Again, a decent branding of the memory sticks helps raise awareness of your company.

Practicability

Several items can cause a surprisingly negative reaction from a participant at your press conference.

Your journalist may have to travel quite a distance back home from your press conference. If it was an international press conference, he will have to pass borders and most likely customs and he will be limited to hand luggage on a plane.

Oversized items should therefore not be considered. A framed picture, for example, may be nice and may fit the theme of your event. But it may be too bulky for transportation.

Other items may be subject to import restrictions in certain countries. You should always make sure your give-away can be taken into any of the countries where your delegates come from.

Another typical example of a not-so-good give-away is alcohol. It may neither support your message nor meet the journalist's taste. And you should always take into account that the journalist may have planned to buy a bottle of their favourite whisky in the airport's duty free shop – and would not be allowed to import more than that one bottle into their home country. We have seen complaints from Scandinavian journalists because of just that, when they received a bottle of wine when departing from a press conference. Because of the high taxes on alcohol in their home countries they wanted to take advantage of the business trip to buy their personal favourite alcoholic brand abroad.

Uniqueness

You should always aim to position your company as something special. You are not just a follower of the industry or a 'me-too' company. You want to position your company as a unique company with certain strengths. You drive the industry rather than being driven by it.

Consequently, you should be inventive when it comes to gifts. Probably the most boring ones are 'yet another pen' or 'yet another T-shirt'. We remember times when a press conference without a T-shirt as a give-away was not a proper event. Journalists must still have piles of T-shirts in their cupboards, wearing them on Saturdays when they mow the grass behind the house – or have their kids wear them after school. A T-shirt as a give-away is probably the opposite of inventiveness.

It is much more interesting to give journalists something that not only reminds them of your message, but is also unique. There are two lines of thought you should keep in mind for finding a special give-away.

The first line of thought is to provide a give-away that cannot be bought in any shop; something that makes you feel privileged to own it. An example could be an item that is autographed by a celebrity. You should consider this when working with a VIP who endorses your products or messages – in advertising, for example.

The second line of thought is to consider something personal. Nowadays it is not difficult to find an agency that can personalize almost any item for your journalists. How about a car model that has your name as a number plate (assuming the idea of a car goes with your message)? Or how about a bottle of olive oil with a label indicating that this bottle was produced specifically for you – your name being on the label (assuming that the oil goes with your messaging and/or you run the event in, for example, Greece)?

Ethics

As stated above, give-aways must not be used as an attempt to bribe a journalist. A gold watch or any other expensive item would therefore be extremely inappropriate. It is probably fair to say that business journalists comply best with ethical guidelines. A German business reporter was quoted in a radio programme that he was already concerned not even to accept a pen if possible.[1]

The problem at international press conferences is the fact that the thresholds from ethical to unethical can vary quite significantly from country to country. The real value of a certain item may not be different from country to country, but common practice may be different from one country to another.

A fine leather briefcase (with an imprint of your company logo) holding the press kit, for example may be considered an acceptable item in some countries, while it would be rejected in others.

It should be noted that ethical standards are particularly high in the USA, where it would even be inappropriate to take a reporter out for lunch for an interview or for exchanging opinions and thoughts. In this context it should be noted that even the question of who pays for the journalists' travel would be answered differently in the USA and in Europe. While it is more or less common practice in Europe for the organizer of the press conference to pay for travel, reporters in the US will pay for themselves to avoid any potential conflict of interest or even dependency on a vendor.

Teaser

In order to maximize awareness for an event, a gift can also be handed out together with the initial invitation.

The give away needs to be different, unique and likely to catch the journalist's imagination. Basically, it needs to make the journalist become interested in learning more about your event. Therefore, the gift needs to be closely linked to the event.

Here a few examples from previous events we were involved in:

- For an event in Dublin, we added an Irish leprechaun (troll) to the invitation.
- For an event introducing a product codenamed Piranha, we produced special ginger bread shaped like a piranha.
- At a tradeshow we introduced mobile solutions. We created awareness for our event with chocolate shaped like a mobile phone.
- At another tradeshow we ran a press conference to which we invited journalists with a letter accompanied by a key. The key then opened a door in a safe. The journalists were so curious to find out what was in the safe that almost three times as many attended the press conference as initially expected.

---

1   Karl Schlieker, business reporter of the Wiesbadener Kurier in the SWR 2 programme 'Achtung, Schleichwerbung. Die Macht der Pressesprecher' on 2 September, 2005.

Minor teasers could also be used as incentives in exchange for a returned feedback form (see Chapter 26). Depending on the quality level of the event, this may be small toys or CDs with local music.

Exhibition products at special prices

It is common practice at trade shows to sell off exhibition products at special prices to visitors at the end of the show. It is particularly interesting for consumer products, but commercial products are often also sold at large discounts if bought directly at the trade show.

In a similar fashion, you can offer used products exhibited at a press conference to journalists. This works if discounts are attractive enough and if the journalists have a personal interest in the products. These offers are not really free gifts, but it is a unique opportunity for the journalists, as they only got access because of their profession.

5 *After the Event*

26 *Feedback Collection*

During a press conference you have several opportunities to collect feedback from journalists. The fact that a press conference is an opportunity for a dialogue rather than a one-way communication is often overlooked (see also the introduction to Chapter 9). Collecting feedback is in fact equally important for your company, since it not only tells you something about your messages, how they are perceived, or how you execute the logistics of press conferences, but it also offers you an external view of the industry, trends and directions – and your company's relative position in the market, as viewed by independent observers of the industry.

It is very important to understand that collecting feedback does not only happen at or after a press conference; you already have an opportunity to collect input during the initial contact and during the invitation process.

For example, you may learn during the invitation that many journalists will not be able to attend because they have already agreed to attend another press conference by another vendor. Maybe you are lucky and you even learn which vendor has invited them to a press conference. If so, then this may be an indication that you have to watch out for a competitive move that could directly affect your own announcement strategy and your own message. In that case, you had better prepare respective drawer statements on anticipated moves by your competitors.

Formal feedback

During the event itself, you have several opportunities to collect formal feedback from the journalists.

An obvious one is to make an interview a true dialogue rather than a Q&A session. You certainly answer questions from a journalist, but you also request feedback or ask for the journalist's opinion. This technique should consciously be used in an interview, but you should not undermine the main purpose of the interview. Also, you should not start asking questions yourself only because you are not able to answer the journalist's questions.

There is a school of thought that you should not get involved in such a two-way discussion with a journalist at all. We disagree with this strict approach. We believe there is room for a discussion during an interview – as long as the length of the given time slot allows it and as long as the journalist opens up to the discussion. The discussion should obviously not be forced upon the journalist nor should it conflict with the desire of the journalist to collect information. In other words: The primary reason for the interview should not be compromised.

The second formal way of collecting feedback from journalists is to use feedback forms. You can use feedback forms in different ways or on different levels. Either you ask them to fill in a single feedback form for the entire event, or you provide feedback forms for each session.

For example, if you run a main press conference and several workshops and/or product demonstrations and/or breakout sessions, you may want to offer feedback forms for each activity. This should give you detailed feedback on each topic. Experience shows, however, that journalists do not really appreciate spending too much time filling in feedback forms.

Best practice is to have a single form available for the entire event. And it must be as brief as possible. You should not exceed a double-sided A4 (or letter size) page. It is important to explain the return process clearly to the audience. You may even offer a little incentive in return for a filled-in form.

Please find a sample feedback form on the following pages.

It is obvious that you cannot ask questions in a formal feedback form in the same way as in an informal discussion.

In a feedback form, you address the following topics:

- Value of the presentations (content and presentation format/style)
- News value
- Value of the overall event and of individual activities
- Personal impression and perception
- Event logistics.

You may add a question on plans to write articles on the news disclosed at the events. But we recommend that you do not put this question in the formal questionnaire – especially at international press conferences, since in some regions this question is considered to be inappropriate. It is more suitable to ask questions about intended write-ups at informal occasions like small talk over drinks, during breaks or at dinner.

This questionnaire is designed to gather your views of this press event. It will help us to find out more about your needs and ensure that future events meet your requirements. Please be honest when completing this questionnaire.

Please give marks out of ten for each of the following: (1 = poor, 10 = excellent)

Morning Presentation

	Speaker 1 *Title of speaker 1*	Speaker 2 *Title of speaker 2*
Quality of the presentation:	....	....
The value of the information given:	....	....
The quality of the press material:	....	....
The news value of the briefing:	....	....

Breakout Sessions

	Topic 1	Topic 2	Topic 3	Topic 4
Quality of the presentation:	....	....	....	....
The value of the information given:	....	....	....	....
The news value of the briefing:	....	....	....	....

What were your three key highlights of the event?

1. ....

2. ....

3. ....

How could this event have been improved for you?

....

....

....

Overall Event: **Please tick:**

How would you rate the information value for this event?	1. unacceptable	2. acceptable	3. good	4. very good	5. excellent
Did the trip meet your expectations?	1. unacceptable	2. acceptable	3. good	4. very good	5. excellent
Overall, do you feel that the trip was worthwhile for you?	1. unacceptable	2. acceptable	3. good	4. very good	5. excellent
How satisfied were you overall with the event?	1. unacceptable	2. acceptable	3. good	4. very good	5. excellent

What suggestions would you make to the organizers:

....

....

....

Name: ....

Publication represented: ....

Country: ....

Informal feedback

Most of the time you probably interact with a journalist either on the phone or via e-mail. A press conference is one of only a few opportunities to spend time face to face.

Ideally, you have created an agenda that allows for 'shoulder rubbing' and informal discussions. You may offer a cocktail reception, coffee breaks, dinner, lunch, or other hospitality events. All these activities allow you to spend time with the journalists to learn about them, their opinions and what they have picked up from their readers. We have seen cases where journalists are not very keen to share this information. But most of the time, they are extremely willing to discuss these items.

We have even seen cases where journalists proactively approached vendors to work together. Technical journalists who evaluate products are sometimes especially interested to sit down with engineers from your company to share information in the interest of their readers and to get customer requests built into development plans for future products.

27 *After the Event*

The last journalist has left the conference building, you are exhausted, and you open a bottle of champagne with your colleagues to celebrate. The conference is over.

Is it really?

In fact, it is not.

Not only does your agency need to de-rig the stage and remove all equipment, but you also still have several tasks ahead of you. Not necessarily straight away, but certainly within the next days and weeks.

Initial de-briefing

It is strongly recommended that you do an initial informal de-briefing right after the event – while the memories are still fresh. You should note down any kind of immediate feedback, either from your colleagues directly, or based on informal feedback they have picked up from participants at the event (journalists, guests and executives).

As long as you are still on site you should also run a formal de-briefing with the management of the hotel or the conference centre. Even though they have probably worked primarily with your events agency, you are ultimately responsible for the event, and you should ensure that there are no loose ends left behind. Make sure, for example that the hotel is satisfied with the condition of the venue as you leave it behind. No further cleaning or making good should be needed that would catch you unawares and make an impact on costs. Even though costs may go via your events agency and they have even budgeted for everything, the event was ultimately done in the name of your own company. And it should be part of your corporate responsibility to ensure that no mixed feelings are left behind.

We remember a major press conference in Venice where hanging up several pictures on a wall caused the wall colour to suffer. The request from hotel management to repaint the wall was justified – especially since the hotel was a historic monument – and the cost was actually minor. You should not leave such negotiations to your agency, but show commitment yourself in representing your company.

Follow-ups

Very high on your priority list of action items must be all follow-up activities with journalists. You have probably picked up action items from journalists who attended the event. But there is also an action item related to journalists who did not attend the event.

Remember: When a follow-up is promised you must follow up! Not doing so can be considered a PR crime! With respect to action items that are not followed up, a journalist's memory is similar to that of an elephant.

Typical actions are picked up during 1:1 interviews. Journalists may have requested detailed information that may have required some research and was not available right away. The PR managers who attended the interviews need to collect all these action items and process them immediately. You need to keep in mind that the journalists attended your event and dedicated time out of the office to collect information from you and your company. They are now writing their articles and probably depend on the additional information they requested from you during the interview. You had better provide that information as quickly as possible. Remember that they are competing with many of the other journalists who also attended the press conference and they need to write their article straight away in order not to fall behind.

Another typical scenario is a request during an open Q&A session that either cannot be answered immediately away or that is only of interest to a single journalist, and a lengthy answer would bore the rest of the audience. A typical speaker's reaction is the request to take this question offline. Again, this approach is not a carte blanche to forget about the question and the respective answer, but it is an action item for the speaker to follow up. The follow-up can happen either right after the presentation or – if additional information is needed – in a phone call at a time that is appropriate for both parties.[1]

Typical information requested for follow-ups includes picture material, market data or technology details.

But you also need to follow up with journalists who did not attend the event, especially those journalists who initially wanted to come but cancelled later and must be very interested in your news (otherwise they probably would not even have cancelled, but would have simply stayed away). You should send them the material together with the offer to be available for additional questions if needed.

A little side note related to follow-ups with journalists: it is inappropriate in several countries to thank the journalists for their participation at your press conference. They would feel offended since they did not participate to do you or your company a favour, but because they did their job. They certainly do not want to leave the impression that they only attended because they owe you something. This would obviously be unethical.

After the event is before the event

You certainly want to measure the outcome of the event. You want to see what the journalists have been writing about your announcement. You also want to de-brief with the crew and understand what worked well and what can be improved at the next event.

In particular, the end of this PR project already gives some indication of what to do next and how to approach future PR activities, since PR work is a circle (planning – execution – evaluation – situation analysis – planning – and so on). The outcome of the current press conference should clearly affect the planning of future PR projects.

---

1   This example illustrates that postponing an answer cannot mean forgetting about it. If a spokesperson cannot answer a question, it is right to admit the fact, to refer it to another spokesperson or follow it up in person at a later time, once the information has been gathered.

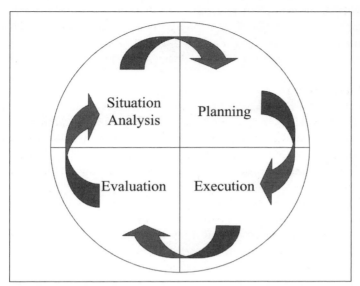

Figure 27.1   PR process

We would like to discuss a few scenarios that you may encounter and that should drive your future PR activities:

1. You have just completed a press conference educating the business press about your business strategy. The event was clearly set up as a pre-cursor to a new drive of your company with new products into new markets. An obvious next step would be to introduce those new products to the trade press.

2. You realize from the feedback that your message did not go down well with your audience. Maybe they bluntly disagreed with your story. In that case you may need to rethink your product development, your marketing strategy, your go-to-market approach or your overall business strategy – depending on what your message and the reaction actually was.

    But the disagreement of your audience could have been caused by some other factors as well. Maybe you simply did not articulate your message well enough or maybe you did not tailor your message well enough for the audience you addressed at your press conference (maybe you delivered a technical message to the business press, or a business message to the lifestyle press). Either way, you need to think of implementing a plan to correct the impression you have left.

3. You realize that the journalists agreed with your strategy, but they demand proof points in the future. In that case you may want to consider a follow-up in a reasonable timeframe, presenting customer case studies or references.

4. You may receive positive feedback, but at the same time the journalists tell you that they hear not so positive comments from your channel partners. In that case your next campaign may address the channel press – or your company makes use of other elements in the communication mix to educate the channel.

All these examples indicate that you want to learn for the future from your recent press conference. A de-briefing should be done formally, documented properly and it should address several aspects.

Internal de-briefing

The objective of a de-briefing is to identify next steps in your PR activities from a content point of view, but also to enhance logistical aspects of future activities. You should therefore separate two levels of a de-briefing. Nevertheless, it is strongly recommended that you do not separate them during the de-briefing itself, since this would slow down the feedback process for the participants.

In a de-briefing session you want to collect all feedback from your company's participants at the event, but also from your supporting staff from external agencies. All the feedback is based on personal impressions and on informal discussions with the journalists during and after the event. This part of the de-briefing should be done rather like a brain-storming session where initially all feedback is put on the table in an unmediated way. Just collect feedback without arguing or commenting on it.

The formal feedback forms should be evaluated in parallel. It would be interesting to see if the 'objective' feedback is in line with the 'subjective' impression the staff have collected. Regardless of whether it is in line, be careful not to draw conclusions too quickly! Only make decisions for next steps after having consulted all sources. This includes:

- Journalists' formal feedback, in feedback forms, for example.
- Subjective impressions based on individual experiences;
  - From PR staff
  - From executives and spokespeople
  - Based on informal discussions
  - Based on discussions in 1:1 interviews.
- Media analysis (see also next chapter).

On the content and the message of your press event you want to collect feedback addressing the following items:

1. Was the content understood by your audience?
2. Were the journalists able to articulate your main messages?
3. How did they rate the content?
4. Did they compare your announcement with similar news they received from your competitors?
5. Did they share your company's direction and strategic vision?
6. Was the content relevant to their readers, that is, will they cover it?
7. Was, in the journalists' opinion, anything missing in the announcement?
8. Was, in their opinion, your content consistent in itself, with earlier messages and also with other information they learned from your company?
9. Did they share feedback from third parties, for example from industry analysts?
10. Do they think you will be successful?

But you also want to learn how you can improve the running of press conferences. Therefore, you should also pay attention to feedback related to the following:

1. Were all logistics to their satisfaction?
2. Did the event meet their expectations?
3. Did they suggest improvements?
4. Did they make a comparison with your competitors' events?
5. Did they get access to the information and the executives they expected?

But also, collect feedback from your executives and spokespeople! Especially, evaluate all notes taken at the interviews. The journalists, the questions and the way they asked them helps tremendously to understand where potential issues are and if the message was received positively or if scepticism was detected.

The consolidated feedback should give you indications in many areas. They include:

- General acceptance of your message. Is your message on target or do you need to refine it?
- Do you reach your audience?
- Are there influencers that you have not addressed yet or that are not convinced yet?
- Was a press conference the right approach in the first place to deliver your message?
- Will you need to do a follow-up with the journalists to close gaps that became obvious?
- Did you receive feedback about your products that you need to pass on to your company's R&D (research and development) department, your marketing department or the sales organization?
- Did you learn about new industry trends or developments that your high-level management or your business development department needs to know about?
- Did you get positive responses that you want to share with your company's employees? (Note that positive responses from the media have a strong impact on the employees' attitude and morale.)
- Do you need to develop your executives and spokespeople to stay on message better?
- Do you need to improve the logistics of the event?
- Did your supporting agencies do a good job?

This list can obviously be continued. It is important to have proper documentation of all inputs. But the final de-briefing document should be the opposite of the initial brainstorming! While you initially allowed all feedback, you now need to condense the feedback to items that are confirmed from various sources, that is, they must be relevant and not be based on individual incidents. Prioritize the feedback and try to identify the top three items. Do not dilute the feedback, since you should focus on the top issues in your future activities. Do not waste your (limited) resources on solving issues that have no impact or address items that are only of secondary importance. Target your PR resources on those items that maximize the benefit for your company.

Media analysis

Measuring the results of the press conference should happen on several levels. The classic 'Lindenmann model' describes three levels in great detail; the output, outgrowth and the outcome levels. As described in *Media Relations Measurement: Determining the Value of PR to Your Company's Success* (Ralf Leinemann and Elena Baikaltseva),[2] you should pay attention to two more levels describing internal company topics and your relationship with the journalistic community (see Figure 27.2).

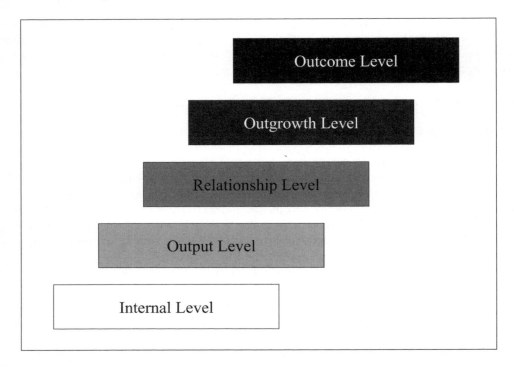

Figure 27.2   Lindenmann model (enhanced)

We'll briefly describe all five levels and provide examples of what to pay attention to specifically when measuring a press conference:

1. *Internal level.* On the internal level we measure internal company goals. For example, we want to have all speakers at a press conference attend media training before presenting or going into an interview. Another example for an internal goal would be to have a certain number of interviews with a certain speaker to position that executive in the media, and potentially position him or her as a specialist for a well-defined topic.

    Other internal goals may include budget goals, technical excellence, internal communication, compliance with internal guidelines and policies, preparation, and so on.

2. *Output level.* On the output level, basic aspects of PR are measured. At a press conference,

2   Gower Publishing Ltd, 2004, ISBN 0 566 08650 6.

this would include aspects such as the number of journalists attending, the number of interviews done with company executives, or the number of articles written by attending journalists after the event.

3. *Relationship level*. On the relationship level, your relationship with the media community is measured. On this level you should try to answer questions like: Are you and is your company accepted by journalists? Do they trust you? Do they ask your opinion on developments in the industry? At press conferences, a first indication of their willingness to talk to your company is the journalists' reaction to your invitation.

4. *Outgrowth level*. On the outgrowth level the focus is on the content and on the question of whether the content is understood by your audience, that is, the journalists. You would no longer simply ask whether a journalist has written an article. Neither would it be sufficient to ask for the rating of the article, that is, if it was negative or favourable to your news. The question would rather be whether the article addresses the content, the message, and especially the focus you intended. You may ask questions like: Is the headline the intended one?

5. *Outcome level*. On the outcome level, the changed behaviour of your target audience is evaluated. This could apply to the journalists and their attitude towards your company, or their readers and for example their buying behaviour.

    If you refer this to the journalists, you may want to compare their behaviour towards your company before and after a press conference.

    If you refer this to their readers (which is the actual understanding of this level per Lindenmann himself), that is, your potential customers, then you would examine their awareness of and preference for your company's brand and/or products.

More details on PR evaluation will be discussed in the following chapter.

28 *Media Analysis**

* Major parts of this chapter are taken from *Media Relations Measurement: Determining the Value of PR to Your Company's Success (Ralf Leinemann and Elena Baikaltsevea)*, Gower Publishing Ltd, 2004.

In 2004, we supervised the running of an international press conference held in Greece. The event was designed to address a significant audience from across Europe, Middle East and Africa. It was developed to host up to about 220 to 230 journalists with very different backgrounds. The heterogeneous audience represented consumer and B2B ('business-to-business') publications; they represented trade publications focusing on different markets, and technical and consumer lifestyle publications.

The press conference was the seventh in a series of annual events. It had become reasonably popular in the industry. Journalists registered well in advance, even though they may have not even received an invitation at that point. In 2004 it became very obvious that the event had developed some dynamics of its own. Word of mouth propaganda had raised interest with so many journalists that the number of planned slots turned out to be insufficient to facilitate all interested journalists. At the end of the day, more than 260 journalists actually attended the event.

It is obviously a nice challenge to have more demand for your news than you anticipate. But you still need to make tough decisions. If budgets are too tight, you may need to 'uninvite' journalists. If budgets allow you to accommodate all registered journalists, you still need to enhance the event agenda to meet the needs of the increased number of participants. You still want to run an event that allows for interaction and relationship building and allows your staff to look after all individuals at the event. You want to avoid creating a 'zoo'.

But most importantly, the decision to either 'uninvite' journalists or to increase the number of slots at the event is dependent on the goals you had set for the event.

If the main goal was to reach as many journalists as possible, then the decision would be an easy one. If the goal was to spend as much time 1:1 with the journalists as possible, then you may have already thought of alternatives, since more journalists obviously means less interview time per individual journalist. You will notice that both these goals are very tactical goals that are addressed on Lindenmann's 'output level'. There may also be an aspect of the 'relationship level' in here, as defined in the enhanced Lindenmann model.

We saw in the previous chapter that the enhanced Lindenmann model can be broken down into five levels. Goals can be defined on any level, but it probably goes without saying that the most rewarding goals are set on the two higher levels, the 'outgrowth level' and the 'outcome level'.

This little example already shows how goals and measures define the planning and execution of a press conference. In more general terms, measuring a press conference can be considered a superset of measuring an individual press interview. At the same time, measuring the results of a press conference is measuring the results of a special PR campaign or a part thereof. The main difference would be that a press conference is an event at a defined point in time whereas a PR campaign can last for a longer period. Even though a press conference is a single event, it should not be viewed as such in the context of the overall communication process. A press conference needs to be integrated into the overall communication strategy of the company. It needs to be consistent with earlier PR activities and it needs to be in line with other communication activities of the company.

For example, your messages need to be consistent over time and across the company. Also, you need to select from your various communication tools (press release, interview, press conference,...) consistently, depending on your specific announcement. For example, you do not necessarily want to announce a minor product enhancement in a worldwide press conference, while letting the world know about your company's new CEO only in a brief press release. Or in other words: you select your communication tactics depending on the news value of the content of your announcement.

Before we go into the details of measurement criteria, we need to acknowledge that there are two fundamentally different press conferences that cannot be treated with the same measures.

The first type is probably the most common one. This is a press conference in an environment that you do not have complete control over, for example a press conference held at a major trade show. Here you typically compete with other press conferences held by many vendors. The attending journalists have not come to the event specifically to see your company's presentation and are completely free in deciding what event they want to go to and what to skip. Journalists will not register up front to attend your event as in the above example, but you typically only learn about their participation at the event itself.

The second type provides your company with exclusive access to invited journalists. You may have brought them to a special location, so you have a captive audience. The entire event follows your predefined agenda. In such an environment you obviously have much more access to the individual journalists. You can allocate dedicated time to presentations, special interest group breakouts, interviews or product demonstrations. There is hardly an escape route for your journalists.

As discussed before, we can measure the results of a press conference on several levels. A good tool to achieve additional data from the participating journalists is a press questionnaire. A good tool to collect data on what has been published in the media is a clipping service and, ultimately, a detailed media analysis.

We want to discuss the five levels described in the enhanced Lindenmann model one after the other.

Internal level

A typical first internal goal is to see your participating executives being happy. However, before you join in their enjoyment, you should double check the cause of their excitement. It could easily be that their general happiness is caused by some very individual subjective incidents at the event. Maybe they were just delighted about the number of journalists that attended the event – but a closer look may show you that you missed the intended target audience. Or, an executive was particularly happy about a particular interview, which was not representative of the entire event.

Internally you may also want to check if all logistics went smoothly. Did the AV equipment work properly? Did transportation work as planned? Was the press kit ready in time and handed out to everybody? Was the timing of the event okay? The number of logistical aspects to look after is endless. It is important to remember not to get lost in measuring them. Even though they are important, you did not invite the journalists to enjoy a glass of champagne served with style.

One internal criterion that should be of interest, though, is the number of interviews facilitated at the press conference. Vendors often make the mistake of believing a press conference is a 1-hour presentation – full stop. Far from it! The presentation can only be the appetizer – and in fact it should be done in less than one hour. The main course for the journalists is delivered exclusively to the individual in a 1:1 interview or in a Q&A session. So, the number of interviews that were executed on the back of the initial presentation is typically a good measure of the true interest of the journalists. The more interviews that were conducted, the more you can be assured that your message was put across and well understood. Still, the pure number of interviews conducted is a very mechanical measure that can only be an initial hint right after a press conference. It certainly requires a more detailed evaluation on one of the later levels.

Tactical or output level

Probably the most basic tactical measure for a press conference is the number of journalists attending. (By the way, your immediate check should be to compare the number of journalists attending with the number invited – see also below.) If only mass awareness of your announcement is key, this criterion might be an easy one to measure. Nevertheless, it does not necessarily translate into good bottom line results. It is more or less just a 'bums-on-seats' approach that can be achieved by flying journalists to a beautiful venue – a place they cannot really say no to – and wining and dining them. This approach should not really be considered to be PR; even though the selection of an appropriate environment is important for an announcement, it should not become a purpose in its own right. It should only support the announcement and not become bribery (see also the Chapter 12).[1]

It is much more important to have the right target audience at your event. Therefore, a more realistic approach is to identify the journalists and publications beforehand and compare afterwards who from your initial wish list actually attended. When you do this comparison, do not just compare the names of the publications, but also the level of seniority of the participating journalists. You may discover that all your target publications attended, but only junior journalists were sent. You should accept this as proof that they did not expect significant news to break at your event.

Relationship level

Despite the fact that you may often hear that relationships cannot be measured, there are many ways of measuring your relationship with the journalists.

The first opportunity to have some feedback is before the event itself by having a careful look into the journalists' reaction to your invitation. Do they respond immediately? Do

---

[1]   Note that a good venue cannot excuse poor content!

they confirm their attendance right away? If so, it would mean that they trust you. They are convinced that they will not be wasting their time attending your event. They have probably had a good experience with your company before and know for sure that you only request their attendance at an event when you really have something important to share with them. You should always keep in mind that attending a press conference is a significant investment by the journalists. They will only dedicate that much time to your event if they can be sure that there is a return on that investment.

Apart from looking into the number of confirmations it would also be interesting to see what the reasons are for not attending. Do they even come back to you at all? And if so, is the negative response to your invitation a valid one or just a polite excuse leaving the impression that they consider other activities to be more important than to attend your event? If they simply cannot attend your event – maybe just for logistical or personal reasons or because that time slot is already booked – a journalist would still be interested to receive the information in a timely fashion and/or follow up at another time with a briefing (a telephone interview, say) by one of your company's spokespeople.

It should also be noted that the number of confirmations can indicate if the topic of the press event was explained and positioned correctly in the invitation, or if the information in the invitation letter was not triggering any interest at all to attend.

At the event itself, it is always important to collect feedback from the journalists. This can happen either informally through small talk during a break or over lunch or dinner, or in a very formal way, with the help of a feedback form, for example (see Chapter 26).

If you prefer the informal way, you must ensure that you have a sufficient sample that you can derive a conclusion from. Also, you must listen and document the feedback very carefully. And, you must ensure that the feedback is collected in a consistent way, that is, you should ask the same questions tofthe various journalists you talk to. Ideally, you would collect feedback not just by yourself, but also with the help of some of your colleagues. That way, there is a better chance to avoid you just hearing what you want to hear. And the journalists may be more or less open with different people.

Another measure could be the level of engagement you see from the journalists at the event. Do they interact with your spokespeople and look for discussions? This would be a very good sign for them being interested in the topic and the particular announcement. Or do they stay passive? In that case they probably could not connect with your message. Either you did not adapt your message to their respective fields of interest or your announcement was simply not as important as you initially thought. It could also be that you simply set too high expectations beforehand.

CULTURAL ASPECTS

At this point it is important to note that there are cultural differences that you need to pay attention to. Delivering the same message with the same speakers to journalists with the same fields of interest could cause very different reactions in different countries. The obvious challenge would be language barriers. Assume you deliver your message in English somewhere in Europe. In the UK, you would have no issues whatsoever; in Scandinavia you should feel comfortable as well. But the more you go south or east in Europe, the more you need to be prepared to acknowledge that your audience would prefer the content to be delivered in their local language.

But even if we disregard the language challenge, there are still cultural differences that cause your audience to react differently to the same presentations. For example, Finnish or

Dutch audiences are typically more conservative and do not show too strong a reaction in either way to your announcement. On the other side of the spectrum you may find the British media being very outspoken and direct – despite the fact that the British in general are typically considered to be more conservative than others.

If your announcement is related to technology, you will also discover that there are country dependent differences in Europe. Journalists writing for the same type of publications from different countries will perceive the same presentation differently. Typically, the British press is interested more in business aspects, while the French or Russian press is on the other side of the spectrum, being more interested in technology details. (We have attended international press conferences where English journalists left the room and complained afterwards that the content was far too 'techy'. At the same time, their French colleagues who write for publications with a similar focus and a similar target audience in their country would have liked to see even more technical details of the products. Apparently, when that happens your press conference was the right compromise for an international audience...)

Another aspect that is subject to cultural differences is the question of whether you are given access to an article for proofreading prior to publication. In several countries you would probably not even ask a journalist for that favour, but in some other countries journalists would be comparatively open to having you check an article for correctness before it goes to print.

ATTITUDE AND PERCEPTION

The attitude and perception of a journalist can be positioned in a two-dimensional plane (see Fig. 28.1).

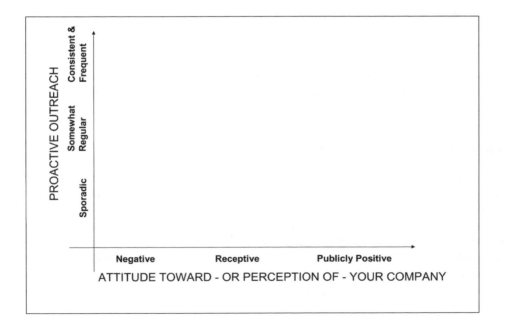

Figure 28.1   Attitude/perception grid

Filling this figure in is still to some degree subjective, but it helps significantly to follow individual journalists as they move around this grid over time. Your objective should always be to move a journalist who you consider to be important for your business to the upper right-hand corner of the figure.

Depending on the current status, that is, the current position on the figure, and the identified reasons for being there, several trajectories are possible for developing the relationship with a journalist. A very typical trajectory would be to initially intensify the communication with a journalist, that is, move them up in the figure.[2] This will not change their attitude immediately, that is, you should not expect them to move horizontally straight away. What you should see – if you have done your job well – is a move towards the right that follows with a more or less significant latency. This effect is well known in physics and called hysteresis. It applies to many biological or physical systems that operate with a built-in memory – including humans.

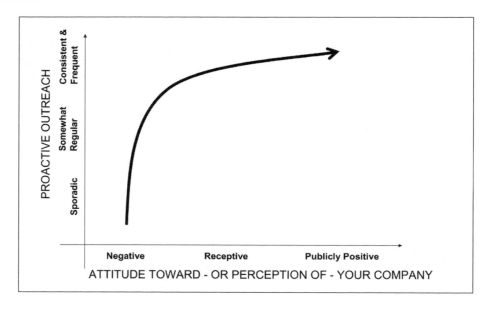

Figure 28.2   Attitude/perception grid – relationship development

In the same fashion, journalists should remain positive for a while even though you may need to reduce the number of contacts with them for a time. Dissatisfaction should only become apparent later.

Alarm bells should ring when a journalist suddenly starts to move left. In that case you or some of your messages have probably upset him or her. In a good relationship this should not catch you by surprise, but you should be aware of it straight away and be able to react immediately.

---

2   Never forget, the time journalists spend with you, they do not spend with your competition.

TRUST

Another approach to measuring the level of your or your company's relationship with a journalist or a publishing house would be to introduce an index for *trust*. We should be aware of the fact that this is an abstract value that you need to fill with life depending on what you consider to be important to achieve your overall goals. We need to warn you, however, not to misunderstand the term 'trust'! Do not mix it up with expectations towards journalists that would require them to compromise their independence!

Trust, as we want to understand it, includes a journalist's qualities such as:

* Openness towards messages from your company
* Being unprejudiced
* Giving fair coverage
* Not being opinionated
* Taking second opinions where appropriate
* Sharing values with you and/or your company
* Ideally, admitting the importance of the company's business and its presence in the market.

You should expect to be able to influence a journalist's trust in many ways. An obvious one is to stay in close contact with them. Figure 28.3, however, shows you that the frequency with which you meet the journalist is not the only influencing parameter. If it were, all journalists would appear in a narrow band along the diagonal in the figure.

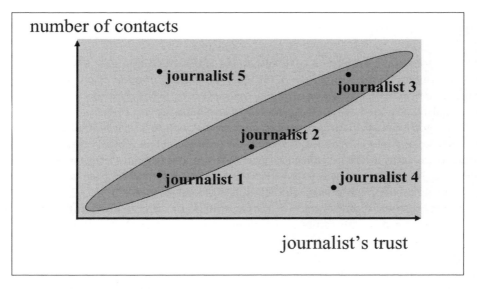

Figure 28.3   A journalist's trust

In Figure 28.3, Journalists 1 to 3 seem to follow the pattern that their relationship with you is directly dependent on the number of contacts you make with them. Staying in contact makes you a good source for the journalist because you are probably easy to access and a source that provides good information for the readers.

Journalist 4 puts a lot of trust in you even though the number of contacts is low. You can speculate why this is the case. Maybe the content you provide, whilst it does not fit with the focus of the particular publication, is of personal interest. Maybe that journalist trusts all vendors. Maybe the quality of your contacts compensates for the low number you have made. For example, you may have given this person exclusive access to a high-level executive at some time. But, whatever it was, you should try to identify the cause for their behaviour and transfer it to your relationship with other journalists, if possible.

Journalist 5 is at the other end of the spectrum. You seem to spend a lot of time working with them and developing a good relationship, but it does not seem to pay off. Maybe this journalist writes opinionated articles against your company or products, or writes about topics without even considering your company (even though you are a major player in that field). Maybe it is editorial policy not to cover product launches – but unfortunately that is the only thing you offer. Again, many reasons could have caused that behaviour. Maybe your competitors' PR organization has been very good in influencing this particular journalist. Or you need to look for an answer within your own organization and you need to ask yourself questions like 'Do I provide the right services and/or messages to the journalist?' or 'Did I annoy them at some time?'.

Journalist 5 is the one you should focus your attention on, since this is probably the person who can be most damaging to your company.

Outgrowth level

When it comes to measuring the coverage, all the standard criteria such as number of articles or tone of the individual articles come into play again. The number of criteria by which you can measure the coverage is almost endless. In this context we suggest that you consult a book that is dedicated to media analysis (Leinemann and Baikaltseva, 2004).

Before you start evaluating coverage, you need to define a process that gives you access to the articles as well as TV or radio coverage. If your event was a local one with, say, twenty journalists, you may be able to collect the articles yourself. If you ran a major international press conference similar to the one referred to at the beginning of this chapter, you are dependent on a professional clipping service, which you need to sub-contract.

The task of the clipping service is not to evaluate or rate the articles, but simply to get access to them for you. This can be a major undertaking in itself. In the above example, there may have been several freelancers at the event, and quite a few of the journalists would write more than one article as a result of attending the event. Simple mathematics would tell you that you should expect hundreds of articles from the event.

In order to detect all articles, it is essential to provide the clipping agency with a sophisticated brief. The keywords they should look out for need to be carefully selected. Typical keywords include:

* Product names
* Spokespeople names

- Your company name in combination with the event theme
- Your company name in combination with the event location
- Keywords describing your strategy
- Your company name in combination with the name of a guest speaker.

It is important not to include generic coverage in this clipping brief. Articles that were not generated by your press conference (but appeared accidentally at the same time) must not dilute your results!

There are a few aspects you may want to look at specifically after a press conference.

For example, you should evaluate the degree to which the text of the articles actually referred to the press conference itself. Was the location mentioned? Was a specific spokesperson quoted? Was the theme of the event referenced? Were certain exhibits you had on display at the event referred to?

And, last but not least, was the article accompanied by picture material that either you provided to everyone or the journalist took personally?

If you do not see any reference to the event, you may want to ask yourself whether the same coverage could not have been achieved in a different, maybe less expensive, way. Could the distribution of a press release have achieved the same results? Why did you provide a photo opportunity that was not used?

But the outgrowth level does not only describe the collection of the coverage and some basic evaluation. The outgrowth level primarily addresses the question of whether the journalist indeed understood your message – and reported it in a way you had planned. Here you should ask yourself questions like: Is the article focusing on the main topics delivered at the press conference? Did the journalist understand the message but consciously decided to question it?

Probably the simplest way of getting an answer to these questions is to look at the headlines that were published. During your planning phase you should have defined those intended headlines (see Chapter 4). You should evaluate now whether the actual headlines reflect your initial wish list.

Outcome level

Let us not forget that the ultimate goal is to influence the readers of the articles and the listeners/viewers of the radio/TV coverage you generate through your PR activities. Therefore, the ultimate goal would also be to measure these people's attitude change.

The ideal situation would obviously be to make a direct connection between your press conference and your company sales figures. This is a very ambitious goal that is extremely difficult if not impossible to achieve for an individual press conference. Since your potential customers are influenced by many factors – articles generated by your press conference being only one of them – long-term trends need to be evaluated that allow the measurement of awareness and preference trends.

Nevertheless, there are certain scenarios that do allow conclusions to be drawn about the impact of a press conference on your customers.

One scenario could be the following: You have introduced a product without accompanying the launch with a press conference and you have launched another product supported by a press conference. Assuming both products are comparable (addressing the same markets, audiences, competitive situation, and so on), the different successes of the products may be tracked back to the different awareness you have generated with and without a press conference. However, this approach is not only very academic, but also requires you to be able to exclude any other factor that could have caused the different market acceptance – a difficult task to accomplish.

Appendices

A *Checklist for Preview Trip*

In this appendix we provide a checklist to be used on preview trips to a venue that you are considering for your press conference. Note that several items appear more than once in different contexts in this list.

The list is in two parts. The first part ('Location') addresses more generic questions and topics linked to accommodation. The second part ('Conference venue') focuses on the venue used for the press conference itself. It may or may not be integrated into the hotel used to accommodate the participants.

Location

		✓	✗
1.	**Linking of location to message and theme**	☐	☐
1.1.	Appropriate style	☐	☐
1.1.1.	Rural versus city	☐	☐
1.1.2.	Modern versus historic	☐	☐
1.1.3.	High-class versus moderate	☐	☐
1.2.	Country	☐	☐
2.	**Attractiveness of location**	☐	☐
2.1.	Uncommon location	☐	☐
2.2.	Weather at time of event	☐	☐
2.3.	Other events at same time	☐	☐
2.3.1.	Pro: could attract more participants	☐	☐
2.3.2.	Contra: crowded environment	☐	☐
2.3.3.	Contra: no facilities available	☐	☐
2.4.	Attractive environments for social events	☐	☐
2.5.	Lifestyle	☐	☐
2.6.	Possibility of indoor and/or outdoor activities	☐	☐
3.	**Hotel (accommodation)**	☐	☐
3.1.	Availability of hotel rooms	☐	☐
3.2.	Sufficient number of rooms and suites	☐	☐
3.3.	Proper style of hotel rooms	☐	☐
3.4.	Availability of conference facilities	☐	☐
3.5.	Proximity of accommodation and conference facilities	☐	☐
3.6.	Proximity of hotel and location for social events	☐	☐
3.7.	Availability of local transportation	☐	☐
3.8.	Hotel service	☐	☐

3.9.	Availability of backup hotel nearby	☐	☐
4.	**Pricing**	☐	☐
4.1.	...of venue	☐	☐
4.2.	...of transportation	☐	☐
4.3.	...of accommodation	☐	☐
4.4.	...of social events		
4.5.	...of other local services		
5.	**Transportation**	☐	☐
5.1.	Easy access for all participants	☐	☐
5.2.	Direct flights from most European airports	☐	☐
5.3.	Short distance between airport and venue	☐	☐
5.4.	Flexibility		
6.	**Local infrastructure**	☐	☐
6.1.	Public transportation service	☐	☐
6.2.	Availability of hotel shuttle	☐	☐
6.3.	Power stability	☐	☐
6.4.	Customs requirements	☐	☐
6.4.	Availability of parking		
7.	**Security**	☐	☐
7.1.	Political stability	☐	☐
7.2.	No threat of acts of terror	☐	☐
7.3.	Low likelihood of environmental hazards	☐	☐
7.3.1.	Earthquakes	☐	☐
7.3.2.	Severe storms	☐	☐
7.4.	Protection against theft	☐	☐

Conference venue

1.	**Transportation**	☐	☐
1.1.	Distance from nearest airport	☐	☐
1.2.	All facilities within close vicinity	☐	☐
2.	**Appropriate style**	☐	☐
2.1.	Link to message and theme	☐	☐
2.1.	First impression	☐	☐
2.1.1.	Rural versus city	☐	☐
2.1.2.	Modern versus historic	☐	☐
2.1.3.	High-class versus moderate	☐	☐
3.	**Local staff**	☐	☐
3.1.	Friendly	☐	☐
3.2.	Helpful	☐	☐

3.3.	Capable	☐	☐
3.4.	Sufficient resources	☐	☐
3.5.	Language capabilities	☐	☐
4.	**Conference facilities**	☐	☐
4.1.	***Required rooms***	☐	☐
4.1.1.	Presentation room	☐	☐
4.1.2.	Breakout rooms	☐	☐
4.1.3.	1:1 interview facilities	☐	☐
4.1.4.	Room for technical demonstrations	☐	☐
4.1.5.	Press room	☐	☐
4.1.6.	Back office	☐	☐
4.1.7.	Rehearsal environment	☐	☐
4.1.8.	Space for welcome desk	☐	☐
4.1.9.	Space for 1:1 desk	☐	☐
4.2.	***Basic requirements***	☐	☐
4.2.1.	Closed environment, no access to public	☐	☐
4.2.2.	Ideal: all facilities are close to each other	☐	☐
4.2.3.	Ideal: all facilities are on the same floor	☐	☐
4.2.4.	Access to bring in large demo equipment, if required	☐	☐
4.2.5.	Low noise level	☐	☐
4.2.6.	All 1:1 facilities can be managed from a single 1:1 desk	☐	☐
4.2.7.	Environment for picture opportunities	☐	☐
4.3.	***Required within the rooms***	☐	☐
4.3.1.	Basic requirements	☐	☐
4.3.1.1.	Height of rooms	☐	☐
4.3.1.1.1.	Must be sufficient for stage	☐	☐
4.3.1.1.2.	Must allow for use of cameras from the back of the room	☐	☐
4.3.1.1.3.	Must allow for good air quality	☐	☐
4.3.1.2.	Visibility for audience	☐	☐
4.3.1.2.1.	Pillars	☐	☐
4.3.1.3.	Air condition	☐	☐
4.3.1.3.1.	Effectiveness	☐	☐
4.3.1.3.2.	Low noise level	☐	☐
4.3.1.4.	Room size	☐	☐
4.3.1.4.1.	Size sufficient for expected audience	☐	☐
4.3.1.4.2.	Sufficient space for a stage	☐	☐
4.3.1.4.3.	Space for video equipment	☐	☐
4.3.1.4.4.	Space for back projection	☐	☐
4.3.1.4.5.	Space for TV media	☐	☐
4.3.1.4.6.	Space for AV centre	☐	☐
4.3.2.	Technical details	☐	☐
4.3.2.1.	Lighting	☐	☐
4.3.2.1.1.	Lights can be dimmed	☐	☐
4.3.2.1.2.	Integrated spot lights	☐	☐
4.3.2.1.3.	Curtains can be closed if required	☐	☐
4.3.2.2.	Power	☐	☐

4.3.2.2.1.	Power outlets	☐	☐
4.3.2.2.2.	Power adaptors	☐	☐
4.3.2.2.3.	Power backup generator, if required	☐	☐
4.3.2.3.	Projection screen	☐	☐
4.3.2.4.	Integrated audio system	☐	☐
4.3.2.5.	TV	☐	☐
4.3.2.6.	Data projector	☐	☐
4.3.2.7.	Overhead projector	☐	☐
4.3.2.8.	Flipcharts	☐	☐
4.3.2.9.	Internet access	☐	☐
4.3.3.	Furniture	☐	☐
4.3.3.1.	Chairs	☐	☐
4.3.3.2.	Desks	☐	☐
4.3.3.3.	Podium	☐	☐
4.3.3.4.	Flexibility to change seating per special needs	☐	☐
4.3.4.	Environment	☐	☐
4.3.4.1.	Temperature	☐	☐
4.3.4.2.	View from window	☐	☐
4.3.4.3.	Noise level	☐	☐
4.4.	**Security features**	☐	☐
4.4.1.	Protection against theft	☐	☐
4.4.2.	Fire	☐	☐
4.4.3.	Other (earthquake precautions, for example)	☐	☐
4.4.4.	Medical first aid	☐	☐
4.5.	**Business centre**	☐	☐
4.5.1.	Copy facilities	☐	☐
4.5.2.	Fax	☐	☐
5.	**Local office supplies and copy shop**	☐	☐
5.1.	Distance from conference facility	☐	☐
5.2.	Pricing	☐	☐
5.3.	Availability of 24-hour service	☐	☐
5.4.	Capabilities (colour, formats, binding, stapling…)	☐	☐
5.5.	Delivery service	☐	☐

B *Cultural Influences**

* This appendix is based on the Diploma Thesis of Bettina Schoeppe, Fachhochschule Aalen, 2003, in cooperation with Hewlett-Packard GmbH, Germany.

Communication specialists need to take into account cultural influences on relationship building and on communication itself. This is true for PR in general and for press conferences in particular. In cooperation with Hewlett-Packard, the Fachhochschule Aalen investigated the influence of cultural aspects on PR in the IT industry in Europe (Bettina Schöppe, 2003). In this diploma thesis, the impact on international press conferences was investigated in detail.

The results of the research were based on interviews with almost 20 Hewlett-Packard PR managers from across Europe, more than 25 European PR agencies and almost 100 journalists following the IT industry.

The idea of the research was to find out whether journalists from different regions or countries have different needs to be addressed at international press conferences. It also investigated whether the requirements of journalists from different regions match the typical stereotypes or prejudices one has.

We want to cover parts of the research in this chapter, since the findings have some interesting impact on conducting international press conferences in Europe.

General findings

The research done with the journalists was based on interviews and on questionnaires filled in by journalists at international press conferences run by HP. The journalists were segmented into five groups representing five European regions:

*   British Isles: UK and Ireland
*   Northern Europe: Denmark, Norway, Finland, Sweden
*   Central Europe: Germany, Austria, Switzerland, Belgium, the Netherlands
*   Southern Europe: France, Italy, Spain, Portugal
*   Eastern Europe: Czech Republic, Hungary, Poland, Russia.

The interviewed journalists represented IT publications (about 75 per cent) and the business press (about 25 per cent).

The survey had some very interesting findings. One of the biggest surprises was the fact that the journalists were willing to spend more time out of the office to attend a press conference than initially expected – assuming obviously that strong and relevant content is provided.

The second finding was that in the eyes of a journalist, the perfect schedule of a press conference should offer:

- 42 per cent of the time dedicated to briefings
- 37 per cent dedicated to breakout sessions
- 21 per cent dedicated to 1:1 interviews.

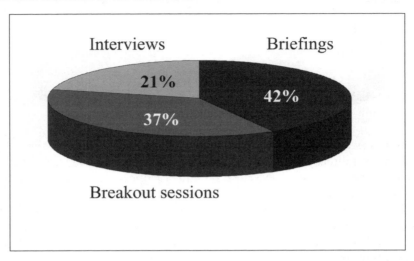

Figure B.1   Perfect press conference schedule (according to journalists)

In this respect, there was no significant difference, by the way, in the responses from the IT journalists and the business press journalists.

It must be noted here that this split represents the schedule for the individual journalist. This does not necessarily represent the time you should dedicate to the respective items in an event agenda. For example, if you have a large audience and only a few spokespeople, you may need to dedicate a significant amount of time to interviews in order to have the average journalist spend 21 per cent of his individual time in interviews.

There was a difference in the responses from the two groups (business press and IT press) when asked for the preferred content focus at a press conference. While IT journalists prefer a split along the lines of:

- 54 per cent of the time dedicated to technical and product information
- 18 per cent on promotion and marketing
- 28 per cent on strategy and business updates,

the business press preferred:

- 37 per cent on technical and product information
- 20 per cent on promotion and marketing
- 42 per cent on strategy and business aspects.

It was expected that the journalists would want to have independent opinions and views delivered at press conferences by independent specialists such as industry analysts or other guest speakers. About half the journalists consider such a presentation to be either important or very important.

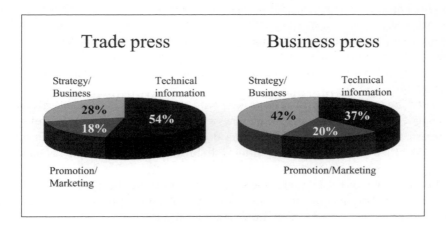

Figure B.2   Perfect content split (according to journalists)

Another finding was related to the perceived best tool to deliver certain messages to the press (see also Chapter 2):

• Strategic announcements should primarily be announced at international press conferences.
• Significant product launches can be done either at local or at international press conferences – or covered with a press release only.
• Industry partnerships should be covered in press releases – or at a local press conference, if a press conference is considered by the vendor.

Interestingly enough, more than three quarters of the interviewees did not consider an online press conference (see Appendix F) to be an option instead of a face-to-face press conference.

Specific regional findings

1. *British Isles* Journalists from the British Isles tend to prefer press conferences with a lot of time spent in briefings. But they are not very fond of breakout sessions. They prefer to interview spokespeople with worldwide responsibility rather than local or European spokespeople. They are most interested of all in conducting interviews.
2. *Northern Europe* Journalists from Northern Europe are the only group that prefers breakout sessions over briefings to larger audiences. They are interested in conducting interviews, but their prime target is spokespeople with European responsibility. Worldwide speakers tend to be the least important ones for them.
3. *Central Europe* Central European journalists tend to have only limited interest in interviews. They prefer a balance between briefings to larger audiences and breakout sessions. Worldwide speakers are the most interesting targets for them; European speakers are the least important ones.

4. *Southern Europe* Southern European speakers have a tendency to listen to presentations in larger audiences. They avoid breakout sessions and are also not too keen to do 1:1 interviews – but when they do, they prefer to talk to European speakers. Local speakers are the least important ones for them (this is something they only have in common with journalists from Eastern Europe, while all other regions value local information significantly higher).

5. *Eastern Europe* Eastern European speakers tend to be the quietest ones – according to this research. They prefer listening to the news as a part of a larger audience, and they are least interested in doing interviews – but if they do, then a speaker with worldwide responsibility would be their prime target. Their interest in breakout sessions is only average.

It becomes obvious that there are slight differences in the needs of journalists from different regions. You may be able to find the cause of some of these differences in different cultural backgrounds. Some of them, however, may also be due to language barriers.

Anecdotal evidence

In this section, we would like to document some observations we have collected over the years. They are by no means representative. However, communication with European PR colleagues seems to support the following points.

We will discuss our observations in no particular order.

- As already discussed in Chapter 28 British journalists in particular are very interested in economic and business aspects of your news. French or Russian journalists tend to be much more interested in technology. French journalists are very interested in gadgets and attractive product features (sometimes more than in benefits for the user). Russian journalists tend to have a very good technical education. They are very interested in understanding technical details, that is, they would like to know what is going on inside a black box, rather than just looking at the benefits for the customer.
- The British and Norwegian press especially appreciate an aggressive tone during a press conference. We would argue that they expect more from you than just being controversial. There seems to be a tendency that they almost expect you to bash the competition, since they would argue that you are not really convinced of your new products if you do not do so. If you use the same aggressiveness in countries like Germany or the Netherlands, however, you should be prepared for journalists to leave the room, since they prefer to receive only plain facts from you.
- Supporting the above research, it is very interesting to notice that especially Italian, but also Spanish journalists often prefer to do interviews in smaller groups rather than 1:1. They are typically accompanied by local PR managers, who host them at international press conferences. Since the PR managers often support the interviews with (simultaneous) translations, we suspect that the request for group interviews is at least to some degree caused by language barriers.
- We mentioned in Chapter 11 that journalists who are invited by vendors to a press conference typically expect to get their travel paid by the inviting company – at least in Europe. In fact, this is correct for the trade press in most of Europe, Middle East and Africa.

The business press tends to cover these expenses itself. The lifestyle press is at the other end of the spectrum, typically expecting a vendor to pay. In general, there also seems to be a trend for the trade press to make journalism more independent from vendors. This trend has become most recognizable recently in Sweden and the UK in particular.

- Journalists from different countries seem to show different levels of openness in their feedback. Journalists from Finland, for example, tend to be very quiet initially. You cannot really be sure how they rate the news. Journalists from other countries tend to show their agreement or disagreement much more openly.

C *Views of a Journalist*

In this appendix, we try to put ourselves in the shoes of a journalist. How does he or she actually perceive a press conference?

The important word here is 'perceive', since it is – as always – perception that makes reality. The perception is influenced by several parameters that are unique to the individual journalist.

First of all, journalists is embedded into their personal history. They may have had good experiences with your company before and therefore trust your judgment and are more than happy to attend your press conference. They know from experience that your company has always delivered good content that is relevant to the magazines they write for, or rather for their readers.

On the other hand, they may have had a bad experience with your company in the past. Either your company has misled them at some time, or they are not convinced that your company provides added value to their readers. It could also be that there was a personal issue at some point in time that a journalist has not forgotten about. Sometimes it is small incidents that upset them. Maybe they did not get the news they were expecting at a previous event, maybe there was an issue with the hotel room at a previous press conference with your company, maybe they got economy flight tickets when they expected business class, maybe you had failed to respond in time to their queries, maybe they did not get the interview they requested some time ago. The list is endless.

It is important to remember that journalists are only human. They come to your event with a certain expectation that you had set and that is based on their experience. And sometimes that expectation is even more of a prejudice. You had better know about this up front, so you can react to concerns proactively at the event. And, you can prepare your speakers and executives for potential issues so they act accordingly.

It is important to keep track of journalists' attitudes. Especially when you are working for larger corporations, the attitude may have been formed after a contact with a different part of your company that is not in your own direct control. In that case, a single database containing information about journalists is recommended across the entire company. It should be maintained by all PR teams in the company.

A journalist's thoughts – part 1

The invitation to your press conference has just arrived.

'Oh no, the fourth invitation to a press conference just this week. I do not believe I can afford the time. I have already decided not to attend the other three. Why should I go to this one?'

'Hm, it is this company that made that bold announcement a year ago. They had planned to become market leader within twelve months. That should be about now. Let me see, maybe they want to give a business update. Maybe they want to announce that they have achieved their goal. Well, the invitation does not say anything about that. Apparently they only want to introduce a new range of products. Maybe I should go and challenge them. Maybe I should remind them of what they said a year ago. This could result in a very interesting article for my readers. Actually, it would be interesting, regardless of the company's response.'

In this case it is obvious that the journalist is interested to attend not so much because of your invitation, but because of a personal agenda. This person is clearly driven by his or her readers, and believes that your event will provide the raw material for an article that will interest them.

The journalist agrees to attend the press conference and – because of those objectives – requests an interview with the CEO of the company. That is confirmed soon afterwards.

Three weeks later the journalist travels to the press conference.

'Wow, they are having the event in one of the most expensive locations in Europe: the most prestigious hotel in St. Moritz. Impressive! Looks like they indeed have a reason to celebrate. They have probably achieved their ambitious forecast. This would really make a good story. Looks like a nice couple of days are coming up. Maybe I can even do some skiing, once I am there…'

Your company's history and the selection of the venue have certainly created a certain expectation. You had now better deliver against it. If you do, you seem to be on to a winner. If you don't, then you seem to have a major challenge ahead of you.

A journalist's thoughts – part 2

The invitation to your press conference has just arrived.

'Oh no, not yet another invitation to a press conference. Who is this from? PR agency. And who do they represent? Not sure. Ah, okay, now I see. What do these guys do again? I am not sure. Let me see, what do they want to announce? All the invitation says is *Invitation to press conference*.'

The invitation ended up in the wastebasket right after these thoughts.

In this example, almost everything was done wrongly. Apparently, there was no relationship with the journalist yet. The invitation was basically a cold call. It was not visible immediately that your company was the inviting entity. Your PR agency issued the invitation in your name, but they were more prominent on the invitation than your own company.

But the worst crime you committed was that there was no hint in the invitation about what to expect at the event. It would have been a mystery tour for the journalist, who cannot afford to gamble with precious time.

A journalist's thoughts – part 3

The journalist has just arrived at the airport and is looking for the ground transportation to the event venue.

'Where are they? They were supposed to be here and pick me up. I have already been searching for them for almost a quarter of an hour. I hope they manage their business better than this press conference…'

Not a good start into the event. Your logistics show room for improvement. The real problem is that the journalist looks at your event as one single experience. Logistical problems have a negative impact on perception just as flawless execution leaves a positive impression.

The above is not just fiction. We know of an extreme case of a European journalist who wanted to attend a press conference in New York in the late 1990s. He did not find the organizers at JFK airport, so he decided to immediately book himself a seat on the next flight back home.

While this journalist did not make it to his event in New York, we hope that the journalist in this example made it to the press conference – and that the content delivered there more than made up for the logistic flaws – and finally wrote a positive article about the your news.

A journalist's thoughts – part 4

The main presentation has just finished.

The journalists leave the presentation room either to file a story right away by phone or by Internet, or they head for interviews. One of them has doubts…

'This was interesting news. They actually delivered a very good overview of what is currently happening. I am just concerned that they stayed at a comparatively high level. They did not really go into details. There were a lot of bold statements, but I am still missing the proof points. The guest speaker they had was good, but I am left with the impression that he was too close to the family. He only repeated what this company had to say. To me he did not look independent. It was a bit cheesy, I think. Also, I am surprised they did not allow for any questions at the end. Are they afraid of open discussions? Let's see if they can shed some more light on details in the interviews.'

It indeed looks as though you delivered a press conference that left some strange aftertaste. I do not want to say that your honesty is in doubt, but at least your openness is questioned. You certainly left the impression that you were trying to hide something. You almost triggered the thought that there must be something somewhere that you do not want the journalists to know about.

We would argue that you have indeed done too much marketing around your messages. The journalist called it 'cheesy'. The danger is that your approach can also be interpreted very quickly as arrogant. You certainly do not want to leave that impression.

A cause for these thoughts could have been that you tried to run a press conference without having sufficient content to justify it. You have then artificially blown up the story like a balloon. And now you run the risk that this balloon is about to burst.

A lot now depends on the interviews. If your spokespeople are not equipped with more details to support your message, then you will run into significant challenges. On the other hand, if they can share detailed proof points, then you should be able to save the day – at least with those journalists who were patient enough to interview your speakers. You may need to follow up with those who left the event right after the presentations.

A journalist's thoughts – part 5

The press conference has just ended.

'I am confused. What did they want to tell me? They announced a business update in the invitation, but they basically just did a product launch with a lot of details. I have not heard any business results. Do they have anything to hide?'

It looks as though your messaging was not consistent. Whatever caused the inconsistency, there is no excuse for it. You misled the audience. You certainly lost trust and you should expect issues when you invite them to another activity in the future.

'My readers are not really interested in product details. I would not know what to write. Maybe I can secure an interview with one of their business managers, so I can at least get something out of this.'

You should expect an interesting interview with this journalist, who will most likely ask questions that you may not be prepared for.

D Industry Analyst Briefings

Press conferences and briefings for industry analysts have a lot in common. But there is also a significant number of differences that one should be aware of. In this appendix, we discuss industry analyst briefings in comparison to press conferences. This means we do not want to address individual analyst briefings (just as we do not discuss individual press interviews), but events for a larger audience.

What is an industry analyst?

It is important not to mix up industry analysts with financial or security analysts. Security analysts consult with investors, industry analysts consult with customers and/or vendors.

Industry analysts exist today in almost every market. They typically specialize in a certain vertical industry or in a certain customer segment. We shall have a look at the IT industry as an example.

Technology has become more and more complicated over time – and so have business processes. The number of options to implement IT infrastructures, solutions built on top of them and business processes has increased immensely. As a result, corporate decision makers have had to become specialists in topics that require highly specialized training, such as storage infrastructures, network management solutions and high-availability technologies – to name just a few.

Politicians have become more and more dependent on special committees. Similarly, corporate managers hire consultants to advise them before they make purchasing decisions. These consultants have traditionally been their own employees, that is, specialists who had to work with the equipment that was about to be bought.

The opinion of company employees, however, was dependent on individual experience, often a lack of willingness to change and potentially a narrowed view of the world. Consequently, companies involve external consultants more and more often before major decisions are made.

Another reason for bringing in external consultants is the fact that more and more processes within a corporation have become interdependent. This includes supply chain management across multiple suppliers, go-to-market strategies across multiple vendors or interconnections across multiple levels of the CIM (computer integrated manufacturing) hierarchy.

Classical industry analyst companies employ staff on two different levels. The first level is consultants. They focus on solving individual companies' issues. They for example get deeply involved in specific projects such as business re-engineering. The second level is analysts. Analysts focus more on strategic approaches. They try to determine or predict industry trends. Their research is the basis for the consultants and their clients. You could say that industry analysts do research, while consultants do applied work.

When planning a briefing for analysts, it should be taken into account that analysts and consultants will require different treatment. However, it is most likely that you will address industry analysts only with your briefings. They will absorb the information and package it for their consultants and their clients.

There is a second segmentation of industry analysts you should be aware of. Different analyst companies typically focus on different clients. Some analyst companies have specialized in selling their services (basic research and consulting) to businesses, typically to larger enterprises. Some other analyst companies focus more on selling basic market data such as market share analysis back to vendors as inputs to their business intelligence units. Again, it should be taken into account that 'strategists' have different needs from 'number crunchers'.

Analysts and journalists

It should become obvious in this appendix that analysts and journalists have different interests. Thus, they need to be treated differently. Apart from the fact that they address different clients, they also need to manage information differently.

Journalists are news driven, and they have limited space in a magazine or limited time on TV to articulate the news. Analysts typically articulate their thoughts in research notes, papers or speeches. They certainly spend more time on compiling information than the average journalist does.

But it is interesting to note that the border between the journalist community and the analyst community is not always a very clear one. Some analyst firms publish monthly newsletters that can in fact hardly be distinguished from 'normal' magazines. Content can be similar, style can sometimes be similar (even though much more facts-based); even the structure can sometimes be similar, occasionally even allowing for advertising space. Only the distribution model for the publications is normally different to normal magazines.[1]

You need to make sure that you have a clear understanding of what the interest of these analysts is and, for example, to what degree they honour NDAs (see also below). If in doubt, it would be better to invite them to press conferences than to analyst briefings. But these decisions should be based on experience with the individual analysts. A generic answer cannot be given.

The same generic statements cannot be made with other individuals or small firms that define themselves as analyst houses, but operate in a different way. In certain industries there are individuals as influential as analysts, but they are for example university professors, artists or other celebrities, or they are members of public bodies. Despite the fact that they can have a tremendous influence on your target audience – ultimately your customers – you must address them in a different way; neither in a press conference nor in an analyst briefing.

Industry analysts show another pattern that is not too common for journalists: many analyst companies operate on an international basis, or they address topics in an international context. In Europe, for example, many analysts tend to have an international responsibility. Journalists, on the other hand, typically have a local focus, writing for a local or national publication. The number of true pan-European publications, for example, is fairly limited. Typically the number is limited to a few business titles and some special interest magazines.

---

1   By the way, some journalists try to go the other way, in that they try to position themselves as specialists who can offer services similar to those of industry analysts.

But normally, the interest in local content and language barriers drive the press to address a national audience only.

An immediate conclusion from the international scope of industry analysts is the fact that briefings in the English language are common. Press conferences, on the other hand, should always take into account potential language barriers that either require audiences to be addressed on a national basis in the local language or require simultaneous translations of presentations.

Why brief analysts?

Industry analysts are typically embedded into networks with financial or security analysts, but also with the press. Before journalists publish significant news, they typically consult with specialists to get a second opinion on what they have learned from another source. It is, for example, common practice for many journalists to call an industry analyst and ask for an opinion on a product launch they have just learned about.

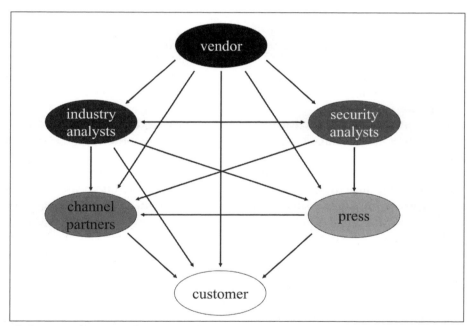

Figure D.1   Industry analyst network

An immediate conclusion is to invite analysts to press briefings just like journalists. Sometimes, this makes sense. But for most news announcements you should consider a more sophisticated approach.

We will see in the next sub-chapter that analysts require a different approach to the news from the media. The simple fact that you need to adjust your content to the target audience requires separate treatment for analysts. A second reason is related to timing. You certainly want to give analysts an advantage over journalists. You want to give them the chance to digest the news first and to draw appropriate conclusions so they can later – on public announcement of the news – share their results with journalists and with the public.

There is in fact yet another reason for briefing analysts up front. This reason would not justify an analyst briefing to a broad audience. Some companies provide very early information to selected analysts in return for getting their opinion on their message. They basically use the analysts as a sounding board. In some cases an analyst has signed a non-n NDA and is paid for message testing; in other cases the analyst provides an opinion for free in return for getting early access to information – still honouring the embargo date.

Briefing analysts prior to journalists has three advantages:

1. You can tailor the news to the specific needs of an analyst. Typically, they are interested in more background information and more technical details.
2. If the reaction of the analysts to your announcement, is positive you may want to invite some of them to your press conference later on as external references.
3. You give analysts the chance to consult with their clients in a more proactive way. Assume that a client is to make a buying decision that could be significantly influenced by your upcoming announcement. In that case the analysts can make use of their knowledge and consult the client to wait for your announcement (not necessarily pre-empting your announcement – depending on the NDA you have with the analysts).

How to brief analysts?

We have already learned about the timing of analyst briefings relative to public announcements to the press. It is recommended that you do an analyst briefing about two to four weeks prior to the public embargo date.

Disclosing information before the official launch date obviously requires an NDA with the analysts. Under normal circumstances this should not be a formal written NDA – as you would have with journalists – but a 'gentlemen's agreement', which should be sufficient if the relationship between your company and the analysts is close enough. Most analysts would not break the agreement, since they understand clearly that they should not expect an invitation to any future event in that case, that is, they would be cut off from the life-blood of their job.

In general, openness is one of the key differences between communication with journalists and communication with analysts. With journalists, you are always on the record. You should expect that anything could be published that you say in a formal interview, in a presentation, and even in an informal discussion over dinner.

But, with the analysts, you and your executives should expect the communication be to more a peer-to-peer discussion. The discussion is often an open dialogue about respective views of the industry.

Still, the agenda for an analyst briefing is similar to the agenda of a press conference. You allow for presentation time and for time spent 1:1. If you announce new products and the products would justify a presentation, it is recommended that you do a product demonstration. As usual, showing a product in use says more than 1000 words – and the consultants especially will appreciate a demonstration.

One of the most important things to remember when presenting to analysts is to present facts.[2] There is a significant difference between what journalists want to hear and what analysts

---

2   The entire environment of an analyst briefing is typically much more factual than a press conference. While you need to pay attention to decoration at a press conference, for example, you do not need anything like that at an analyst

are interested in. For journalists you need to focus your message on up to three main points that you want to get across. Ideally you want them to appear in their headlines afterwards.

You need to be prepared for the fact that analysts can follow much more complex topics. Obviously, you still want to get your company's view across – and ideally see it confirmed by the analysts' opinion. But you can go into detail and provide a lot of background information as appropriate. It is in the nature of an analyst to absorb as much information as possible – from as many sources as possible.

But it is also in the nature of analysts to draw conclusions themselves. So, you should not 'package' your message tightly or try to 'sell' a certain opinion. An analyst will definitely not appreciate such an approach. While spinning a story is a common tool to address an audience of journalists, it is not recommended with analysts.

Finally, you need to select your executives presenting at an analyst event carefully. Chief Executive Officer or General Manager level is always appropriate. But while you may want to have marketing managers complementing them at press conferences, you should also consider sales management at analyst events.

Agenda of an analyst briefing

It should be noted up front that analyst briefings to larger audiences are rather uncommon. In comparison, individual briefings, for example on the phone, are much more common. So, you should limit face-to-face analyst briefings to very important announcements only – or run annual (or regular) analyst meetings with your company independently of major announcements.

When planning analyst briefing you must always take into account that the time of analysts is precious. You can basically consider time to be their most precious resource. Many analyst firms in fact pay their analysts based on the amount of their time sold to their clients for consulting.

You should therefore consider short travel times when selecting a venue for the briefing. Many analyst communities in Europe are clustered in certain cities (depending on the respective industries they are active in). You should consider running your briefing in those cities, so that the analysts can come by car or even local public transportation.[3]

A typical agenda then may look like this:

10:00	Arrival
10:30	Presentation
12:00	Product demonstration
13:00	Lunch
14:00	1:1 opportunities with selected executives
	(Optional: parallel roundtables or special interest groups)
17:00	End.

---

briefing.

3   By the way, whenever you have an event where analysts – or journalists at a press conference for that matter – come by car, you should have tickets available to cover their parking expenses. With any major hotel it is no problem to get these pre-paid 'free-exit tickets' for the hotel garage.

E *Detailed Cost Breakdown*

In this appendix, we list typical cost items for a press conference. For most press conferences, this list may be far too detailed. Consider it to be a checklist or a menu you can select from; you are not forced to take every single course of action.

Preparation:

Budget item	✓ or ✗
Message development & content definition	
Media training for executives	
Theme and logo creation	
Preview trip	
Invitation process	
Speech writing	
Internal (employee) communication	

Production of PR material:

Budget item	✓ or ✗
Media alert	
Press release(s)	
Background material & white papers	
Photo material	
Executive biographies and photos	
References and customer case studies	
By-lined articles	
Press kit folder	
CD ROM production	
Website development for online press kit	
Hardcopy press kit production (prints and collating)	

Logistics:

Budget item	✓ or ✗
Journalists' flights to destination airport	
Ground transportation between airport and venue	
Ground transportation to social events such as dinner)	
Conference room booking	
Breakout room booking	

Interview rooms booking	
Press room booking	
Accommodation for all participants	
Catering: Breakfast, lunch, dinner	
Coffee breaks between sessions	
Onsite support as needed (travel desk, registration desk, and so on)	
Hostess support as needed	
Badge development and production	
Gifts	
Optional: Social programme	

Event production:

Budget item	✓ or ✕
Stage design and creation	
Room decoration	
Signage	
AV equipment (sound, lighting)	
AV equipment (speaker support)	
AV equipment (microphones for Q&A session)	
Set-up of breakout rooms and interview rooms	
Set-up of press room	
Optional: Special effects	
Optional: Simultaneous translation service	
Optional: Set-up of product demonstration area	

Press room:

Budget item	✓ or ✕
Network connections	
Computer and printer equipment	
Copier	
Fax	
Document shredder	
Telephone lines	
Refreshments	
Development of customized screensaver	
Production of customized mouse pads	
Technical support	

Guest speaker:

Budget item	✓ or ✗
Travel expenses	
Accommodation	
Catering	
Rate for presenting	
Optional: Rate for preparation and briefing	

After the event:

Budget item	✓ or ✓
Press clipping service	
Media analysis	
Internal (employee) communication	

F *Online Press Conferences*

As we have already seen, online press conferences are not necessarily the preferred way of communication for journalists. In the appendix on cultural influences (Appendix B), for example, we referred to a study that was done in Europe, where only a very small minority of journalists (less than 25 per cent) considered online press conferences to be an option for replacing face-to-face press conferences.[1]

Nevertheless, it is probably fair to say that the adoption of online press conferences will grow over time. It will probably grow at different speeds in different communities. This means that during the transition time, you need to make sure you understand what audience you can reach and where you may need to do a follow-up with a traditional press conference or traditional communication tools.

The required infrastructure may include comparatively advanced PCs and software tools to access the online conference. Since journalists do not necessarily have the latest PCs with the latest operating system and the most advanced software packages, you need to ensure that your online press conference demands only very little of the journalists' PCs. The more you demand advanced installations on the PC, the more you will lose your target audience – even though you may make it very easy to download the required software from your server.

Even more challenging is the fact that you do not have control over the network capabilities the journalist is using to access your conference. More or less everything is possible from access via modem to high-speed office access. You should adjust the amount of transmitted data to the lowest performing connection. This limits the tools you may want to use. Consider video streaming as an example. The live video transmission will catch a journalist's attention only if no jerky images are received. A static image that only changes every few seconds, however, is rather frustrating. So, using live streams only makes sense when you can be sure that all participants are connected via a high-speed network.

Online press conferences would be supported by a phone or an online-based conference (VoIP[2]) call. Your journalist would therefore require access details for the web-based service and for the phone-based conference call. Make sure you put all the required details into a media alert that is distributed a few days before the actual press conference.

The media alert functions in a similar way to an invitation letter. However, it already demonstrates one of the most significant disadvantages of an online press conference. It is a very anonymous exercise. We mentioned earlier that a press conference is one of the very few communication tools that allow you to meet a journalist in person (rather than only exchanging information by e-mail or on the phone). The online press conference eliminates that advantage.

---

1   It should be noted that this study was conducted with journalists following the IT industry. You may assume that these journalists are the most advanced in making use of modern technology. So, you may conclude that in other industries the adoption of the Internet for press conferences is even lower than in the IT industry.

2   Voice over Internet Protocol (VoIP) eliminates the need for two separate connections (PC, phone), but it requires a headset connected to the PC and you may face security issues.

We must admit that an online press conference also has advantages. One of the most obvious ones is probably saving time. There is no travel needed, and journalists can simply disconnect as soon as they believe they have the information they want. But we are certainly not friends of online press conferences. We believe that the disadvantages outweigh the advantages – up to now at least. And we fully appreciate that journalists apparently think along the same lines.

We know from experience that the attendance rate of journalists at online press conferences is significantly lower than at face-to-face press conferences. The rate has increased over recent years, but it is still at a level that you would not make your communication strategy dependent on just online communication.

We believe that there are only a few occasions where online press conferences – or online communications in a wider sense – are reasonable. We will discuss two examples that are successful for more or less the same reason.

If you have a defined target audience that you share information with on a regular basis, then an online press conference may be a very suitable way of getting the information across. Examples for this regular communication may be the quarterly earnings announcements or a regular update on a certain project (maybe the preparation of a major sports event, monthly communication of market share data or product shipment data, or the like).

A second example would be an even more regular way of communication, which actually already goes beyond the scope of a press conference. You may for example want to offer chat sessions with selected executives on a weekly basis. You could rotate your spokespeople and change the topic every week. If this were a very regular service, you would certainly have a considerable audience subscribe to it.

The two examples above have one thing in common. They both describe a *regular* service.

We are convinced that one of the reasons for journalists not yet feeling comfortable with online press conferences today is the fact that the technology is not yet easy to use. So they would not want to go through the hassle of setting everything up for just a single press conference. But if they benefit from a single set-up over multiple occasions, then there is a certain reward for that work, or some 'critical mass' that justifies the effort.

What to pay attention to for online press conferences

One of the issues we have discussed already is the fact that you have an anonymous audience. You should do whatever possible to get some personal note into the activity. One of the most important requirements is that journalists identify themselves when registering for the conference call. This would not only allow you to track their participation, it would also allow you to watch out for future articles and in general it would tell you something about their areas of interest.

But the need for registration should also be driven by the need for security. You do not want the whole world to participate in your online call, but only those press representatives you have designed the event for., A facilitated phone conference service is therefore often used. This service can also mute all participants except the speaker, but allow un-muting on request, for asking a question, for example.

Your conference tool should provide several features:

- The tool must be able to display messages as needed. For example, you have to start two minutes later than advertised. If you do not send a message out indicating the delay, you could lose a significant part of your audience immediately. Remember that patience hardly exists when using the Internet. It does not improve significantly with online press conferences.
- The software should provide tools offering interaction like a chat-like service that allows journalists to submit questions.
- The phone-based conference call should allow you to mute the audience since the noise level could be very disturbing. Still, every journalist should be given the option to un-mute his line to submit questions.
- The tool should be able to record the presentation for future downloads. This would then be offered to journalists who were not able to call in live.
- You offer the slides as downloads. At a live press conference you have offered them in a press kit as well.

Your spokespeople need to pay attention to some special considerations as well. The audience will not see them (unless you offer a live stream). Typically, the journalists only stare at some slides that are forwarded every few minutes. In other words, your spokespeople need to act like radio hosts. This has a few implications:

1. You must start on time. In a face-to-face press conference you can afford to start a few minutes late. If you did the same in an online press conference, you would already have lost a significant fraction of your audience.
2. Spokespeople cannot rely on body language. They only have their language as a tool they can use. Some speakers are natural talents. But typically you should be prepared to offer special training to your executives.
3. Using online communication, a high attention level is maintained for only 90 seconds.[3] Attention drops considerably after that period. Speakers must take that into account to grab the audience's attention using appropriate speaking techniques.

Also, you need to take into account that journalists who attend an online press conference could be (and typically are) distracted by what is going on in their environment. They may need to respond to colleagues or check their e-mail while listening to your press conference.

Bottom line: You do not control your audience. You do not control the atmosphere in which your message is received. There is a tremendous threat that the news does not come across properly.

---

3   By contrast, the attention level remains high for about 20 minutes when listening to a face-to-face presentation.

Bibliography

1. *Handbuch der Public Relations*, Albert Oeckl, Süddeutscher Verlag München, 1964, ISBN B 0000 BM2Z 2
2. *Publicity – How to: Write a Press Release, Prepare a Press Kit, Run a Press Conference, Write a Letter to the Editor, Organize a Media List*, Martin Pollack, Alliance Pub, 1989, ASIN 0 9368 3613 X
3. *Publicity Power*, Charles Mallory, Crisp Publications, 1989 (German: PR-Power, Ueberreuter Verlag, ISBN 3 9012 6092 7)
4. *Crossing the Chasm*, Geoffrey A. Moore, HarperCollins, 1991, ISBN 0 8873 0519 9 (paperback: 0 8873 0717 5)
5. *How to Promote, Publicize, and Advertise Your Growing Business: Getting the Word Out without Spending a Fortune*, Kim Baker and Sunny Baker, Wiley, 1992, ISBN 0 4715 5193 7
6. *International Public Relations*, Hugh M Culbertson and Ni Chen, Lea, 1996, ISBN 0 8058 1685 2
7. *Dictionary of Event Management,* Joe Goldblatt and Carol McKibben, John Wiley & Sons Inc, 1996, ISBN 0 4712 8792 X
8. *The Handbook of Strategic Public Relations and Integrated Communications*, Clarke L. Caywood, McGraw-Hill (first edition), 1997, ISBN 0 7863 1131 2
9. *Communicate Clearly,* Robert Heller, Dorling Kindersley, 1998, ISBN 0 7513 0630 4
10. *Perfect PR*, Iain Maitland, Intl Thomson Business Press, 1998, ISBN 1 8615 2221 5
11. *Value-Added Public Relations*, Thomas L. Harris, NTC Business Books, 1998, ISBN 0 8442 3411 7 (hardcover), ISBN 0 8442 3412 5 (paperback)
12. *Inside the Tornado*, Geoffrey A. Moore, Capstone, 1998, ISBN 1 9009 6158 X (paperback)
13. *The Complete Guide to Publicity*, Joe Marconi, McGraw-Hill Trade, 1999, ISBN 0 8442 0091 3
14. *Value-Added Public Relations: The Secret Weapon of Integrated Marketing*, Thomas L. Harris, McGraw-Hill (first edition), 1999, ISBN 0 8442 3412 5
15. *Effective Public Relations*, Scott M. Cutlip, Allen H. Center, Glen M. Broom, Prentice Hall; (Eighth edition), 1999, ISBN 0 1354 1211 0
16. *Энциклопедия Этикета*, Иван Панкеев, Издательство Олма-Пресс, Москва 1999, ISBN 5 2240 0017 3
17. *Company Internal Communication*, Tatiana Fish, 1999, Hewlett-Packard GmbH, Germany
18. *How to Run a Successful Conference*, John G. Fisher, Kogan Page, 2000 (2nd edition), ISBN 0 7494 3406 6
19. *Event Planning: The Ultimate Guide to Successful Meetings, Corporate Events, Fundraising Galas, Conferences, Conventions, Incentives and Other Special Events*, Judy Allen, John Wiley & Sons, 2000, ISBN 0 4716 4412 9
20. *The Future of Teledemocracy*, Ted Becker and Christa Daryl Slaton, Praeger Publishers, 2000, ISBN 0 2759 6632 1

21. *Public Relations Kit for Dummies*, Eric Yaverbaum and Robert Bly, For Dummies; Book & CD edition, 2000, ISBN 0 7645 5277 5

22. *30 Minuten für erfolgreiche Presse- und Öffentlichkeitsarbeit*, Jens Ferber, Gabal Verlag, 2000, ISBN 3 8974 9044 723.

23. *Grundwissen Öffentlichkeitsarbeit*, Werner Faulstich, UTB Wilhelm Fink Verlag, 2000, ISBN 3 8252 2151 2

24. *Planning and Managing Public Relations Campaigns*, Anne Gregory, Kogan Page, 2000, ISBN 0 7494 2991 7

25. *Effective Public Relations*, Moi Ali, Dorling Kindersley Ltd, 2001, ISBN 0 7513 1290 8

26. *The Publicity Handbook, New Edition: The Inside Scoop from More than 100 Journalists and PR Pros on How to Get Great Publicity Coverage*, David R. Yale and Andrew J. Carothers, McGraw-Hill; 2nd edition, 2001, ISBN 0 8442 3242 4

27. *The International Dictionary of Event Management*, Joe Goldblatt, Wiley, 2001, ISBN 0 4713 9453 X

28. *Special Events: Twenty-first Century Global Event Management*, Joe Goldblatt, Wiley, 2001, ISBN 0 4713 9687 7

29. *Public Relations on the Net: Winning Strategies to Inform & Influence the Media, the Investment Community, the Government, the Public & More*, Shel Holtz, American Management Association; 2nd edition, 2002, ISBN 0 8144 7152 8

30. *The PR Practitioner's Desktop Guide*, Caroline Black, Hawsmere Publishing, 2002, ISBN 1 8541 8260 9

31. *The Fall of Advertising and the Rise of PR*, Al Ries and Laura Ries, Harper Business, 2002, ISBN 0 0600 8198 8

32. *Media/Society: Industries, Images and Audiences*, David Croteau and William Hoynes, Pine Forge Press; 3rd edition, 2002, ISBN 0 7619 8773 8

33. *Now Is Too Late: Survival in an Era of Instant News*, Gerald R. Baron, Financial Times/Prentice Hall; 1st edition, 2002, ISBN 0 1304 6139 3

34. *Qualitative Research Methods in Public Relations and Marketing Communications[1]*, Christine Daymon and Immy Holloway, Routledge, 2002, ISBN 0 4152 2274 5

35. *The Chasm Companion*, Paul Wiefels, Capstone, 2002, ISBN 1 8411 2468 0

36. The Press Conference: When to Hold It and How to Do It Right [download: PDF], Joan Stewart, Breakthrough Consulting, 2003, ISBN B 0000 892Q T

37. Manieren, Asserate Asfa-Wossen, Eichborn, 2003, ISBN 3 8218 4739 5

38. *Primer of Public Relations Research*, Don W. Stacks, Guilford, 2002, ISBN 5723 0726 9

39. *The New PR Toolkit: Strategies for Successful Media Relations*, Deirdre Breakenridge, Thomas J. Deloughry, Tom Deloughry, Financial Times/Prentice Hall; 1st edition, 2003, ISBN 0 1300 9025 5

40. *In The Court of Public Opinion: Winning Your Case With Public Relations*, James F. Haggerty and James Haggerty, Wiley; 1st edition, 2003, ISBN 0 4713 0742 4

41. *Media Training 101: A Guide to Meeting the Press*, Sally Stewart, Wiley, 2003, ISBN 0 4712 7155 1

42. *Public Relations: Contemporary Issues and Techniques*, Paul Baines, John Egan, Frank Jefkins, Butterworth-Heinemann, 2003, ISBN 0 7506 5724 3

43. *Public Relations*, Philip Henslowe, Kogan Page, 2003, ISBN 0 7494 4072 4

44. *Cultural Influences on Public Relations in the Information Technology Industry in Europe*, Bettina Schöppe, Diplomarbeit Fachhochschule Aalen (in cooperation with Hewlett-Packard

---

[1]   With very detailed bibliography on the topic of research, evaluation and analysis.

GmbH, Germany), 2003

45. *Public Relations in Practice*, Anne Gregory, Kogan Page, 2003, ISBN 0 7494 3381 7
46. *Getting Free Publicity*, Pam & Bob Austin, How To Books Ltd, 2004, ISBN 1 8570 3972 6
47. ПИАРЩИК, Michael Willard, Vidalia House Publishing, 2004, ISBN 9 66788905 X
48. *Public Relations – Perspektiven und Potenziale im 21. Jahrhundert*, Tanja Köhler, Adrian Schaffranietz (Hrsg.), VS Verlag für Sozialwissenschaften, 2004, ISBN 3 5311 4035 3
49. *Media Relations Measurement: Determining the Value of PR to Your Company's Success*, Ralf Leinemann and Elena Baikaltseva, Gower, 2004, ISBN 0 5660 8650 6
50. *When it Hits the Fan*, Michael Bland, Knowledge Nugget Guide, 2004, ISBN 1 9015 3407 3
51. *Teach Yourself PR*, Angela Murray, Hodder Education, 2005 (first published in UK 2001), ISBN 0 3408 8688 9
52. *PR на 100%: Как стать хорошим менеджером по PR*, 3-е изд, Альпина Бизнес Букс, Москва 2005, ISBN 5 9614 0148 0

Index

About the Authors

Dr Ralf Leinemann has more than 15 years of experience working in international PR, marketing and business development departments in the high-tech industry. He holds a PhD in Physics from the University of Tübingen, Germany. He joined Hewlett-Packard in 1989, initially in technical marketing for real-time computer systems. Afterwards, he did product marketing for workstations and industrial systems. He then did business development for technical systems with a focus on the telecom industry, before he moved into Public Relations. He started his career in PR as the PR manager for HP's computing systems in EMEA (Europe, Middle East and Africa). In that role he managed all external communication for that business in EMEA. He then integrated all communication for HP's business-to-business (B2B) solutions. He is currently the Communication Manager for Hewlett-Packard's Imaging and Printing Group in EMEA with a focus on the consumer space. In 2003, he was entered in the *Who's Who of Professionals*.

Elena Baikaltseva has been Public Relations and Marketing Communications Manager for Advanced Micro Devices (AMD) in the representative office in Moscow since 2001. She has eight years' experience in communications functions, working for the international high-tech corporations Hewlett-Packard and AMD, and collaborating with PR agencies. Her responsibilities today include PR for AMD in Russia and the CIS countries with a strong focus on consumer markets. She graduated from the Molodyezhi Institute in 1995 and has a Higher Education Degree in Management and Administration. Since 1995 she has worked at Hewlett–Packard in various marketing and communication positions, focusing primarily on enterprise market segments. She started her career in PR initially as PR manager for the HP Enterprise Computer Systems Organisation, a role which later developed into PR Professional for HP Russia, responsible for planning, development and execution of marketing communication and public relations programmes for all HP product categories. Elena Baikaltseva has vast experience in the management of integrated marketing campaigns and in the integration of international and regional PR projects of different scales.

The authors jointly published *Media Relations Management: Determining the Value of PR to Your Company's Success* in 2004 (Gower Publishing Ltd., ISBN 0 566 08650 6).